THE CONFLUENCE OF WISDOM ALONG THE SILK ROAD

Omar Khayyam's Transformative Poetry

M. Vaziri
University of Innsbruck, Austria

Series in Literary Studies

VERNON PRESS

Copyright © 2022 Vernon Press, an imprint of Vernon Art and Science Inc, on behalf of the author.

All rights reserved. No part of this publication may be reproduced, stored in a retrieval system, or transmitted in any form or by any means, electronic, mechanical, photocopying, recording, or otherwise, without the prior permission of Vernon Art and Science Inc.
www.vernonpress.com

In the Americas:
Vernon Press
1000 N West Street, Suite 1200,
Wilmington, Delaware 19801
United States

In the rest of the world:
Vernon Press
C/Sancti Espiritu 17,
Malaga, 29006
Spain

Series in Literary Studies

Library of Congress Control Number: 2021941350

ISBN: 978-1-64889-378-0

Also available: 978-1-64889-257-8 [Hardback]; 978-1-64889-316-2 [PDF, E-Book]

Product and company names mentioned in this work are the trademarks of their respective owners. While every care has been taken in preparing this work, neither the authors nor Vernon Art and Science Inc. may be held responsible for any loss or damage caused or alleged to be caused directly or indirectly by the information contained in it.

Every effort has been made to trace all copyright holders, but if any have been inadvertently overlooked the publisher will be pleased to include any necessary credits in any subsequent reprint or edition.

Cover design by Foaad Farah.

This book is dedicated to Razia, Nadia, and Shukria, Afghan sisters orphaned since 2002 who, against all the odds, have created a life for themselves in Kabul. Now all in their twenties, Razia is a Montessori preschool teacher, and Nadia and Shukria are midwifery students. Their will to seize life and go forward should enliven courage and optimism in those of us who sometimes lose hope.

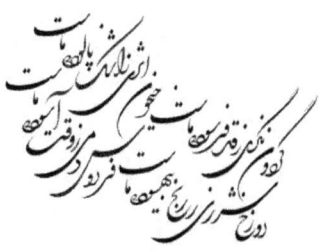

The cosmos in commotion is an echo of our degenerating body;
The Oxus River is an expression of our untainted tears;
Purgatory is but a flare of our futile anguishes;
And paradise is made up of the moments of our tranquility.

- Khayyam

Table of contents

List of Figures	ix
Prelude	xi
Part I: Interwoven Philosophies of Life	1
Chapter 1 A Nexus of Wisdom on the Silk Road	3
Chapter 2 Life is Like a River: Heraclitus and Khayyam	39
Chapter 3 The Liberated Drunkard: Daoism and Wine in the *Rubaiyat*	51
Chapter 4 Self-Rule, Joy and Emptiness: The Bedrock of the Buddhist and Khayyamian Paths	67
Chapter 5 The Immortal Clay: An Echo of the Chandogya Upanishad in Khayyam's Allegory	89
Part II: Therapeutic Approach: Four Essays	97
Chapter 6 Poetry-Philosophy as Medicine: A Historical Background	99
Chapter 7 The Entrapped Mind and Psychosomatic Alarms	113
Chapter 8 Wisdom Therapy and Khayyam's Poetry	121
Chapter 9 Khayyamian Thought as a Psychological Alternative	141
Conclusion	149

Part III: The Quatrains	151
Chapter 10 **The Flow of the *Rubaiyat*: New Translation and Classification**	153
Bibliography	175
Index	185

List of Figures

Figure 1: Map of the Silk Road. 7

Figure 2: *Hich* – Nothingness. 172

Prelude

Personal remarks

In the first quarter of the twenty-first century, tumultuous events have befallen our modern world ranging from expansionism, dictatorship, religious fundamentalism, gender inequality, human rights violation, refugee crises, climate change, the lingering effects of colonialism, and the Coronavirus pandemic, as well as the age-old human problems of poverty, angst, insecurities, and existential confusion. The beginning of the twentieth century also saw similarly serious global circumstances when in the first quarter of the century, the world experienced devastation due to World War I, colonialism, ongoing slavery, and the Influenza pandemic of 1918-1920 (Spanish flu), which is estimated to have infected almost one-third of the world population with about 50 million deaths, followed by a stark economic depression.

In the face of those seemingly hopeless events at the beginning of the last century, some in society sought psychological solace in a variety of ways. Perhaps feeling the need for a fresh start and different answers, people began exploring new realms in order to change things for the better, including Eastern spirituality, philosophy and countercultural pursuits as means of transformation and self-therapy. Poetry, literature, music, art, and cinema also became agencies of adjustment in order to heal psychological wounds and engage in soul-searching.

Post-WWI, one particular book gained increasing attention among such seekers—the *Rubaiyat* of Omar Khayyam. This collection of poetry offered a simple message of living a joyful life. A large number of translations enabled widespread reading of the 900-year-old *Rubaiyat*, and Omar Khayyam clubs sprang up in America and England, evidence of how much people craved his message during a dark time.

In our new century, we are again walking a thin existential line in safeguarding our vulnerable social and individual psyches. And once again, the philosophical poetry of Khayyam is proving to be effective in keeping psychological turmoil at bay. His poetry often prompts a paradigm shift in readers towards viewing the world in a realistic and joyful light. It entails taking an uncorrupted, secular look at nature the way exactly as it presents itself, bringing thinkers closer to nature and appeasing their confusing fears and beliefs. Prescient Khayyam was aware that if such confusing fears are removed, natural joy gradually takes their place. Khayyam's poetry, in fact, was much more than just poetic lines. It presented a philosophy of life.

Perhaps Khayyam's philosophical poetry resonates so much for us because Khayyam himself also lived during a very tumultuous period. His verses were composed during critical times, for critical times, especially for people struggling with the politics of the day while doubting the meaning of their own lives. Khayyam was well aware that the combination of sociopolitical and psychological factors can deeply entangle people in life's quandaries, and issues of Khayyam's world in the twelfth century were not all that different from those we face today.

Other great thinkers have also offered philosophy combined with poetry as a counterbalancing force. Laozi (Lao Tzu) and Zhuangzi (Chuang Tzu), the founders of Daoism, wrote their treatises between the sixth and fourth centuries B.C.E, during China's brutal state wars and the accompanying repugnant bloodshed and inflammatory politics of the day. Laozi and Zhuangzi invited people to focus instead on character-building and psychological peacefulness rather than the agonies of war.

The same reformative stance was taken by the first century B.C.E. Roman poet and Epicurean philosopher Lucretius. He composed a 7,400-lined poetic treatise not only releasing people from fallacious religious understandings about the workings of nature, but also advising Romans to seek their own pleasure in life and liberate themselves from the shackles of the Roman imperial ambitions. Lucretius's rebellious position has had profound application in inculcating a deeper understanding of life and death, as well as valuing life in its given beauty. He encouraged people to diligently take care of themselves rather than to be politically or socially manipulated.

The poet Khayyam also encouraged emancipation from shackles of all sorts, whether political, religious, social, or psychological. The eleventh and twelfth centuries were a period when the military demagogies of the Seljuq Dynasty, Ismaili militias, ambitions of outside power contenders, and the gloomy prospect of a fanatical religious culture loomed over people's sense of well-being and security. Given the desperate psychological necessity, he wrote the *Rubaiyat* for people during these times, but in fact, the religious environment was too sensitive for the poems to be openly circulated, and few of his contemporaries had the chance to benefit from it. But fortunately, it survived, and his message has been highly relevant ever since.

Besides being a poet, Khayyam was a mathematician. His empirical, rationalist nature rebelled against unsubstantiated theories and claims regarding the reason for existence, the role of god, and beliefs of an afterlife as promoted by religion. His empirical poetry stood the test of time by pointing to nature and its verifiable body of unbreachable laws. The only verifiable purpose for life that Khayyam could identify was to do one's best to live with a relaxed, painless, and joyful state of being in this abundant world for as long as one's life lasted.

The prescient language of the *Rubaiyat*, even after 900 years, still echoes the same longings most of us seek in this life. Khayyam warned that if self-care is neglected and postponed to some obscure notion of 'tomorrow,' the pleasure of living in the now is irreversibly lost. He poured out Zen-style verses to remind readers that each moment of life is complete in itself, by itself, and that the incompleteness manifests itself only in the mental states of people who are not yet aware. The natural world lives independently for itself, unattached to our feelings of pain and joy, and in Khayyam's view, acknowledging this liberating fact is the first step towards having a pleasant life.

Khayyam's message offers a philosophical and universal mandate that is both transformative and therapeutic. The rediscovery of Khayyam's legacy is a rediscovery of the rational wisdom of the ongoing human odyssey. His poetry is not merely for reading and understanding in the moment, but it is for developing an integrative knowledge of life—for implementing it and taking it one step further, beyond an intellectual understanding, towards 'post-understanding.' The present book with its intertwined subjects of anthropological philosophy and therapeutic philosophy presents a more modern approach towards the *Rubaiyat* not only to better understand Khayyamian thought and its cultural interconnections today, but also to offer a new perspective on using his poetry for personal transformation, particularly in difficult times.

The Confluence of Wisdom

This book is a first effort to trace the themes of the *Rubaiyat* back to powerful Hellenic, Chinese and Indian philosophical traditions by uncovering surprising parallels in original works by Heraclitus, Zhuangzi (Daoism), Nagarjuna (Mahayana Buddhism), and the Upanishads. Given the healing power of the ideas within such ancient wisdom traditions over the course of centuries, connecting them with the central themes of the *Rubaiyat* enables us to look at Khayyam's work in a therapeutic light and see the *Rubaiyat* as a source of wisdom therapy and a psychological alternative.

In general, there have been two dominant approaches to Khayyam as a philosopher, and the two somewhat contrasting approaches have inadvertently overlapped each other. In one approach, Khayyam is seen as a scholastically conformist philosopher feasibly influenced by mysticism and the author of six treatises closely oriented to the Aristotelian-Avicennian-style of classic "*falsafa.*" But in the other approach, he is seen as a freethinker with a hidden life, secretly pouring out verses about a naturalist-hedonist philosophy in creating what would eventually become the *Rubaiyat*. The present book focuses on this second approach because the first approach is insufficient to support or explain the wide-ranging themes of the *Rubaiyat*.

There are numerous publications on Omar Khayyam and many translations of his *Rubaiyat*. But the idea and methodology of the present book are radically different because the narrative takes a wider approach, situating Khayyam and his ideas in the cultural corridors of the Silk Road through exploring his cosmopolitan and inclusive positions. The book presents in three parts: first, the transformative ideas of Khayyam in connection with four ancient schools of philosophy; secondly, the therapeutic aspects of Khayyam's poetry; and finally, a fresh translation of the *Rubaiyat* with a unique classification of his quatrains.

Part I entails an investigation of the cultural and intellectual interactions among the major cities of the Silk Road, particularly in the Central Asian-Eastern Iranian region of Khayyam's birth. Since his hometown of Nishapur was situated at the intersection of the Iranian, Indian, and Chinese worlds and Greek philosophical works were also readily available, it is highly probable that Khayyam studied and perhaps even borrowed from the philosophies of Heraclitus, Zhuangzi, Nagarjuna and the Upanishads. The similarities to these works that echo in the *Rubaiyat* hint at the interconnections among ancient wisdoms circulating freely along the Silk Road over the centuries.

In Part II, four essays explore therapeutic perspectives that broaden the psychological utility of Khayyam's poetry. They show how Khayyam counted on the power of words and images for the deconstruction of unreason and the process of unshackling the mind from misleading perceptions of reality and explain how these are themselves powerful steps to alleviating existential discontent. Khayyam's bluntness about inescapable natural laws is a reminder to turn off the "hot" cognition which generates overpowering emotions and unfounded beliefs and, far more gravely, can breed stressful states.

His verses simultaneously turn on a "cold" cognition, cooling down the mind for a judicious accessing of the true nature of existence while also energizing an appreciation for life the way it flows. The cold cognition that Khayyam turns on praises the beauty of life for what it has for us here-and-now, rather than focusing on what it lacks or for all that has gone. Khayyam declares the perspective of happiness to be inherent in us; it simply has to be reawakened. We are reminded to enjoy the day at hand—'carpe diem therapy.' It is actually this aspect of his poetry that contributed to the reputation of hedonism associated with the *Rubaiyat*. But more than merely being a hedonist, Khayyam was a pathbreaker in terms of being aware of how one lived daily life. What was called 'hedonism' was, in fact, Khayyam's approach to living a life in the moment with a balanced appreciation for the nature of reality. In addition, the philosophy of life in his poetry became a conduit for alternative social thinking, stepping outside of dogmatic and tyrannical cultures. Khayyam himself epitomized the counterculture movement of his time by valuing logic and rationality over the claims of culture.

The impetus for a fresher translation of poems that comes in Part III was not only to bring the words and ideas of Khayyam in Persian[1] closer to the meaning Khayyam most probably intended, but also to contextualize his ideas in the nexus of the philosophies prevalent on the Silk Road during his time. In addition, a new re-classification of the verses of the *Rubaiyat* divides the quatrains into five sections following Khayyam's stepwise approach to life. The order of the five categories highlights the expected progression of life and the human experience of it and Khayyam's corresponding recommendations. The aim here is to correct misinterpretations of Khayyam being either depressing and nihilistic, or frivolously hedonistic. Such extreme or one-sided views of Khayyam are not keeping the whole body of his work in view and have thus been detrimental to a fuller understanding of his philosophy and stance on existential issues. In fact, Khayyam's *Rubaiyat* represents a broader balanced picture of life, presenting two sides of the same coin: not burying joy under the sting of death, nor covering up the pain of death by imagining endless joy. In an image arising from his Silk Road roots, Khayyam described life as a steady stream of "caravans" of people who are born on earth for their impermanent stay to simply to take delight in the flowing joy of now before moving on.

Taken all together, this volume presents two major layers of Khayyam's work. The *outer* layer or the 'skin' is an anthropological study connecting the origins and similarities of Khayyam's intellectual ideas and inspirations to other ancient cultures and philosophies. This goal leads us to embrace an intercultural approach in exploring the larger context of philosophical ideas on the vibrant culture of the Silk Road.

The *inner* layer of this study, or the 'heart,' concentrates on the key existential messages of the *Rubaiyat*. This includes the archetypal messages of the *Rubaiyat* and their interpretation in the context of what matters in life, regardless of where and when. The essence of these inner meanings, as extracted from the entire premise of the *Rubaiyat*, lies in the cultivation of contentment while living in harmony with nature.

Acknowledgements

This book evolved to become what it is because of the inspirational and continuous dialogues with my wonderful life partner, Allison. She made her immense contribution by reading and editing various drafts of the manuscript.

In this project, the enormous intellectual support and inspiration of Professor Reinhard Margreiter deserve heartfelt thanks. His philosophical insights over

---

[1] As for the translation of original quatrains of Khayyam, I have translated the entire 143 *Rubais* from Sādiq Hedayat, *Tarāneh-hāye Khayyam*, (Tehran: Entesharat Javidan, 1934).

the course of the years, and in this book, in particular, have enriched my research and interpretation of intercultural philosophy as a whole.

In reading various chapters of the manuscript and guiding me to deeper and better arrangements of the ideas, I must sincerely thank Professor Graham Parkes—a prominent expert of Zen-Daoist and Nietzschean-Heideggerian philosophies—, who has taught in the US, Britain, Ireland and China. In addition, I am indebted to my intellectual mentor Professor Michael Morony, a veteran of Near Eastern Studies at UCLA, who read the Silk Road chapter and made very important suggestions. Professor Ramin Mojtabai, a professor of psychiatry and mental health at the department of Johns Hopkins University with an in-depth understanding of Persian culture and literature, deserves profound thanks for reading the entire therapeutic section of this book and making incisive recommendations. I am thankful to Dr. Ernest Abel, a psychiatrist, friend and former classmate at the Universität Innsbruck medical school, who read a segment of the therapeutic section and made constructive comments. I would also like to thank my dear colleague, Professor Marie-Luisa Frick, for her continuous intellectual encouragement.

I am profoundly grateful for the meticulous proofreading and correction of the manuscript in its entirety by my wonderful and respected friends, Virginia and Jean-Michel Bock. I must also thank Sydney Schardt for her valuable last-minute input about the book's title and subtitle. I never adequately thank my childhood friend, Dr. Asghar Feizi, for sharing ever-continuing and ever-inspiring conversations about the themes of every book or article I write. I am pleased to acknowledge and appreciate the years of vibrant communication and significant correspondence of ideas about the *Rubaiyat* of Khayyam with my long-time friend, Mrs. Shahrzad Esfarjani. The image of '*hich*' (nothingness) in this book is her artwork. It is absolutely my great pleasure to acknowledge Dr. Uta Maley, a wonderful friend, for her heartwarming support in my university and intellectual life.

In manifesting the project of this book, I must thank the enthusiastic support of Ellisa Anslow, Commissioning Editor, and Argiris Legatos, Editorial Manager and other team members at Vernon Press, for their diligence. Finally, the cover design, as well as the Persian calligraphy in the opening page of the book, are the expressive and artistic work of Foaad Farah, to whom I am grateful.

Mostafa Vaziri
Casablanca and Innsbruck - Spring 2021

Part I:
Interwoven Philosophies of Life

Chapter 1

A Nexus of Wisdom on the Silk Road

Prelude

In the eleventh-twelfth centuries, the region of Khurasan in northeastern Iran was the birthplace and home of Omar Khayyam, a brilliant polymath who specialized in algebra, geometry, physics, music theory, astronomy and meteorology. Renowned for his work in cubic equations as well as his development of a 1,000-year calendar, Khayyam was driven to describe existence scientifically and mathematically. But like many others, he yearned to understand the world philosophically. In pursuit of this endeavor, he dedicated himself to philosophy and expressed his deep realizations primarily through poetry.

Khayyam's celebrated work of poetry, the *Rubaiyat*, is made up of 143 quatrains (in S. Hedayat's version)[1] which probe why we are here, seeking rational explanations of nature while proclaiming a life joyfully lived as the ultimate significance. Even after almost nine hundred years, these poems are still impacting our understanding of the material world, inspiring our vision of existence, and modeling the psychology of living a worthwhile and positive life beyond the boundaries of religion and sectarianism. Any ethnic or religious labels such as "Arabic-Islamic philosophy," "Persian," or other faith-based attribution to Khayyam and his work should be considered suspect. In fact, his wisdom as offered in his *Rubaiyat* manifests the "Wisdom of the Silk Road," multifaceted, inclusive and cosmopolitan.

Khayyam lived in the vibrant city of Nishapur, a significant commercial, political and intellectual hub along the Silk Road. This location is not insignificant: in tracing the sources of inspiration and creativity in Khayyam's poetry and worldview, it behooves us to lay out three aspects relevant to his philosophy: First is to establish on an inferential basis how it was that the

---

[1] 143 quatrains according to the version of Saḍiq Hedayat, *Tarāneh-hāye Khayyam*, (Tehran: Entesharat Javidan1313/1934), which is used in the present book. On the question of the accurate number and in regards to the authenticity of some of the quatrains, Mehdi Aminrazavi deserves credit for saying it is not the messenger who is important here, but the significance of the message itself which we are dealing with. The Khayyamian School of Thought is being analyzed here, not necessarily the poet himself. Mehdi Aminrazavi, *The Wine of Wisdom: The Life, Poetry and Philosophy of Omar Khayyam*, (Oxford: Oneworld, 2007), 13–14, 97–8.

literati such as Khayyam of Central Asian cities were familiar with much older Greek, Chinese and Indian cultures and philosophies. From this connection, it can be inferred that the scientifically- and philosophically-inclined Khayyam of Nishapur most likely came in contact with those intellectual spheres.

The second aspect is to explore the role of Khayyam as a freethinker who was living at the nexus of tension between the religious establishment of the time and innovative thought. As has often happened throughout history, freethinkers try to disseminate new reflections while the conventional religious views consider such moves as heresy, dissent and threats to religion. This intellectually xenophobic attitude of the religious establishment existed during and after Khayyam's lifetime, and in fact, can still be seen today, thus lending Khayyam's life a very real and present-day significance.

Thirdly, we will analyze how Khayyam's brilliant and open mind interwove with his exposure to ancient philosophies that arose outside of yet passing through Nishapur, including Heraclitan philosophy, Daoism, Buddhism Nagarjuna and Upanishadic knowledge. Consequently, these philosophical elements manifested themselves in various ways in his worldview and his poetry. We will see how his natural tendencies toward freethinking in combination with influences from these ancient philosophies resulted in his powerful poetic, philosophical collection of quatrains, The *Rubaiyat*.

As a typical medieval poet, in composing the poems of his *Rubaiyat*, Khayyam did not provide precise references for the sources of his inspiration. Despite the fact that there are many excellent studies available today[2] analyzing Khayyam's biography and poetry, work investigating the *sources* of his intellectual inspirations is still pending. There is no concrete evidence; however, there are resemblances and relationships as suggestions of the influences of these more ancient philosophies on Khayyam's worldview. By utilizing primary sources in order to obtain the most direct interpretation of key concepts in the original works of Heraclitus, Zhuangzi, Nagarjuna, and the Upanishads, and by exploring inferential corroborations regarding the cultural and intellectual circumstances in Central Asia along the Silk Road, perhaps we can appreciate what may have led Khayyam to come under the influence of the ideas of Heraclitus, Zhuangzi, Nagarjuna and the Upanishads.

---

[2] The usual Avicennian or even Aristotelian philosophy is often speculated to be the basis of Khayyam's philosophical pondering; a speculation that can neither be substantiated nor corroborated with the themes of the *Rubaiyat*. It is worth mentioning a highly interesting and original reading and interpretation of Khayyam's *Rubaiyat*, undertaken by Reza Parchizadeh, *The Myth of Xayyam: A Study of Monologism in Persian Discourse*, Saarbrücken: VDM Verlag Dr. Müller GMbH & Co. KG, 2010.

Khayyam, a true child of the Silk Road

Nishapur lay in the center of greater Khurasan. During the Islamic period, Nishapur flourished and was the capital city in several dynasties. The city has an illustrious history that goes back to the Sassanid King Shahpur in the third century. Nishapur served both as a summer retreat, a strategic city on the trade route for collecting custom taxes, and a center for politico-military surveillance of Central Asian competitors. Throughout the centuries, Nishapur was consistently a critical junction point of routes that led off in different directions to destinations along the Silk Road. Caravans came from the east from Khotan and Yarkand, from Turfan and Aksu passing through Kashgar, and continuing to Kokand, Samarqand, Bukhara, and Merv before reaching Nishapur and then moving on toward Western Iran.

Caravans coming from the west came from the eastern Mediterranean regions, passing through Palmyra, Baghdad, Hamadan, Ray, and Sabzevar, then reaching Nishapur before continuing onwards to the east. Thus, this high-profile city of Nishapur in the eleventh century lay between the Indo-Chinese and the Western Asian and Eastern Mediterranean worlds, manifesting tolerance and multiculturalism, holding within it the long-lasting residues of Buddhism, Manichaeism, Hellenism and Indo-Chinese thought.

In Nishapur and Central Asian cities, philosophical and scientific books from the Hellenic and Indian worlds were readily obtainable. The rulers and patricians of Nishapur, in their support of the advancement of science, philosophy and literature and in competition with other important cities on the Silk Road, had to import many texts from the East and the West via the caravans. Works of Greek and Avicennian philosophies and Buddhist and Hindu topics in Soghdian, Uighur and Sanskrit languages were distributed as well as a number of such works in their Arabic and Persian translations (which are now lost to us). Books on Hinduism and Buddhism were available in Arabic and Persian before and during Khayyam's generation, such as al-Biruni's unique and comprehensive eleventh-century treatise on Indian religions. On the subject of Buddhism, the ninth century Abul Abbas Iranshahri and later authors, Marvazi and Gardizi,[3] all living in Central Asia and the eastern Iranian world, produced their Buddhist literature in Arabic and Persian.

Born in 1048, when Nishapur was at its cultural peak, Khayyam grew up in this cosmopolitan city where religious minorities lived, and caravans regularly brought political news and gossip of all sorts from neighboring lands and transported these unique books and treatises. Once Khayyam had become a

---

[3] For more details, see Mostafa Vaziri, *Buddhism in Iran: An Anthropological Approach to Traces and Influences* (New York & London: Palgrave Macmillan, 2012), 115, 138.

renowned scholar in the region, it is highly likely that he would have been among the first to be contacted by couriers as a reliable customer when new books of astronomy, algebra and philosophy arrived. Khayyam also spent time in Samarqand, another significant city situated on the Silk Road strongly associated with the Chinese culture in particular, and which may have also been a conduit for his exposure to texts on Greek, Chinese and Indian thought.

Early on, Khayyam was exposed to Greek philosophy and sciences, as evidenced by his mathematical work in which he fundamentally challenged Euclidean geometry. Someone like Khayyam, who was interested in understanding the order of the world and the laws governing the universe through mathematics, often turned to philosophy when exploring such questions. Questions about space and geometric order led Khayyam to probe Euclidean geometry, and he took on mathematics and physics essentially to achieve a philosophical goal rather than a mathematical one.[4] He presented a theorem and more proofs on non-Euclidean geometry and expanded on cubic equations. In a similarly mathematical style, Khayyam presented a philosophical solution to an age-old human existential problem.

Given that he spent some years in both Samarqand and Isfahan for his successful scientific research on establishing a precise solar calendar, he had extensive access to libraries in those cities. His scientific and inquisitive mind must have led him to study different rational philosophies as well, particularly the principal schools of his time, namely Greek, Indian and most likely Chinese.

As much as innovative ideas and books were ubiquitous and accessible in the cities of Central Asia, rough times for multiculturalism had already begun after the tenth century, when the iconoclastic Muslim Saffarid and Ghaznavid dynasties in Khurasan and throughout the Indo-Iranian world began purging Hindu-Buddhist temples in the area.[5] This was a harbinger of things to come for freethinkers in the region, especially those in Khurasan who dared to target or deviate from Islam. The final blow to freethinking would come from the Seljuqs of the eleventh-twelfth centuries, during the tumultuous days of Seljuq domination when terror and fear were part of the politics of the day.

Thus, as a freethinker, Khayyam was born into a generation that was running against time. Yet despite the risks, radical intellectuality continued to challenge

---

[4] Aminrazavi, *The Wine of Wisdom*, 188-190. Khayyam could be seen as the combination of Isaac Newton and John Locke; his mathematical and intellectual conceptions opened the mind to a universe governed by laws that should be applied to life itself, as they cannot be broken or swayed by one's arbitrary beliefs.

[5] Vaziri, *Buddhism in Iran*, 26.

Islam's parochialism in the cosmopolitan and multicultural cities of the Silk Road. Khayyam, with his celibate, vegetarian lifestyle and distinctive personality, belonged to the counterculture of his generation. Even as a first-generation Muslim,[6] being the son of a Zoroastrian convert to Islam, there is no trace of Khayyam's alleged paternal Zoroastrianism or of Islam in his poetry. In actual fact, neither his nonconformist lifestyle nor his quatrains represented Islamic views or etiquette. It is not surprising then that after his death, when his quatrains came to light, Khayyam became a target of Muslim criticism as reflected in Islamic chronicles such as the thirteenth-century work by al-Qifti, which we shall see below. The tension was very strong between Islamic doctrine and the freethinking represented by Khayyam.

Figure 1: Map of the Silk Road.

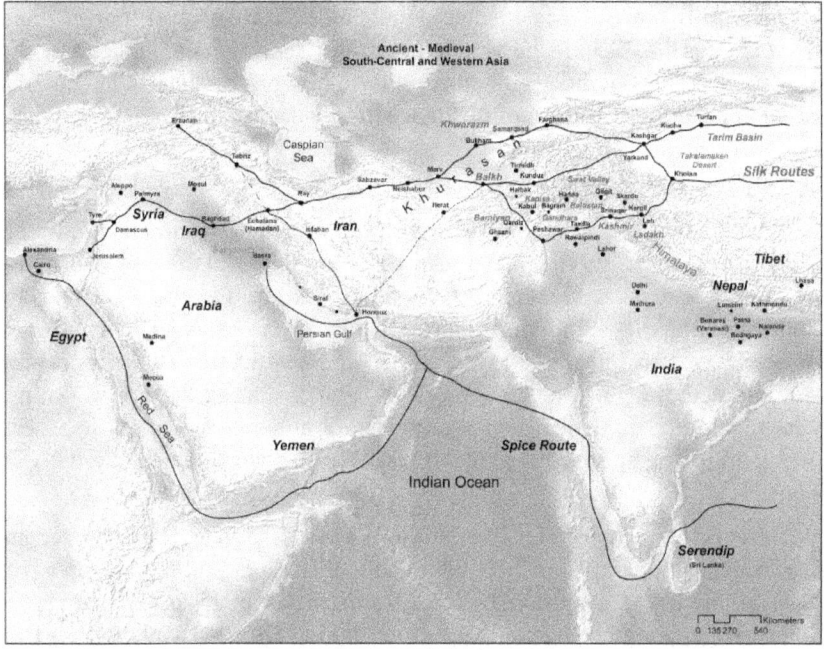

---

[6] Aminrazavi, *The Wine of Wisdom*, 19, Omar Ali Shah based on his contentious manuscript claims Khayyam was a Sufi master, and asserts that he was born to Afghan parents from a Sufi community of Balkh. C. E. Bowen, "The Rubā'iyyāt of Omar Khayyam: A Critical Assessment of Robert Graves' and Omar Ali Shah's Translation," *Iran: British Institute of Persian Studies* 11 (1973): 63-73, Bowen debunks all the arbitrary assertions made by Omar Ali Shah and R. Graves; see also Aminrazavi, *The Wine of Wisdom*, 154-156.

Khayyam was perhaps one of the last of the iconoclastic logicians who rebelled against monolithic and repressive beliefs; being born into a region suffused with diverse religious and philosophical ideas, he relied upon the solidity of science and mathematics in developing his advanced theories and ideas. But growing up in an age of great fear and uncertainty about the future, Khayyam also composed rational poetry which embodied the impermanency of shifting existence, the joy of life and the logic of no life after death—poems which he had to hide until his death. For his generation, he championed Process Philosophy, looking at the unceasingly shifting nature of the world; a world with no absolute fixity in date or station, espousing a philosophy that had been initiated by Heraclitus, Zhuangzi and Nagarjuna, centuries earlier and thousands of kilometers away. Khayyam, the scientist and thinker, leaned towards intellectually inclusive rather than exclusively religious views. In achieving his aims, Khayyam met significant challenges and indeed often feared for his life. Despite the tumult, Khayyam was successful in blending the flowing Hellenic, Buddhist, and other philosophies on the Silk Road before the era of philosophical and scientific silence took over Nishapur and the region.

Trade, politics and philosophies along the Silk Road

In order to fully appreciate the richness of the cultural environment into which Khayyam was born, it is helpful to take an in-depth look at the history of some important exchanges and interactions along and around the Silk Road. By understanding the vibrant and colorful history of the region in the centuries before Khayyam's birth, one can begin to see how the area had been deeply suffused with the powerful human phenomena of sharing, arguing, debating, challenging, and influencing, arising out of trade and military conquests as well as scientific and spiritual pursuits. It was into this world that Khayyam was born.

The geography of the Silk Road in Central Asia of most interest to us covers many key regions along the ancient Silk Road, including present-day areas of northeastern Iran, Afghanistan, Turkmenistan, Uzbekistan, Tajikistan, Kazakhstan and their periphery in Uighur China (Turkistan), Gilgit (Pakistan), and western Kashmir. It was in this complex geography that much of the constructive exchanges and interactions, particularly among the intelligentsia and artists of Iran, Central Asia, China and India, took place. It created a kind of Silk Road pluralism that can still be detected in the background today.[7]

---

[7] See Bert G. Fragner, "Iran, Zentralasien und die Seidenstraße – universalgeschichtliche Überlegungen," in: *Spektrum Iran* 1993 (vol. 6, fasc. 4), 59.

But first, we can acknowledge that it has been persuasively argued that the romantic notion of a single 'Silk Road' is a nineteenth-century European construction. It is true that the term *Seidenstraße* (Silk Road) was coined in 1877 by the German geographer and traveler, Ferdinand von Richthofen (d. 1905), and the criticism against the romantic fascination of an imaginary Silk Road as a unit of study in academia may be justified, along with acknowledgment of the idea that an actual "Silk Road" is not an extra or separate extension of world history.[8] It is also true that this overland trans-Asiatic trade route was never a singular "road." The term "Silk Road" is also anachronous for the eleventh century C.E. It is unlikely that silk was actually still being exported from China to Iran as late as the eleventh century C.E., when it would be no longer appropriate to call it a "silk" road.

As much as it is true that the term 'road' is thus perhaps too specific for a heterogeneous entity too amorphous to have its own distinct historiography,[9] it can be a useful metaphor or image. The central argument is that the roads were used for the diffusion of ideas by the pilgrims, especially between India and China, book traders, artists and others who most likely traveled on the same route as merchants. As a result, this "road" can be conventionally referred to as Silk Road and can be thought of as a cultural conduit that made the transfer of various thoughts and civilizations from one region to another possible over centuries. It is from this perspective that we will utilize the term "Silk Road" in this work.

Perhaps it is helpful to consider the Silk Road as a sort of constellation of cities of high culture as pivot points of intellectual discourse. The Silk Road served as a corridor of exchange in much the same way that the peak of Western scientific and intellectual development in the nineteenth century unfolded along amorphous corridors, in the way that the latest scientific and intellectual ideas were exchanged among Paris, London, Leipzig, Weimar, Berlin, Vienna, New York and Chicago. Through such corridors of creativity, whether on the old Silk Road or in modern Western cities, the intelligentsia of the time could influence and be influenced by sharing books, ideas, and dialogues, even when living far from each other. Consequently, although the Silk Road is traditionally and historically famous as a trade route, and trade did indeed often seem to be the primary activity on the Silk Road, in fact, cultures interacted, and ideas actively melded in the background.

---

[8] Khodadad Rezakhani, "The Road That Never Was: The Silk Road and Trans-Eurasian Exchange," *Comparative of South Asia, Africa and the Middle East* 30/3 (2010): 420-433.
[9] Ibid., 423.

On the façade, for example, the Silk Road trade in Chinese exports of apricot-colored and white porcelain which poured into Iran by the ninth century[10] and the Uighur miniature motifs that were sold in Nishapur seemed like entirely commercial ventures. But such trade, in fact, became the impetus for traders of China to settle down in the areas of the Silk Road, bringing their cultures with them.[11] Thus these caravans coming and going to distant lands, as H. W. Haussig puts it, transported not only their material products but also their immaterial culture and civilizations indirectly.[12] The trade corridor became a cultural and philosophical corridor.

1. Pre-Islamic intermingling

Through the centuries, commerce across the Silk Road, particularly the trade between China and Central Asia, brought about demographic and cultural changes. For example, commerce between the Sassanid Empire of Iran and China in the fifth and sixth centuries brought goods from the western territories and Iranian provinces into the heart of China.[13] This commercial channel also opened the way for Zoroastrianism, the official religion of the Sassanid Empire, to arrive in China early in the sixth century, during which time Zoroastrianism attained a degree of official recognition in northern China.[14] Over time, the rearrangement and intermixing of populations resulted in the relocation of a large number of Central Asian Soghdian people to Tang China by the eighth century.[15]

More consequential than Zoroastrianism in China was the arrival of Manichaeism via the Silk Road. A form of hybrid doctrine between Christianity and Buddhism founded in the third century by the prophet Mani, Manichaeism would have an enormous religious influence in Asia, even though it would ultimately become an extinct religion.

---

[10] J. M. Rogers, "Chinese-Iranian Relations ii. Islamic Period to the Mongols," *Encyclopedia Iranica* Vol. V, Fasc. 4 (December 15, 1991, October 14, 2011): 431-434.

[11] Hans Wilhelm Haussig, *Die Geschichte Zentralasiens und der Seidenstraße in islamischer Zeit*, (Darmstadt: Wissenschaftliche Buchgesellschaft, 1988), 18, 91.

[12] Ibid., 125, 230, 252.

[13] Edwin G. Pulleyblank, "Chinese-Iranian Relations i. In Pre-Islamic Times," *Encyclopedia Iranica*, Vol. V, Fasc. 4, (December 15, 1991; October 14, 2011): 424-431.

[14] Ibid., see also, Jacques Gernet, *A History of Chinese Civilization*, (New York: Cambridge University Press, 1982), 283, 286.

[15] Kevin van Bladel, "Eighth-Century Indian Astronomy in the Two Cities of Peace," in *Islamic Cultures, Islamic Contexts: Esaays in Honor of Professor Patricia Crone*, edited by Behnam Sadeghi, Asad Q. Ahmed, Adam Silverstein, Robert Hoyland, 257-294, (Leiden: Brill, 2014,) 270.

It was geographical proximity that led to the extensive intermingling of Buddhism and Manichaeism in China and Tibet,[16] and the cross-influences with Daoism (developed into Zen-Buddhism) slowly became more evident. Via the Silk Road, the influential Manichaean doctrine was brought into Uighur regions (western China) and then into China in the sixth century C.E. Upon the conversion of the Uighurs from Buddhism to Manichaeism, Manichaean temples were slowly established in different cities of China.[17] In order for the Manichaeans to integrate into Daoist Tang China, the process of syncretism began, with their prophet Mani depicted as the re-manifestation of Laozi, the founder of Daoism and Manichaeans sometimes presenting themselves as Daoists and other later times as Buddhists. Manichaeans sustained their survival in China as an underground cult, at times existing under the guise of Buddhism. Even though Manichaeism, as a widespread and yet ultimately doomed religion, expanded among Chinese populations and court elites and endured for almost 800 years (possibly as late as the sixteenth century[18]), it gradually survived only in small pockets throughout the land before fading away completely.[19]

Manichaeism was quite strong in Central Asia for centuries. Initially, the persecution of the Manichaeans by the Sassanid dynasty of the third century in Iran pushed this community to Central Asia (as well as North Africa). Manichaeans maintained their stronghold in Nishapur and Samarqand until the tenth-eleventh centuries when Nishapur was one of the main eastern Iranian centers, which was gradually purged of Manichaeism.[20] Consequently, most of Manichaeism's patriarchs and adherents headed toward China and Tibet.[21]

As the Silk Road became a conduit for the movement of missionaries and the flight of ideas from one region to another, the development of additional syncretic movements took shape. Bodhidharma was a legendary personality in

---

[16] Barrett, "Tang Taoism and the Mention of Jesus and Mani in Tibetan Zen," 56-58.

[17] Sammuel L.C. Lieu, "Manicheism vi. in China," *Encyclopædia Iranica*, (2002). http://www.iranicaonline.org/articles/manicheism-v-in-china-1. (Accessed December 4, 2020).

[18] See David Scott, "Manichaean Views of Buddhism," *History of Religion* 25/2 (November 1985), 114.

[19] Pulleyblank, "Chinese-Iranian Relations i."

[20] Dinavari Manichaean groups concentrated in Samarqand and Nishapur, see Werner Sundermann, "Dīnāvarīya," *Encyclopaedia Iranica*, (1995/ Last Updated: November 28, 2011). (Accessed December 2010/ and November 25, 2020). For discussion of cross-influences between Manichaeism and Buddhism, see Vaziri, *Buddhism in Iran*, chapter 3.

[21] T. H. Barrett, "Tang Taoism and the Mention of Jesus and Mani in Tibetan Zen: A Comment on Recent Work by Rong Xinjiang," *Bulletin of the School of Oriental and African Studies* 66/1 (Feb. 2003): 56-58.

the sixth century who single-handedly spearheaded the combining of philosophies. As a 'Buddhist-Daoist' monk who arrived in China around 520 C.E. from India, or perhaps Central Asia[22] (possibly explaining why he was known as the "blue-eyed bearded monk"), he innovated through his teachings a hybrid of Buddhism and Daoism. From the end results of his effort, we learn that Bodhidharma must have mastered Buddhism and Daoism in the form of a new path called Chan (Zen). The melding of the two schools of philosophy aimed to put the mind (Buddhism) in harmony with nature and effortless existence (Daoism). Bodhidharma lived in China for nine years, where he became known as the first Zen patriarch.[23]

Only the presence of a conduit for the flow of thoughts and ideas such as the Silk Road corridor explains how Bodhidharma may have had a knowledge of Daoism outside of mainland China. It could be that the Daoist Tang imperial rule shared borders with Buddhist Central Asia and Kashmir, facilitating the awareness and study of Buddhism and Daoism by the adepts such as Bodhidharma in Central Asia or northern India.

Bodhidharma may be seen as a sort of predecessor of Khayyam. Both men benefitted from the exchanges among schools of thought in the region, ultimately combining different philosophical traditions and distilling them down to a few concise and inspiring concepts—short stanzas. This is to say, neither Bodhidharma, the pioneering Zen patriarch, nor Khayyam, the metaphorically masterful poet, seemed to need lengthy, pedantic discourses to transmit their teachings.

Another very significant culture and philosophy exchanged via the corridors of the Silk Road was Buddhism itself. Buddhist art and philosophy evolved and spread throughout the Central Asian region and along the Silk Road between the first and eighth centuries. Many aspects of Buddhism that we associate with

---

[22] The legendary Bodhidharma, credited with bringing new meditational techniques to China in 520 C.E. Founding Chan (Zen) Buddhis in China, Bodhidharma is believed to have come from the Iranized areas of Central Asia; either Soghdiana or Khotan. See, Jeffrey L. Broughton, *The Bodhidharma Anthology: The Earliest Records of Zen*, (Los Angeles, Berkeley: University of California Press, 1999), 54. See also, Vaziri, *Buddhism in Iran*, 22.

[23] The bridging of Buddhism and Daoism in China during the Tang (618-906) and the Song (960-1279) dynasties continued, resulting in the propagation of Chan/Zen Buddhism until the Mongol invasion in the thirteenth century, when the centers of Zen were transferred to Japan. (The Tang dynasty, however, underwent a doctrinal swing, at one point favoring the popular Buddhism and then around the middle of the ninth century launching a crushing campaign against it.). See Book Review by Alan K. L. Chan, *Taoism Under the T'ang: Religion and Empire During the Golden Age of Chinese History* by T. H. Barrett in *China Review International* 7/2 (Fall 2000): 392-395. See also: https://www.britannica.com/topic/Buddhism/Central-Asia-and-China. (Accessed November 23, 2020).

today, in fact, arose out of the Central Asian region and had an enormous influence on that area at the time. Innovations in art and iconography in Buddhism were the outcome of the fusing of Indian with Greek and Persian art styles in a school of art known as Gandhara in Taxila, in present-day northwestern Pakistan near southeastern Afghanistan. Innovating the classic representational statue of the Buddha in a seated lotus position and in standing positions was the creative work of the Gandhara school. It was in the same region, near the Swat Valley, that great Buddhist philosophers and yogis such as the fourth century's Vasubandhu and Asanga shaped the Yogacara sub-school of Mahayana Buddhism, and eventually developed Buddhist psychology on a more concrete level. The famous master Padmasambhava, also from the Swat Valley, was an important Tantric and Yoga master who systematized Vajrayana Buddhism, which he later successfully established in Tibet around the mid-700s.

Buddhist thinkers and missionaries traveling to and from the Silk Road cities of Peshawar, Kapisa, and Balkh to the Swat Valley and its periphery engaged the Buddhist adepts in debates between the sub-schools of Mahayana, namely Yogacara and Madhyamika (whose founder was Nagarjuna, to be discussed in Chapter 4). The influence of the work of these thinkers can be felt even today in modern Buddhism - the impact of their revolutionary philosophies must have been massive in the region at the time.

The flow of both material and immaterial elements from China to Turkistan, Central Asia and later to the Near East took on great significance in post-Sassanid times and during the early Islamic period. By the eighth century, the looming presence of the mighty Chinese Tang Dynasty at the borders of Central Asia was as much about politics as it was about the trade of porcelain, silk, and paper. Ultimately, border clashes between Chinese and Muslim armies led to the victory of the Muslims (under General Ziad ibn Saleh) over the Chinese at Taraz (Talas) east of Samarqand in the year 751. The battle of Talas resulted in the permeation and transfer of the Chinese paper industry to Samarqand.[24] Then following the battle of Talas, Abu Muslim, the Central Asian hero of the revolution against the Umayyad Caliphate in Damascus, in 754, having heard of immense wealth and industry in that land, considered invading China via Kashgar, but the invasion never happened.[25]

Despite this tension, diplomatic relations between the Caliphate of Baghdad and the Tang dynasty survived. The exchange of embassies and cultural gifts

---

[24] Reported in *Laṭā'ef al-ma'āref* by *Ṭa'ālebī* (d. 429/1038; p. 140), quoted in, Rogers, "Chinese-Iranian Relations ii. Islamic Period to the Mongols," 431-434.
[25] van Bladel, "Eighth-Century Indian Astronomy," 267-8. ' a'

continued even to the point where astronomy was imported all the way to Baghdad from China.[26] Later Baghdad court astrologers, Nawbakht and Abu Sahl, mention the knowledge of Chinese and Indian astronomers, especially noting the Indian master astrologer Gautama Siddhartha who had come up with a new calendar rendering Sanskrit terms of the planets and had established scientific methods in the Tang court.[27] So even during tumultuous political episodes, the productivity of intellectuals, artists and scientists continued as caravan traders transported books, treatises, and other goods east and west.

2. Intermingling after 700 C.E.

For most of its history, Central Asia has been an epicenter and collection point for rich philosophical ideas. The transport to and translation of Indian and Central Asian texts in Baghdad in the late eighth and early ninth centuries invigorated the intellectual and scientific atmosphere in both the Near East and Central Asia. This was facilitated by a politically powerful family in Baghdad, the Tokharian Barmakids. This family had close ancestral ties to Central Asia, having originally come from Buddhist Kashmir and Balkh during the sixth to seventh centuries. It was under the supervision of the Barmakid family and Central Asian artists that the new capital of the Abbasid Caliphate, Baghdad, was established in 762 C.E. Year later in Baghdad, it would be this Central Asian family that sponsored the delivery and translation of texts from Central Asia and India to Baghdad, including Buddhist texts. This transference also enhanced the expansion of different kinds of sciences and the introduction of Buddhism into the Islamic world from Balkh and Kashmir to Baghdad:[28]

> "The Buddhist ancestry of the Barmakids seems to have stimulated interest in Indian sciences during the age of translation in Baghdad in the late 8th century. Yahyā [Barmaki] became even more successful than his father, Khālid, and sponsored Sanskrit translation in the 'Abbāsid court at Baghdad, motivated in part by a personal interest in Indian and Buddhist work."[29]

---

[26] Ibid., 266.
[27] Ibid., 277-9.
[28] Kevin van Bladel, "The Bactrian Background of the Barmakids," in *Islam and Tibet— Interactions along the Musk Routes*, edited by Anna Akasoy, Charles Burnett, and Ronit Yoeli-Tlalim, 43–88, (Surrey: Ashgate, 2011).
[29] van Bladel, "The Bactrian Background of the Barmakids," 74-86, quoted by Vaziri, *Buddhism in Iran*, 96.

The reach of Central Asia appears in other curious ways. In fact, the name that the caliph al-Mansur originally gave to his new capital in 762 C.E. was not Baghdad, but *Madinat as-Salam* (The City of Peace). However, this Arabic-Islamic name for the city would not stick. The choice of site for the capital was, in fact, not even in the Arab heartland but was near Ctesiphon, the old capital of the Sassanid Empire, where Baghdad was already the name of a market town (monthly market) in the Sassanid period.[30] And even more surprising for an Islamic city, the name that took precedence over the Arabic "*Madinat as-Salam*" had Iranian-Asian connotations: the word 'bagh' (*bhag*) in both Middle Persian and Sanskrit means 'god,' and 'dad' (*daad*) means 'gift' (given)—a rather non-Arabic, non-Islamic choice for the name of the city where the new caliphs were supposed to begin their preaching and carrying out of Islamic affairs.

The intellectual connections between Central Asia and the Islamic world were strong for several decades, with extensive translations of Indian and Soghdian scientific and philosophical works, as well as the Greek books (translated by the Christian Syrians who knew Greek and Arabic), undertaken in the *Bayt al-Hikam* (the Center of Knowledge 'and Translation') in Baghdad, under the directorship of the astute and qualified philosopher, al-Kindi (d. 873). The selection of translated books ranged from topics on mathematics (especially the Indian numeral system), medicine (*Carakasamhitā*, or The Compendium of Caraka),[31] and Buddhist philosophy and Buddha legends.[32] Many such books were written in Sanskrit and other Central Asian languages, which were then translated into Arabic.

The propagation of Hellenic philosophical and scientific works in the Islamic world also picked up momentum, with a widespread translation movement beginning in the eighth century. Soon after its distribution via the Silk Road, the Hellenic philosophical tradition, particularly that of Aristotle, was elaborated and commented upon by philosophers of Baghdad and Central Asia such as al-Kindi (d. 873), al-Farabi (d. 951) and Avicenna (d. 1037). The intellectually vibrant atmosphere of philosophical debate and scientific inquiries from the ninth through twelfth centuries marked an important period of history in the Near East and Central Asia.

---

[30] Michael Morony, "Iraq i. In the Late Sasanid and Early Islamic Eras," *Encyclopædia Iranica*, Vol. XIII, Fasc. 5, pp. 543-550, available online at: https://www.iranicaonline.org/articles/iraq-i-late-sasanid-early-islamic. (Accessed March 15, 2021).
[31] Dominik Wujastyk, "From Balkh to Baghdad: Indian Science and the Birth of the Islamic Golden Age in the Eighth Century," *Indian Journal of History of Science* (December 2016), 3.
[32] See Vaziri, *Buddhism in Iran*, 43-46.

After the tenth century, the political and intellectual decline of Baghdad began. At the same time, the surrogate and fanatical Muslim dynasties strengthening in the eastern Iranian and Central Asian territories in the tenth and eleventh centuries became a greater and greater threat to the region's scientists and philosophers, causing the gradual decline of Balkh, Bukhara, Samarqand, Herat, Nishapur and other cities that once flourished along the Silk Road.[33]

The decline of Indian philosophies including Vedanta, Shaivism, and Buddhism as well as the waning of Zoroastrianism, Mazdakism, Neoplatonism, Pantheism, and Buddhism in Central Asia and Nishapur[34] were also due to the rise of Islam, and the large-scale conversion to Islam largely replaced such philosophies and traditions. For example, at the time of Omar Khayyam, the population in his city of Nishapur was still mainly Zoroastrian, Christian, Jewish, or possibly even Buddhist,[35] but the Turkish Seljuq dynasty of the eleventh through twelfth centuries in the Eastern Iranian and Central Asian territories began the persecution of many Buddhists, Manichaeans, and Christians, sending them underground.[36]

Despite such persecution and the resulting limited physical presence beyond the eleventh century in Central Asia, remnants of Buddhism continued to influence the Central Asian and Iranian world, still existing but under an Islamic guise with the term 'Buddhist' having been rendered unmentionable in Islamic sources.[37]

3. A Golden Age, with or without Islam?

The era encompassing the ninth to twelfth centuries, with so many remarkable achievements in science and philosophy, is commonly known as the "Islamic Golden Age." This classical orientalist designation of an "Islamic Golden Age" or "Islamic Civilization" is often used to represent the achievements of Islamic lands versus Christian lands, yet is remarkably imprecise. Such labels ignore

---

[33] When the decline became inevitable in Central Asia and the Islamic world altogether, the appearance of scientists and astronomers in later centuries such as Nasir al-Din Tusi (d. 1274) and Ulugh Beg (d. 1449) (both from Khurasan), were rather scattered and disjointed scientific endeavors with so much gaps and interruptions between them.
[34] Rothfeld, Otto. *Umar Khayyam and His Age*, (Bombay: D. B. Taraporevala Sons & Co. 1922), 20-22.
[35] Richard Bulliet, *The Patricians of Nishapur: A Study in Medieval Islamic Social History*, (Cambridge: Harvard University Press, 1972), 15.
[36] Richard N. Frye, *Bukhara: The Medieval Achievement*, (Norman: University of Oklahoma Press, 1965), 115.
[37] See Vaziri, *Buddhism in Iran*, chapters, 4, 5, 6 and 8.

the fact that many of the achievements and innovations of the time stemmed from outside the Islamic doctrinal domain. In fact, such advances often lacked any sort of "Islamic" component in an accurate sense. Implementing a more realistic historical and anthropological perspective entails assessing what various Muslim people have done throughout history, rather than what "Islam" per se has done. Islam doesn't act. People do.

Furthermore, these haughty designations gave more ammunition to the propagators of Islam conceived in modern times to appropriate the history of sciences such as medicine, mathematics, astronomy, musical sciences, as well as philosophy and mystical practices, claiming that such advances belonged to the ingenuity of original Islam. In fact, they stemmed from foreign sources in Central Asia, Iran, India, China, Greece and elsewhere. Certainly, between the tenth and twelfth centuries, genius mathematicians, astronomers, clinicians, musicologists, and philosophers in the Islamic world drew upon translations of "foreign" treatises to generate new edifices of science and philosophy. However, although this work occurred in lands controlled by Muslims, the work itself was not Islamic per se. Prominent scholars in Central Asia and culturally significant cities of the Silk Road who were towering prodigies in math and science such as al-Khwarizmi, al-Farabi, Avicenna, al-Biruni and Omar Khayyam, all happened to be living in an Islamic environment, but their work was largely unrelated to Islam or their own Muslim identity.

The label of the "Islamic Golden Age" can instead most accurately refer to a period of Baghdad's free atmosphere of intellectuality with only two tolerant caliphs, Harun al-Rashid (the fifth Abbasid caliph, born in Rayy, Iran) and al-Mamun (the seventh Abbasid caliph, born in Baghdad), who altogether reigned from just 786 to 833. Under their brief patronages, the massive translation movement took place, translating ancient Greek and Indian treatises into Arabic.

Certainly, this movement was a tremendous contribution to the world of science, literature, and philosophy. But after this period, with the decline of tolerance in Baghdad and the rise of fanatical surrogate dynasties in the eastern territories, many scientists, philosophers and mystics often clashed with the champions of puritan Islam in the Islamic heartland. Hence in actual fact, the multi-century claim of an "Islamic Golden Age" is a misleading characterization since it was almost exclusively due to the openness of those two progressive caliphs whose governments lasted just forty-seven years.

Fragmented scientific, philosophical, and medical innovations continued to occur in a scattered fashion, initially tolerated by the Islamic Abbasid Caliphate. But gradually, the powerful grip of Islamic theologians slowly and steadily tightened, and those imported, translated foreign texts came under closer critical scrutiny. Such texts began to be seen as heretical, clashing with

Islamic monotheism and prophecy. Ultimately, scholastic Islam purged and banned many of the translated materials in a move towards censorship. And this restriction of thought would soon spread outwards. Even before the invasion of the Mongols in the thirteenth century, the rise of Islamic conformism in the cities of Balkh, Bukhara, Samarqand, Herat and Nishapur had already precipitated their fateful cultural decline.[38]

Great thinkers in these Central Asian regions read the translated treatises in Arabic, drawing upon them and writing their own discoveries also in Arabic. But they and their non-religion-based works were far removed from the "Islamic" world of state-sponsored theologians. One could say that these geniuses were the agents of a Central Asian Enlightenment, not the products of an "Islamic" or "Arab" Golden Age. Frederick Starr (2015), in his scholarly book on the Central Asian Enlightenment, introduces a significant paradigm shift, covering the resourcefulness of the area in trade, culture, science and civilization between the eighth and twelfth centuries.[39] Starr strengthens the argument that, in fact, it was a Central Asian Golden Age that was appropriated and was given an Islamic or Arabic label.

In other words, those who wrote their scientific, literary and philosophical works in Arabic in far distant lands like Central Asia during the almost 500-year-rule of the Abbasids of Baghdad should not be cataloged under the obsolete label of an Arab or Islamic "Golden Age." So many of these thinkers belonged to the outskirts of the non-Arabic-speaking geography, and some may have only nominally been Muslims, some perhaps even not at all. At times, many of them were barely tolerated in the Muslim world for their research and scientific inquiry. Some were even harassed or executed by the Muslim autocrats, and often their nonconformist philosophical works were destroyed or went missing. It therefore demands taking a new perspective when looking at the history and thriving cultures of Central Asia, thousands of kilometers away from the center of Islam. The work of these great thinkers should not be labeled "Islamic" any more than the work of Isaac Newton should be labeled "Christian." This makes perfect sense when considering, for example, the work of Omar Khayyam, whose genius in math as well as his poetry and philosophical thinking were not at all along Islamic doctrinal lines.

---

[38] See footnote 33.
[39] Frederick Starr, *Lost Enlightenment: Central Asia's Golden Age from the Arab Conquest to Tamerlane,* (Princeton, NJ: Princeton University Press, 2015). 'Arab' or 'Arabic' should be viewed as uniquely designations for those who wrote their works in Arabic language, not ethnic. But often times, in modern-Orientalist scholarships, the term 'Arab' for the medieval Islamic period has erroneously been regarded as an ethnic designation in order to have it contrast with the Persian ethnic group – in either case, it's misplaced.

The transmission of Central Asia's ancient cultural richness during the Islamic period, when Arabic had become the lingua franca throughout a decentralized political geography, in modern times misled a large group of social scientists, modern orientalists included, to concoct the concept of an "Islamic-Arab" golden age. Some other orientalists preferred to distinguish the Central Asian achievements under the designation of "Iranian" as opposed to "Arab"—a narrative that is also highly misleading and anachronistically nationalistic, and its linear historical construction is nothing but imagined and illusive.[40] In retrospect, Central Asia was an area that, long before the coming of Islam, had been a bedrock of intellectual and cultural richness;[41] Islam did not make it so.

It is remarkable to note that the native Arabic speakers of the Arabian Peninsula, where Islam and the Arabic-language Koran are believed to have originated, hardly took part in the translation movement or in the innovation of scientific and philosophical ideas. The earliest Arab-Muslim military conquests seemingly demonstrate little but pillaging, taking slaves (*mawali*—slaves of non-Arab origin) and burning libraries, even though initially some biased historians and chroniclers took the liberty of painting a positively glowing and pious picture of such invaders.

Pure Islam did not begin its history with philosophy, sciences and music; all these subjects were imported into the Islamic world from foreign sources, in a sense rescuing Islam from its rudimentary parochialism. But to reconcile such foreign ideas with the rigid Islamic doctrinaires required clever ways of fusing these imported ideas with Islam. As one example among many, tying the ideas of Greek rationalism together with the notion of the revelation in Islam became a popular innovation among clever thinkers, giving rise to the Mu'tazila school of thought in Iraq between the eighth and tenth centuries.

But with the passage of time and the growing rigidity within Islam, any such innovative ideas (*bid'ah*) that came from outside of religion were judged to have violated the precepts of pure Islam and were therefore subject to punishment according to the jurists and scholastic leaders. Gradually, authors of all sorts began avoiding the mention of any foreign or imported sources in their works in order to avoid the label of *bid'ah* (unless they were actually refuting these

---

[40] See Mostafa Vaziri, *Iran as Imagined Nation: The Construction of National Identity*, (New Jersey: Gorgias Press, 2013; first published New York: Paragon House, 1993).

[41] Frederick Starr in a YouTube interview provides a criticism and the shortcoming of his own book, pointing to the fact that he should have expanded the narrative of his book prior to the 8th century despite the paucity of historical documents. For his interview see https://www.youtube.com/watch?v=RymZTJmUEAw&t=1026s. (Accessed January 6, 2021).

foreign ideas). Therein lies the contradiction: on the one hand, Islam would have liked to take credit for the achievements of the scholars from the so-called Golden Age, but on the other hand, these scholars' innovative ingenuities (*bid'ah*) in science, music, philosophy and art were considered antithetical and heretical.

In a move that cast a pall on free thought, labels such as *kufr* (unbelief), *kāfir* (unbeliever), *ertidād* (apostasy) and *murtadd* (apostate) in Islam[42] began to be applied to literati, even though arbitrarily against those who had not been publicly tried and branded as an apostate. Guidelines were laid out by the ninth-century theological schools of Shafei and Hanbali and modified in the eleventh century by al-Ghazali, which explained exactly how to assess the levels of unbelief expressed by Muslim thinkers and how such thinkers would then be subject to condemnation as apostates.[43] According to the scholastic Sufi-theologian and contemporary compatriot of Khayyam, al-Ghazali (d. 1111), philosophy itself represented a deviation from accepting the Muslim faith;[44] therefore, a suspicion of apostasy was seen as imminent with the practice of philosophical thinking and writing. This harsh position taken against the philosophers and even mathematicians, chemists, and scientists in the Islamic world meant that either scholars would be at dangerous odds with local jurists and central theocratic authorities, or free intellectuality had to be abandoned altogether. It became clear that forcing the choice of abandoning a scientific career in Iran and Central Asia made the religious enthusiasts bolder. Due to Sunni and Shi'i jurists such as Ahmad ibn Hanbal, Musa Nowbakhti, Imam Shafi'i, Ahmad ibn Thawabah, al-Ghazali, Jahiz, and several other theologians, declaring logic, mathematics, geometry, astronomy and even medicine to be works of evil that interfere with God's will, these sciences came to a halt, and Khayyam found himself in the middle of this dogmatic war against scientific methods and intellectualism.[45] After these consequential *fatwas*, the world of Islam said goodbye to sciences and gradually entered into the period of dark ages.

---

[42] For a historical perspective on apostasy in Islam, see David Cook, "Apostasy from Islam: A Historical Perspective," *Jerusalem Studies in Arabic and Islam* 31 (2006): 248-288.
[43] Frank Griffel, "Toleration and exclusion: al-Shāfi'ī and al-Ghazālī on the treatment of apostates," *Bulletin of the School of Oriental and African Studies* 64/3 (Oct., 2001): 339-354.
[44] Ibid., 339-340.
[45] Mehdi Aminrazavi, "Reading the Rubā'iyyāt as "Resistance Literature"," in *The Great 'Umar Khayyām: A Global Reception of the Rubáiyát*, A. A. Seyed Ghorab (editor), 39-53, (Leiden: Leiden University Press, 2012), 41.

Thus, the Islamic prophetic saying exhorting Muslims to seek knowledge even if they have to bear the burden of journeying to China—a saying which had been used to justify the past translation movement—was no longer accepted or valid. Instead, this useful prophetic saying was replaced by another convenient saying from the prophet in order to enforce faith and eradicate scientific inquiries: "There is no benefit in the science of medicine, and no truth lies in the science of geometry, the science of logic and natural sciences are heretical, and those practicing them are heathens."[46] This anti-scientific attitude would ultimately block the patronage of the sciences all the way up and down the Silk Road, even in Khayyam's city of Nishapur.

Any philosophies and philosophical debates in the cities along the Silk Road that strayed outside of Islamic doctrine, be they Buddhist, Hellenic, Manichaean or Chinese, gradually came to be labeled as *kufr* (unbelief). A fervent campaign to purge Islam of the infiltration and influence of these 'foreign' philosophies and 'heretical' religions was carried out between the tenth and twelfth centuries, focusing on Mazdakism, Mithraism, Zoroastrianism and various denominations of Hinduism, especially after hardcore theologians of various schools made their theological positions clear, that philosophers and scientists lean toward apostasy and unbelief. The Islamization campaign was not without resistance in Central Asia and Iran and led to political and even military confrontations (i.e., by the Mazdakites) in efforts to combat the theocratic Muslim rulers. Due to the censorship and oppressive atmosphere, some even wrote books anonymously. For instance, the tenth-century *Ikhwan al-Safa* (Brethren of Purity) was a group of freethinkers (perhaps Ismailis) who wrote their 50 Epistles about many interesting scientific and philosophical topics without wishing to be identified.[47]

***

The dilemma of Islam and heretical philosophy on the Silk Road

The tension heavily damaged the burgeoning achievements of scientists and philosophers. Among those who heightened this tension and made Khayyam fear for his life was al-Ghazali. This prominent Sufi who became an anti-philosopher lived and studied in Khayyam's hometown of Nishapur, then taught in Baghdad before returning to Nishapur years later. An intellectual clash between the two became unavoidable.[48] Al-Ghazali wrote a famous anti-

---

[46] *Rasā'il ikhwān al-ṣafā,'* vol. 4, (Beirut:1957) p .95, quoted by Aminrazavi, "Reading the Rubā'iyyāt as "Resistance Literature","," 42.
[47] See Ali Asghar Halabi, *Gozîdeh Rasā'il Ikhwān al-Safā*, (Tehran: Entesharat Asātir, 1380/2001), see also Vaziri, *Buddhism in Iran*, 56.
[48] Ernest Trattker, "'Umar Khayyām-Poet III Against al-Ghazali," *The Muslim World* 53/2 (April 1963): 120-126.

philosophical book, *Incoherence of the Philosophers* (*Tahafut al-falasifa*), harshly criticizing and refuting the renowned polymath scientist Avicenna, Aristotelian philosophy, and philosophical concepts such as arguments for the world's pre-existence, which clashed with the Islamic belief in God as the creator of all. Interestingly, as much as al-Ghazali refuted philosophy and philosophical thinking, he himself co-opted strategies that cleverly drew upon philosophical approaches in order to support his dogmatic beliefs, contributing to the tension between philosophy and religion of the time. Al-Ghazali attempted to use philosophical approaches to resolve the contradiction between reason and revelation by delegitimizing philosophical arguments that did not align with Islam, ultimately influencing many in the Muslim world for centuries to come.[49]

Almost half a century after his death, al-Ghazali's *Incoherence of the Philosophers* was met with a crushing response from the greatest expert of Aristotelian work and thought, the Andalusian polymath Ibn Rushd (Averroes) (d. 1198), under the title of *Incoherence of the Incoherence* (*Tahafut al-tahafut*). In this work, Averroes argued that al-Ghazali's first incoherence was that he did not understand Aristotelian philosophy properly to argue against the ideas. Al-Ghazali's second incoherence was that he misunderstood Avicennian ideas, which themselves were philosophically weak. Averroes concluded that al-Ghazali's philosophical naiveté led him from one incoherence to another. Ultimately, Averroes' rationalistic, pro-Aristotelian and secular ideas gained greater attention in Christian Europe than did al-Ghazali's anti-Aristotelian arguments (though the Christian priest and philosopher, Thomas Aquinas (d. 1274) was influenced by and integrated al-Ghazali's polemical rhetoric[50]). Nevertheless, Aristotelian ideas and Averroism ultimately prevailed. Their claims that reason and philosophy are superior to faith eventually became sources of inspiration in the later Middle Ages and during the Renaissance.[51]

Al-Ghazali and Khayyam were living in the same city, and it is certain that the two men met and exchanged intellectual challenges [52]—al-Ghazali, in his youth, apparently attended Khayyam's lessons. In later years, Khayyam as a

---

[49] Frank Griffel, "al-Ghazali," *The Stanford Encyclopedia of Philosophy* (Summer 2020 Edition), Edward N. Zalta (ed.), https://plato.stanford.edu/archives/sum2020/entries/al-ghazali. (Accessed November 25, 2020).

[50] Among many articles on the subject, see David B. Burrell, "Ghazali and Aquinas on the Names of God," *Literature and Theology* 3/2 (July 1989): 173-180.

[51] "Latin Averroism," *Encyclopædia Britannica* (April 28, 2009). https://www.britannica.com/topic/Latin-Averroism. (Accessed November 30, 2020).

[52] Mohammad Afshin Vafai, "در خیّام از نویافته رباعی دو - غزّالی محمد امام و خیّام عمر رابطهٔ از ایتازه آگاهی غزّالی رثای," (New Information Concerning the Relationship between Omar Khayyam and Imam Mohammad al-Ghazzali (Two Newly Found Quatrains by Khayyam Elegizing Ghazzali), *Pazhoheshhaye Iranshenasi*, 2/7 (Fall 1396/2018), 6-7.

rationalist thinker was at odds with al-Ghazali, someone who disliked philosophy and philosophers as well as mathematics and mathematicians. One could say that Al-Ghazali did damage the Central Asian philosophical tradition during and after Khayyam's time. According to al-Ghazali, mathematics and the sciences were used to try to explain an existence which in fact, should remain sacred, a mystery of God's creation. Al-Ghazali had made his strict religious position quite clear, speaking out against those who imported such scholarly ideas perceived as unbelief (heresy) into Islamic thinking, acts which Khayyam may certainly have been guilty of in his work in mathematics, and geometry in particular. In his book, *The Decisive Criterion for Distinguishing Islam from Clandestine Unbelief* (*Faysal al-tafriqa bayna l-Islâm wa-l-zandaqa*), Al-Ghazali claims:

> "Teachings that violate certain 'fundamental doctrines' (*usûl al-'aqâ'id*) should be deemed unbelief and apostasy. These doctrines are limited to three: monotheism, Muhammad's prophecy, and the Qur'anic descriptions of life after death."[53]

As we will see later in his quatrains, Khayyam completely ignores or, in some cases, even runs counter to all three of these doctrines that al-Ghazali considered to be inviolable. According to Khayyam's *Rubaiyat*, there is no creator per se, no prophet to guide humanity but one's own rational mind, no mention of a sacred book sent by God, and certainly no life after death. Thus, Khayyam fundamentally demythologizes the connotation of god, which is central to Islamic thought.[54]

It is not difficult to see how al-Ghazali and other creationist theologians clashed with Khayyam's skepticism, naturalism, materialism, pragmatism and hedonism. Against the uncompromising fanaticism of major Islamic legalists and jurists with their anti-intellectual and anti-rationalist *fatwas*, Khayyam composed his rational poetry in secret as "resistance literature" to challenge the hegemony of those who had suppressed the freethinking and freedom of speech.[55] On the other hand, by quoting some of his quatrains, several medieval scholastic authors cataloged Khayyam as a materialist-naturalist thinker and criticized him for selfishly following his logic instead of the teachings of the prophets.[56]

---

[53] Griffel, "al-Ghazali,"
[54] Paolo Imperio, "Omar Khayyam il vino mistico della conoscenza," *Secreta Magazine* 1 (2013), 22.
[55] Aminrazavi, "Reading the Rubā'iyyāt as "Resistance Literature"," 39-41.
[56] Vafai, "خیّام عمر حکیم رابطه از اینتازه آگاهی," page 2.

Considering the focus of al-Ghazali and others in attempting to enforce adherence to Islamic doctrines at a time and place when political and military forces were also gathering fearsome strength on the horizon, Khayyam's commitment to free thought becomes even more impressive. Being a true child of the Silk Road conduit of thought and culture, it is highly likely that Khayyam imported pre-Socratic, Buddhist, Daoist, and perhaps Manichaean or other gnostic and secular sources into his poetry; his cosmopolitan upbringing enabled him to see beyond the limits of religious dogma. Khayyam's oblique and asymmetrical thinking would almost certainly have earned him the label of apostate and an unbeliever. Since his quatrains were released after his death in a scattered fashion from different sources, he escaped with his life—but not with his reputation, especially among the medieval scholastic thinkers, as we shall see later.

Despite the muscular efforts of Muslim theologians such as al-Ghazali, the influx of ideas from other concurrent or preceding religions could not be completely controlled in the region. As a result, much blending of beliefs occurred in the constellation of cities that made up the Silk Road, just as had been happening over the centuries before Islam arrived. However, it was not a smooth process, and Muslim rulers of the region often tried to suppress and delegitimize such influences. Ultimately though, it was impossible to stem the flow of ideas in such a vibrant part of the world.

Syncretism and the construction of Islamic tradition

Due to its political and military superiority and dominance over many religious communities, Islam had become a complex and self-righteous religion. The inner view of the zealot literalists and exegetical authors was that their divinely conceived religion was pure, free from the influences of other religions, philosophies and cultures. Such Muslim thinkers and authors invented Muslim legends about heroes, victorious holy battles and their infallible saints. They also developed polemical techniques, denying that any preexisting high cultures prior to Islam were worthy of praise. This was to be expected when a monolithic religion such as Islam imposed its censorship laws on people who did not share the same values and had no power to assert themselves. As a result, a cultural remaking unfurled through attempting to destroy all non-Islamic traces or transmuting them by giving them Islamic identities.

A clear-cut example of this transmutation can be seen with the preexisting carved footprints of the Buddha, especially along the Silk Road in Central Asia, which were and still are highly respected objects of veneration for the Buddhists around Asia. But during the Islamic era, they were claimed to be the footprints of Islamic saints turned into shrines instead, with absolutely no Koranic or prophetic precedence. Moreover, most of the shrines with Buddhist footprints that were transformed into those of Muslim saints coincidentally lie along the road between Silk Road towns and on the Spice Route shores in Iran, which Buddhist missionaries originally frequented.[57]

Additional cases of Islamic syncretism abound. One example is the influence of pictorial-oriented religious teachings. Islam's ban on pictorial representation was circumvented particularly by the Shiites of Iran, with their drawings of pictures of Islamic saints. This practice had already been in use for centuries in the region: Buddhists, centuries earlier, had employed a pictorial strategy instead of relying on written materials to teach and propagate religion. They seem to have passed down the practice to the Manichaeans and the third-century Manichaean prophet Mani, who was himself an artist-painter who produced the *Arzhang* (now lost), a book of religious illustrations using painting and calligraphy as a means of propagating his teachings.

This tradition eventually influenced the iconographical culture of Shiite Islam, inspiring the tradition of producing miniatures and portraits of their saints, even including the Prophet of Islam, despite the formal Islamic injunction against human representations. Even the halo of light motif often used in portraits of the Buddha and Mani was employed in portraits of the Prophet of Islam and Shiite Imams. This process is an example of a chain of inter-borrowings along the Silk Road, showing that despite overt resistance towards outside influences, the crusaders of original Islam gradually imitated and integrated many non-Islamic elements into what became known as the Islamic culture of towns along the Silk Road.

Reconciling the doctrine of Islam with the non-monotheistic Greek and Indian philosophies became more challenging. In the early centuries of Islam, it was controversial to quote pre-Socratic Hellenic philosophers whose philosophies were primarily based on atheism, rationalism, atomism and materialism, all of which could hardly be reconciled with the Islamic creationist theology. If some of these philosophers, such as Heraclitus, were quoted, the commentary was flavored with explanations that added references to God, prophecy, or other concepts which would reconcile the ideas with monotheism and Islam. For example, Heraclitus became known among the Muslim writers mainly as the author of a cyclical ontological system beginning and ending with God conceiving the world in terms of light, an ontological system that was unknowable to humans.[58] As we shall see in the next chapter, this was a

---

[57] Vaziri, *Buddhism in Iran*, chapter 5, pages 67-80. The Buddha's footprint in Sri Lanka is similarly claimed to be Adam's footprint; a legend fabricated in the ninth century, pages 68-9.
[58] Carmela Baffioni, "pre-Socratics in the Arab World," in *Encyclopedia of Medieval Philosophy* Lagerlund H. (ed,) (Dordrecht: Springer, 2011). https://doi.org/10.1007/978-1-4020-9729-4_416.

misrepresentation of non-theistic Heraclitan philosophy, designed to make it suitable for the domestic consumption of scholastic Islamic philosophers.

The Silk Road and religious dissent before Khayyam

Omar Khayyam was far from the first to hold philosophical views antithetical to the Muslim establishment. He was preceded by other giants who blazed a path of free thought in Central Asia. One of the earliest nonconformist heretical stances taken against puritan Islam in Central Asia occurred in the city of Tirmidh (in present-day Uzbekistan) by the dissident thinker and theologian Jahm b. Safwan (d. 746). Jahm's frequent encounters and debates with Buddhist and Indian thinkers in Tirmidh (with an extensive Buddhist tradition) are believed to have influenced the development of his own philosophy of materialism and rationalism, which did not align with Islamic doctrine. (See also the cross-influences with the Mu'tazila school). Jahm faced Muslim thinkers in formidable arguments, in which he denied the knowledge and even the existence of God, and claimed that the Koran was not eternal.[59] Certain non-Arab scholars formed a group of his followers called the Jahmiyya, which lasted for some centuries. The Jahmiyya continued for a period of time to cause considerable intellectual challenges to Muslim scholars in Khurasan and different parts of Iran.

Another nonconformist philosopher-physician, Abu Bakr al-Razi (d. 925), who lived in the two Silk Road cities of Rayy and Baghdad, seems to have embraced pre-Socratic atomism and rationalism and in ensuing years developed his own anti-creationist and anti-prophetic discourses, which were naturally counter to Islamic doctrine. Even though his philosophical works went missing or were destroyed,[60] Razi's work continued to trigger critical debates within Islam even after he died. Those who read Razi's work and

---

[59] Shlomo Pines, "A Study of the Impact of Indian, Mainly Buddhist, Thought on Some Aspects of Kalām Doctrines," *Jerusalem Studies in Arabic and Islam*, 17 (1994), 184. Joseph van Ess, "Jahm b. Ṣafwān," *Encyclopœdia Iranica*, XIV/4, pp. 389-390, available online at http://www.iranicaonline.org/articles/jahm-b-safwan. (Accessed January 6, 2021). W. M. Watt, "The Political Attitudes of Mu'tazilah," *Journal of Royal Asiatic Society* 1, no. 2 (April, 1963), 40. See also Georges Vajda, "A propos de perpétuiteé de la reétribution d'outre-tombe en théologie musulmane," *Studia Islamica* 11 (1959), 29–30.

[60] In various medieval chronicles, at least 133 scholarly works by Razi are mentioned which had gone missing, especially those with strong philosophical and so-called heretical contents. See A. S. Bazmee Ansari, "Philosophical and Religious Views of Muhammad Ibn Zakariyya al-Razi," *Islamic Studies* 16, no. 3 (Autumn 1977), 157-58.

polemicized against him, such as Maimonides and Avicenna,[61] developed philosophies that, in some ways, were swayed by Razi's work. (For more on Razi's approach to the rational mind and philosophical treatment, see Part II, Chapter 6 of the present book).

Another freethinker was an important rebellious intellectual and author from Khurasan, Ibn al-Rawandi (d. 910). He criticized the blind belief in the prophets and spoke out against the contradictions within Islam and the Koran itself.[62] Al-Rawandi discussed four dogmas in general, but principally he aimed to disparage Islam by 1. denying the truthfulness of revelation and prophecy; 2. claiming religion to be a human invention; 3. declaring the supremacy of reason over faith; and 4. rejecting the scenarios of an afterlife.[63] He wrote *al-Dāmigh*, parodying the Koran and the wisdom of God.[64] His writings leaned towards rationalism while challenging the dogma of monotheism. His heretical philosophy was not an isolated personal opposition against the dogma of Islam, but rather a synthesis of extra-Islamic ideas which have roots in the past cultures along the trade route, a route he traveled along extensively and where he learned to argue his critical ideas freely. He may have been influenced by the tenth-century Manichaean groups (*Dinavariya*), which were based in Nishapur and Samarqand,[65] or potentially by his Manichaean friend Abu Isa al-Warraq (d. 994) in Baghdad. Al-Rawandi spent the last years of his life living safely in the tolerant Samanid dynasty of Central Asia, which ruled over present-day Eastern Iran, Afghanistan, Tajikistan, Turkmenistan and Uzbekistan.

On the Silk Road, intellectual anti-religious criticisms were not only directed against Islamic doctrine, but also against Judaic doctrine as well. Ninth-century Hiwi al-Balkhi was an iconoclastic thinker and poet born in Balkh who most

---

[61] Mauro Zonta, "Influence of Arabic and Islamic Philosophy on Judaic Thought", *The Stanford Encyclopedia of Philosophy* (Winter 2016 Edition), Edward N. Zalta (ed.), https://plato.stanford.edu/archives/win2016/entries/arabic-islamic-judaic.
(Accessed November 24, 2020).

[62] See Sara Stroumsa, *Freethinkers of Medieval Islam: Ibn al-Rawandi, Abu Bakr al-Razi and Their Impact on Islamic Thought*, (Leiden/Boston/Koln: Brill, 1999).

[63] Ilkka Lindstedt, "Anti-Religious Views in the Works of Ibn al-Rawandi and Abul 'Ala al-Ma'arri," *Studia Orientalia* 111, Helsinki: Published by Finnish Oriental Society (2011), 132, 141-153.

[64] *The Fihrist of al-Nadīm*. Vol. 1 translated and edited by Bayard Dodge, (New York: Columbia University Press, 1970), 420–421; see also Reynold Nicholson, A. *A Literary History of the Arabs*, (New York, 1907), 375; Sara Stroumsa, "From Muslim heresy to Jewish-Muslim polemics: Ibn al-Rawandi's Kitab al-Damigh," *Journal of the American Oriental Society* 107, no. 4 (Oct.-Dec. 1987): 767-772.

[65] Sundermann, "Dīnāvarīya," *Encyclopaedia Iranica*, (1995).

likely was of Jewish lineage.[66] In a rationalistic fashion, he asked two hundred provocative questions as a means of criticizing and pointing out contradictions in the Jewish Scriptures. (His book *Two Hundred Questions* did not survive except as fragments in other works of those who tried to refute him, namely the tenth-century Jewish scholar Saadia Gaon.) Hiwi argued that if the Scriptures have so many discrepancies, they cannot be divine. He fundamentally questioned the miracles of the Torah, like the parting of the Red Sea.[67] He asked shocking questions such as: why did God decide to live among impure human beings, or why did he need sacrifices? Hiwi reasoned that god must be philosophically primitive and ignorant, considering that he sends plagues to humans and claims innocent lives such as in the destruction of Sodom and Gomorrah and other capricious behaviors.[68] Like his anti-Islamic counterparts, he was probably influenced by external schools of thought, but it remains unclear whether the enigmatic Hiwi was influenced by Gnosticism, Manichaeism,[69] or the atheism of Greco-Indian dialectics. Hiwi, a critical intellectual of his time, was refuted for his heresy, but he certainly set a precedent for the emergence of Spinoza, another Jewish philosopher who also challenged Judaic doctrine eight centuries later in Europe.

From the early ninth century until the early twelfth century in the Silk Road's metropolitan cities such as Bukhara, Samarqand, and Nishapur, pioneering religious projects were undertaken under the influence of Central Asian culture: Mohammad's hadith collections were consolidated in Nishapur following the Buddhist model of collections of the Buddha's sutras. In addition, the process of systematizing Arabic grammar, phonetics and syntax was undertaken, inspired by the Sanskrit grammar system.[70] This was a bridging time when groundbreaking thinkers linked their generational ideas with the traditions and philosophies of the past. The interplay of ideas from Hellenic, Manichaean, Indian and Chinese sources not only created challenging intellectual fronts against Islamic and monotheistic thinking, but also inspired alternative and free thought. It was against this background that Khayyam composed his quatrains, which due to their religiously controversial nature,

---

[66] See Judah Rosenthal, "Hiwi al-Balkhi: A Comparative Study," *Jewish Quarterly Review* 38, no. 3 (January 1948): 317-342; see also by the same author, "Hiwi al-Balkhi: A Comparative Study: Christian Heretics Continued," *Jewish Quarterly Review* 39/1 (July 1948): 79-94.
[67] Eliezer Segal, *Ask Now of the Days That Are Past*, (Calgary: The University of Calgary Press, 2005), 45, chapter 7.
[68] Daniel Frank, "Hiwi al-Balkhi EBR," *Encyclopedia of the Bible and Its Reception* 11 (2015): 1199-1200; Segal, *Ask Now of the Days*, 45.
[69] Ibid., 1200; Segal, *Ask Now of the Days*, 46.
[70] Fatullah Mojtabai, *Nahv Hindī va Nahv 'Arabī*, (Tehran: Nashr Karnameh, 1383/2004), 53, 56, 81–99, 156. See also Vaziri, *Buddhism in Iran*, 28, 139.

were kept well-hidden until after his death, but which give us strong hints as to what influenced his thoughts.

Situating Khayyam's nonconformist views

Khayyam's Greek and Avicennian philosophical and intellectual engagements did not endanger his position because Greek philosophy was a familiar tradition in the Islamic setting of his days. But his covert beliefs (which were really *un*beliefs) and some aspects of his lifestyle, including his abstaining from eating meat among other uncharacteristic practices and values (at least from the Islamic point of view), made him a target of suspicion. Ibn al-Qifti (d. 1248), who in his *Tārikh al-Hukama* (*History of Philosophers*) perpetuates the accusation that Khayyam was an apostate, says of him: "Omar al-Khayyami, Imam of Khurasan, was the most learned man of his day. Not only was he versed in all wisdom of the Greeks, but he encouraged the search after the One and preached the elevation and purification of the soul through abstinence from the things of the flesh (vegetarian)...The later Sufis have professed to find in his verses confirmation of their own doctrines, and have discussed them both in private and at public meetings. But their inner meanings are as stinging serpents to the Mussulman [Islamic] law, hence the men of his day hated him and exposed the secrets he would fain have concealed, so that fearing for his life, he controlled his tongue and pen."[71] Ibn al-Qiftī continues by saying that Khayyam was threatened with execution on charges of unbelief (*kufr*) and that this led to his unexpected pilgrimage to Mecca to ease the tension.[72] Perhaps due to the apparent pressure to conform, Khayyam announced that he would go on pilgrimage, but there is actually no evidence at all that Khayyam made the pilgrimage to Mecca.

Ibn al-Qiftī also mentions Khayyam's meditation practice aimed at attaining oneness.[73] This could have meant that he practiced some kind of yoga or some other technique of philosophical contemplation. It is claimed that he believed in some form of reincarnation (although unlikely) but was not interested in discussing any of his ideas in public or teaching them to a large audience, and

---

[71] J. K. M. Shirazi, *Life of Omar Al-Khayyami*, (London & Edinburgh: T.N. Foulis, 1905), 58-9; see also Friedrich Rosen, *Die Sinnsprüche Omars des Zeltmachers*, (Wiesbaden, 2008; first published in Berlin 1919), 114, 128-9.

[72] Sadiq Hedayat, "Muqqadame-yee bar Rubā'īyyāt-i Khayyam," in *Neveshtehā-ye Farāmoush Shodeh-i Sādiq Hedāyat*, edited by Maryam Dānā'ī Boromand, (Tehran: Mo'asseseh Entesharat Negah, 1376/1997), 53-65, 57; Avery, et al., *The Ruba'iyat*, 25.

[73] 'Oneness,' in this case could mean 'Yoga' (union of body and mind/self and the world). Or, it meant attaining *Brahman* in Vedanta philosophy.

thus any true belief would remain unrevealed.[74] Largely it was his distinctive vegetarianism and celibacy, both uncommon among Muslims, that raised suspicion.[75] The opposition against his views became even more apparent after his *Rubaiyat* surfaced decades after his death, perhaps because of his philosophical and unconventional views—more reasons to suspect that he adhered to certain unrevealed extra-Islamic doctrines.

The thirteenth-century historian Shahrazuri reports that, out of suspicion, Khayyam was labeled as an apostate and a "bad man" like Avicenna.[76] Khayyam and Avicenna were lumped together as "bad men" because they both adhered to Greek and other ancient suspicious philosophies. Khayyam apparently shares his fear of the conformists in a quatrain attributed to him:

> The secrets which my book of love has bred
> Cannot be told for fear of loss of head.
> Since none are fit to learn, or care to know
> 'Tis better all my thoughts remain unsaid.[77]

It is therefore not surprising that Khayyam kept to himself out of fear of conformists such as al-Ghazali.[78] However, here is a quatrain that testifies as to how he may have been already framed and labeled during his own lifetime:

> If I am drunk from the Magian wine, so I am.
> If I am an atheist, pagan or an idolater, so I am.
> Every group is suspicious of my position,
> But I am my natural self, so I am.
>
> (*rubai* 74)

It can be just as interesting to note non-influences as it is to note influences: Khayyam is believed to have expressed his admiration for Aristotle as well as Avicenna, and considered Avicenna his intellectual mentor. Yet, as much as Khayyam appreciated Avicenna and may have even studied under the tutelage

---

[74] Alireza Qaragozlu, *Omar Khayyam*, (Tehran: Entesharate Tarhe Nou, 1381/2000), 12, 14, 20-21; see also Hedāyat, "Muqqadame-yee bar Rubā'īyyāt-i Khayyam," 58.
[75] Ja'afar Aghyani Chawoshi, "Āyā Khayyam va Abul 'Alā Ma'arrī Zandīq Budeh-and?" in *Nineteen Maqāleh dar bāreh Hakim Omar Khayyam Neishaburī*, (Khurasan: Neishabur Shenasi, n.d.), 6-7.
[76] Shirazi, *Life of Omar Al-Khayyami*, 52, quoting Muhammad Shahrazurī's *Nuzhat ul-Arwah*.
[77] Aminrazavi, *The Wine of Wisdom*, 48.
[78] Mohammad Mohammadian, "Der oblique Blick: Zum Verhältnis von Philosophie und Religion in den Robâ'iyât von Omar Khayyâm," in *Atheismus im Mittelalter und in der Renaissance*, edited by Friedrich Niewöhner, 95-114. (Wiesbaden: Harrassowitz Verlag, 1999), 99, 105.

of Bahmanyar, an outstanding student of Avicenna,[79] the nonconformism of Khayyam's *Rubaiyat* reveals that apparently, he considered neither Avicennian nor Aristotelian thoughts in his own compositions. For example, despite his apparent admiration for the Aristotelian worldview, Khayyam did not support the notion of the world pre-existing, nor entertain the idea of its creation. In fact, he found both assertions useless in an impermanent human life when striving to be free and happy. The following quatrain is a clear dismissal of the Aristotelian notion of the world being eternal or pre-existing:

> Since our station in this world is impermanent,
> To live without wine and romance is a grave mistake.
> How long should we preoccupy ourselves with questions about whether the world was created or has always been?
> When I pass away it makes no difference, since created and everlasting will be identical.
>
> (*rubai* 93)

As an independent thinker, Khayyam was not a follower of Avicenna or Aristotle. Khayyam avoided oversights, profuse speculations and dogmatic and absolutist assertions that some thinkers and groups upheld, including the philosophical certainties formulated by Avicenna. Khayyam rationalized and measured his explanation of the natural world with a moderate and logical approach, avoiding any flamboyant linguistic twists for the sake of his poetry.

In Nishapur, Khayyam had pioneered an innovative poetical philosophy that could be read or easily memorized generations after his death. His ingenuity was the use of the Persian language to assemble together many interesting and practical ideas that people had hardly read or heard in that language, which back then was a relatively young language in Central Asia and on the Silk Road. Khayyam's poems proved to be controversial, but as a freethinker and a philanthropist philosopher, he aimed to offer liberating ideas to existentially and culturally trapped individuals. Thus, his revolutionary symbiosis of several key dialectics obtained from different philosophical schools prevalent on the Silk Road for centuries seemed designed to make abstruse philosophy intelligible to average people. But since he had to hide his poetry, the average people of his time never had the chance to read it.

***

---

[79] Mehdi Aminrazavi, and Glen Van Brummelen, "Umar Khayyam," *The Stanford Encyclopedia of Philosophy* (Spring 2017 Edition), Edward N. Zalta (ed.), https://plato.stanford.edu/archives/spr2017/entries/umar-khayyam. (Accessed November 25, 2020).

Greek, Chinese and Indian ideas in Khayyam's poetry

In light of what has been discussed above, it is now clear that Khayyam's *Rubaiyat* was penned against a background of multiple potential and important influences in the neighboring regions around Nishapur. As a broad-minded intellectual of his era, it can be assumed that he may have easily informed himself about the Indian and Greek philosophies, just like other Central Asian compatriots. His Central Asian predecessor scholar, al-Biruni (d. 1052), spent more than a decade studying Indian religions and Sanskrit. The eleventh-twelfth-century heresiographer, Shahrastani—a contemporary of Khayyam living in Nishapur—conducted scholarly research collecting material about all the existing and extinct religious and philosophical schools that were known in the world of the twelfth century. His allusion to both conformist and heretical Indian religions and philosophies[80] all the way to Hellenic philosophers included seven pre-Socratic philosophers like Heraclitus, Democritus and Epicurus.[81] Shahrastani's work demonstrates that these ancient personalities and their ideas were known to the literati of the time, such as Khayyam.

Such influences have manifested themselves in either parallel allegories in his *Rubaiyat* or have been fused together as an innovative philosophy—a Khayyamian philosophy. In the next four chapters, there are several potential schools and philosophers to look at that constitute various angles within Khayyam's *Rubaiyat*—all linked to the syncretic culture of the Silk Road. They include:

- Hellenic naturalism of Heraclitus,
- Daoism of Zhuangzi,
- Dialectical Buddhism the way Nagarjuna constructed it and,
- Upanishadic Philosophy - Vedanta

Khayyam truly belonged to a minority of thinkers in the early Persianate world whose poetical philosophy is a synchronization of many elements of thought and wisdom. The appearance and integration of these philosophical elements in the *Rubaiyat* seemed to be well considered, handpicked from the intellectual 'melting pot' of Nishapur. The *Rubaiyat* ushered in a new rational revolution. As much as it sounded heretical and annoyed later religious thinkers, its secular and naturalist approach became a guide for liberated thinkers and later poets.

The enigma of Khayyam's creativity baffled many because his *Rubaiyat* dodges the speculative, idealist, and mystical clichés. He remained disdainful of those

---

[80] Abdulkarim Shahristānī, *al-Milal wal Nihal* (*Tozih al-Milal*), trans. Seyed M. R. Jalali Naini, vol. II, Tehran 1387/ 2008.
[81] Ibid., 168-69, 178-79.

philosophers who claimed to know the secret of existence through clever reasoning techniques. He was equally disdainful of staid philosophy, which could not unshackle humanity from suffering and confusion. His ferocious dislike of wasteful and pedantic philosophy is also apparent in his poetry. Thus, he kept his language down-to-earth and his message straightforward.

***

The next four chapters offer the first effort to bring to light Khayyam's erudition, revealing how the Silk Road intercultural philosophy subtly flourished within him, an anthropological aspect of his poetry that scholarship can devote more attention to. Chapter 2 compares and draws parallels between the ideas of Heraclitus, a pre-Socratic philosopher, and those of Khayyam. The discussion aims to draw out more aspects of pre-Socratic philosophy in Khayyam's work, going beyond its typically addressed Epicurean facets. (In a separate work, Epicurean and Lucretian materialism and naturalism in Khayyam's poetry has been recounted.[82])

According to the Heraclitan notion, material nature and human life both flow like a river. Life in its entirety flows irreversibly forward and never stagnates. Based on this conception, life often looks the same but never is the same—the flow itself is old, but it is always incrementally fresh with each go-around. This imagery takes on poetical brilliance in Khayyam's *Rubaiyat*. *Rubai* (quatrain) after *rubai* portrays how births and deaths are recurrent and how life reconstitutes, continuing in the same rhythm but each time appearing to everyone as if it is the first time. Both philosophers contended that the entire physical existence is in a relentless state of transformation and processing, even though it seems to be virtually the same all the time. It is highly probable that Khayyam may have read and discussed the fragments of Heraclitus and with other Hellenic thinkers whose works reached the Silk Road.

In Chapter 3, the similarities between certain ideas of the Daoist Zhuangzi and Khayyam are explored. The parallel aphorism of the 'drunkard who has sipped wine' by Zhuangzi (as well as Laozi, both founders of Daoism) and Khayyam is of great interest and curiosity. The metaphoric exploits of a 'drunkard' and his 'wine' utilized by Zhuangzi illustrate how a person can forget the egocentric, controlling and anxious self. The path to naturalness that leads to connecting the mind with the greater reality of *Dao* (Path) is the reason why all overpowering emotions and frivolous thoughts will have to be forgotten.

---

[82] See Mostafa Vaziri, *Liberation Philosophy: From the Buddha to Omar Khayyam – Human Evolution from Myth-Making to Rational Thinking*, (Wilmington: Vernon Press, 2019). Chapters 5 and 7.

In the Khayyamian perspective, a natural self is one whose drunken state flows and is in conformity with the flow of nature, the joy of life without extra exertion. The naturalistic content of this self is nothing but lightness, oneness with nature, and making the journey of life in accordance with the principles of participation in life and forgetfulness of the constantly visualizing self that is fleeting in a fleeting world. Thus, Khayyam's poetical philosophy of "wine" finds its elegant parallels in Daoism by reframing for us our drunken self, which is naturally designed to live in the moment without anxiety and grief.

It is not difficult to imagine a scenario of cultural interaction between Daoist philosophers and their Central Asian counterparts like Khayyam, since the highest levels of trade between China and its Central Asian and Western territories took place in the tenth and eleventh centuries, during Khayyam's lifetime and the time when Zen-Buddhism (Daoism + Buddhism) was adopted in China.[83] Thus the interaction of the Tang dynasty with the Central Asian patricians and their cultural influences on the in pre- and post-Islamic literati and mystics is easily conceivable.[84] Although we cannot know with exact certainty that Khayyam in the eleventh century directly encountered Daoist adepts, literature and philosophical concepts in Nishapur, it seems quite plausible especially considering the echoes of Daoist ideas, allegories and ideals of human life that can be found in the *Rubaiyat*. (The use of ubiquitous allegories of 'wine' and 'drunkard' in Sufi-Persian literature starting in Central Asia around the eleventh century calls for a new investigation to search and trace these notions in the mystical and philosophical traditions in the surrounding areas of the Silk Road such as Daoist China).

Chapter 4 explores the parallels between the third-century Buddhist thinker Nagarjuna and Khayyam. Spotting parallels between Nagarjuna's specific model of 'emptiness' as the ultimate bearing of reality and its re-envisioning by Khayyam is invigorating. Nagarjuna's *Madhyamika*, known as *Middle Way*, conveys that the entire physical reality at every given time is in an 'intermediate state' (Sanskrit *madhyamika*)—there is never a finished and absolute product in the universe, although it seems to our sensory system that what we encounter is 'finished.' This relentless mechanism of an intermediate state points to a state of 'no-real' object in the physical world—'no-real' object because the object shifts and is never stabilized.

---

[83] Haussig, *Die Geschichte Zentralasien*, 192.

[84] The cross-influences and similarities between Daoism and Sufism in an already a pioneering and comparative study have been undertaken by Toshihiko Izutsu, *Sufism and Taoism: The Key Philosophical Concepts*, (Berkeley & Los Angeles: California University Press, 1984). Izutsu's study focuses on the similarities between the ideas of Ibn Arabi's Sufiism and that of Zhuangzi's Daoism.

The Khayyamian view of emptiness (Persian *hîch:* empty of inherent identity, nothingness) emphasizes the law of transmutation, which is not far from Nagarjuna's model. Khayyam's adherence to the laws of causality and interdependence is represented by the image of an endless caravan of things appearing and disappearing while one thing gives rise to another, causing the downfall of something else—an impersonal process without interruption and without any mysterious forces such as the gods trying to sway such laws.

On a deeper level, the crux of both Nagarjuna's nirvana-liberation approach and Khayyam's self-rule, joy-and-freedom approach was to live happily in the world and yet remain steadfastly disengaged from its misleading sense of permanence. This meant both men spoke for celebrating life and yet at the same time cautioned their audiences to be mindful of the intermediate state of all things, including human life and existence. They called for a special psychological preparedness at all times, an awareness of the existential gear that constantly shifts without exception, whether the object is celestial or earthly—only the speed of the shift is different.

Could Khayyam have been involved with the world of Buddhism and Nagarjuna? Given the geographical proximity and the timing of the fading of Buddhism in the region, Khayyam's generation may have been the last to have had direct contact with Buddhist thinkers and their literature along the Silk Road in Central Asia since Buddhism lingered in pockets in Central Asian regions up until around the tenth century.[85] One particularly intriguing hint of such contact comes from the Malamati—Qalandari antinomian mystics of Central Asia. From the ninth century onward in Balkh, Nishapur, and other areas in the region, these mystics borrowed some of their practices and beliefs from Indian and Buddhist sources.[86] For example, one Malamati legend tells of a prince in Balkh who left his palace and became a mendicant, nearly identical to the story of the Buddha's life.[87] In the Malamati version, though, this prince from Balkh traveled to Nishapur in the eighth century at the time when Balkh was still Buddhist, and the prince's name was adapted from the Buddha (or bodhisattva) to Ibrahim ibn Adham. The possibility that Khayyam himself may have been a Malamati mystic[88], as has been suggested by some sources, leads to the indirect and yet likely assumption that Khayyam was familiar with Buddhism.

---

[85] Vaziri, *Buddhism in Iran*, 12, 144.

[86] Ibid., 143, 144, 149.

[87] For this legend see Farīd al-Dīn Attār, *Taḏkirat ul-Auliyā*, Edited by Mohammad Este'lami, (Tehran: Entesharat Zavvar, 8th edition, 1374/1995).

[88] Aminrazavi, *The Wine of Wisdom*, 63, 151-2; see also Vaziri, *Liberation Philosophy*, 219-220.

In fact, given the historical and complex anthropological circumstances of the Silk Road in and around Central Asia, it may not at all be unreasonable to assume that Khayyam of Nishapur had a fair amount of knowledge about Buddhism given the fact that books on the topic of Buddhism may have been easily available to him. After all, the dialectics of "emptiness" in Buddhist Mahayana scriptures had their roots in Central Asia around the first century C.E. from when Mahayana emerged in the region. Although it is hard to confirm with certainty the precise geographical origin of the Mahayana's major scripture, the *Prajnaparamita* (Perfection of Wisdom),[89] and it is also difficult to confirm with certainty from which precise sources Khayyam may have acquired the Buddhist limb of his philosophy, the similarities point to at least some sort of crossover or exposure to Buddhist ideas.

An astonishing parallel between Khayyam's quatrains and one of the earliest Upanishads,[90] the Chandogya Upanishad, is explored in Chapter 5. There are over 108 Upanishads (maybe as many as 200), which had begun to be written down as early as 700 B.C.E. in northwest India and the periphery, again another ancient wisdom that arose in Central Asia. They may have still been circulating in Khayyam's region, even centuries later. In the Chandogya Upanishad, the significant allegory of 'the immortal clay' represents the eternal, unborn, undying and unoriginated Brahman from which all things are made and to which all things return. This making and unmaking of 'pots' (all animate and inanimate objects) take place in the universal pottery workshop. The universal clay always remains the same for all the past, present, and future pots. Even though the cycle of change renews time and again, the immortal clay (Brahman) remains the same.

This Upanishadic depiction is nearly indistinguishable from Khayyam's allegories of an immortal clay from which new and impermanent pots are constantly made, then broken down into their raw material, and then returned to being part of the same clay again. In the Khayyamian quatrains, we read that the corpses of the kings and beggars mix and their 'clay' becomes inseparable, being used for making new 'pots,' and the cycle of returning to the immortal clay continues.

Khayyam's inspiration could be a coincidence—or it could be a borrowing inspired from the Upanishad. The question is whether the Upanishadic philosophy (Vedanta) was at all accessible in Khurasan and Nishapur. There is indeed a ninth-century reference, where the message of the Chandogya

---

[89] Tilmann Vetter and Anne MacDonald, "Once Again on the Origin of Mahāyāna Buddhism," *Wiener Zeitschrift für die Kunde Südasiens* 45 (2001): 59-9.
[90] Patrick Olivelle, *The Early Upanishads*, annotated text and translation, (New York & Oxford: Oxford University Press, 1998), 12.

Upanishad was discussed and uttered by at least one mystic, Bayazid from Bastam, the Iranian Khurasan, not far at all from Nishapur. Bayazid Bastami is famous for his self-declaration: "There is nothing but 'god' (the immortal spirit) under this cloak." In other words, he said, "I am That." It was very similar to the Upanishadic "Tat Tvam Asi" ('You Are That', or 'I Am He'). The point was that the conventional self with its body is but an illusion (*maya*), where in fact, 'You Are That' points to a self that is the personification of the ultimate reality (Brahman, or the highest Principle).[91]

Although Bayazid is treated by modern scholars as a Sufi (although 'Sufi' designation for him is totally anachronistic[92]), his teacher was an Indian (Abu Ali Sindhi) and is believed to have been the conduit for this philosophical transference. This important precedent suggests Indian and Vedantic (Upanishadic) influences on the spiritual movements in the early Islamic period in the Eastern Iranian world.[93] Nishapur, Khayyam's home, was actually closer to the Indian world than Bayazid's home of Bastam in eastern Iran, so if the Upanishadic influence reached as far as Bastam, chances are good that it had also already reached Nishapur. (Bastam is 370 kilometers west of Nishapur on the route situated between Sabzevar and Rayy, major cities on the Silk Road.)

The powerful Upanishadic-Vedanta teachings spread far and wide over the centuries in Asia. In the tenth and eleventh centuries in Kashmir, these teachings were incorporated into the spiritual, philosophical non-dualistic school of Kashmir Shaivism. The Upanishads came even closer to the Central Asian and Persianate world when in the mid-seventeenth century, Dara Shukoh, the Mughal prince in India, translated fifty Upanishads from Sanskrit into Persian, which he called *Sirr-e Akbar* or 'Great Mystery.'[94] He pursued the

---

[91] Joel P. Brereton, "'Tat Tvam Asi' in Context," *Zeitschrift der Deutschen Morgenländischen Gesellschaft* 136 (1986): 99–109.

[92] For a discussion about the 'Suficization' of Khurasan in the tenth century, see Vaziri, *Buddhism in Iran*, chapter 8, esp. pages 141-144.

[93] Martino Moreno, M. "Mistica musulmana e mistica Indiana," *Annali Lateranensi* 10 (1946): 103–212. See R. C. Zaehner, *Hindu and Muslim Mysticism*, (London: University of London, The Athlone Press, 1960). See also, Vaziri, *Buddhism in Iran*, 145. For a somewhat counterargument see, Mohammad Hadi Tavakoli, "Barresi Ede'âye Yeksân Engâri 'Fatakunu anta dhaka' dar Bayân Bâyazid Bastâmi va 'Tat tvam asi' dar Chandogya Upanishad," (Investigation of the claim on the identical "takunu anta dhaka" in Bayazid Bastami's statement and " Tat tvam asi " in Chandogya Upanishad), *Journal of Motale'at Erfani* 27 (Spring-Summer 1397/ 2018- Kashan, Iran): 5-30.

[94] Persian translation of Dara Shukoh's Upanishads was translated into Latin by the eighteenth-century Orientalist Abraham Hyacinthe Anquetil-Duperron (1731–1805) which became a literary and spiritual inspiration and source for Arthur Schopenhauer

Upanishadic teachings so that the Muslim scholars could bring the Vedantic world closer to the mystical tradition of Islam. Sadly, the erudite Prince Dara Shukoh was charged with apostasy by his younger brother Aurangzeb. He was put to death, once again demonstrating the extreme tensions that can arise between freethinkers and the religious establishment.

Upanishadic notions had already infiltrated the Islamic world as early as the ninth century. Not always through the front door, but inquisitive seekers allowed it in through the back door. In light of these historical and geographical indications, the similarities between the Chandogya Upanishad and Khayyam's *Rubaiyat* may have been intentional and certainly are not surprising.

The cosmopolitanism of Khayyam

As a freethinker living in a major Silk Road city and absorbing a range of philosophies about life, Khayyam fashioned a coherent and distinctive response to human suffering and the path to happiness. His focus was on humanity outside of parochial beliefs, boundaries and doctrines. He became an altruistic universal philosopher. His education in the cosmopolitan culture of the Silk Road, he probably learned how to deal with the universal human psychological inclinations and address common misunderstandings of the nature of reality through the cosmopolitan views represented by Heraclitus, Zhuangzi, Nagarjuna and the Upanishadic yogis.

Based on his own introspection, he had become aware that humans recurrently face failures because of the negative propensities of their mind on one hand, and because they are entangled with ancestral superstition and ignorance on the other. Khayyam, like Epicurus, knew that humans imagine happiness to be easy to attain, but in fact, most end up with disappointment, and the pain of existence flares up tenaciously. This misfortune and unsound human condition called for an altruistic intervention. The pinnacle of Khayyam's universal poetry is his concern about human psychological vulnerability and the return of anxiety. His reshuffling of a very useful philosophy of life into a poetical language was a work of art that he offered as a bouquet of rhymed stanzas—the *Rubaiyat*.

One cardinal recommendation of simplicity expressed throughout the *Rubaiyat* is to nurture a quiet, observing, and fearless mind that savors the impermanency of life. The essence and source of this simple philosophy of life is Khayyam's virtuous mind, nurtured and cultivated in a culturally fertile geography.

(1788-1860), which led to the authorship of one of his most important literary works: *Die Welt als Wille und Vorstellung*, 1819.

Chapter 2
Life is Like a River:
Heraclitus and Khayyam

"One cannot step twice into the same river… it scatters and again gathers; it forms and dissolves, and approaches and departs."
(Heraclitus, Fragment. 91)[1]

This is Heraclitus's simple formulation of life. Simple and yet profound and nearly perfect as a metaphor: Heraclitus implements the image of a river to represent the process of life and the world, all flowing unidirectionally and irreversibly. The entire physical existence exists in a relentless process of change through opposing forces—a mechanism that keeps things the same yet not the same,[2] yet always compatible, maintaining equilibrium—just like a moving river.

Heraclitus's river also represents time: One cannot look back and retrieve the past; everything is always moving forward. And, just as Heraclitus says it is not possible to step twice into the same river, it is also not possible to come into contact with the same mortal being twice in the same state.[3] Neither a river nor

---

[1] There are three fragments about the 'river' attributed to Heraclitus; the earliest belongs to Plato. The one quoted here is from Plutarch. See Charles H. Kahn, *The Art and Thought of Heraclitus: An Edition of the Fragments with Translation and Commentary*, (New York: Cambridge Univ. Press, 1999; 1979), Fr. LI, 53. The same fragment is numbered B 91 in various literature including in G.S. Kirk, *The Cosmic Fragments: A Critical Study with Introduction, Text and Translation*, (London: Cambridge Univ. Press, 1975; 1954), 381.The fragment is extracted from the writings of Plutarch. For a detailed discussion of the river fragment, see Leonardo Taran, "Heraclitus: The River Fragments," *The Society for Ancient Greek Philosophy Newsletter* 253 (1989). https://orb.binghamton.edu/sagp/253. Latest version of this article by the same author: "Heraclitus: The River Fragments and Their Implications," *Elenchos*, 20 (1999): 9–52.
[2] Daniel W. Graham, "Heraclitus," *The Stanford Encyclopedia of Philosophy* (Fall 2019 Edition), Edward N. Zalta (ed.), https://plato.stanford.edu/archives/fall2019/entries/heraclitus. (Accessed January 5, 2020).
[3] Ibid.

a person remains the same. The entire creation, including the human body and mind, is constantly in a dynamic process of subtle change and adaptation.

Thus, the seemingly simplistic metaphor of a river, in fact, became a rich foundational platform for Heraclitus to develop his far-reaching philosophy, one that exhibits remarkable alignment with Khayyam's approach. We will explore the implications of the notion of irreversible flux in a number of Heraclitus's fragments as well as some of Khayyam's quatrains in order to appreciate the similarity of thought shared by these two giant literati.[4] But before we delve into the worldviews of these naturalist thinkers, let us briefly take a look at Heraclitus.

Heraclitus, a pre-Socratic Hellenic philosopher from around 500 B.C.E., was born and died in the city of Ephesus, which was under the Achaemenid-Persian Empire. His tantalizing philosophy is unsystematic and aphoristic and has survived in over one hundred[5] short fragments in brief references to him in the works of ancient philosophers as well as his short and much-disputed biography in the work of Diogenes Laertius (Book IX).[6] Due to the hermeneutic nature of Heraclitus's sayings, his use of synoptic language has been associated more closely with poetry than prose.[7] Consequently, these aphorisms have long been subject to stimulating analysis and elaboration over the course of the last centuries.[8]

The lucid ideas of Heraclitus are not just for professors of philosophy, but also for every thinking person.[9] His philosophy was so influential around the sixteenth-century French Renaissance[10] and the eighteenth-century Enlightenment period that great thinkers such as Hegel and Nietzsche[11] owe the essentials of their

---

[4] It is highly probable to conceive Khayyam as a philosopher, bibliophile and authority on Avicennian-Aristotelian philosophy to have come in direct and indirect contact with Heraclitus' fragments during the heyday of the Central Asian Enlightenment between the ninth through twelfth centuries, when the manuscripts and intellectual and Greek ideas were abounding.

[5] See Kirk, *The Cosmic Fragments*, index of fragments, vii-ix.

[6] According Charles Kahn and other authors some of the anecdotes about Heraclitus were fabrication. See Kahn, *The Art and Thought of Heraclitus*, 1.

[7] Graham, "Heraclitus," *The Stanford Encyclopedia of Philosophy*.

[8] Kirk, *The Cosmic Fragments*, xi, xiii.

[9] See Hans G. Gadamer on Heraclitus, in *Youtube*: https://www.youtube.com/watch?v=El78l6-pNoM (Accessed on February 6, 2020).

[10] See Françoise Joukovsky, *Le Feu et le Fleuve: Héraclite et la Renaissance française*, (Geneve: Librairie Droz, S.A.,1991).

[11] Artur Przybyslawski, "Nietzsche Contra Heraclitus," *Journal of Nietzsche Studies*, 23 (Spring 2002), 88-95. Howard Williams, "Heraclitus 'Philosophy and Hegel's Dialectic,"

philosophies to Heraclitan influences. Heraclitus is also known to be the founder of process philosophy—a philosophy that is grounded in the pulsating and changing nature of existence.[12]

Rational words about existence: Logos

> "Of the Logos (Word)...men always prove to be uncomprehending, both before they have heard it and when once they have heard it...all things happen according to this Logos..."
>
> (Fr. 1)[13]

Heraclitus introduced his notion of *logos* ("word-language") as a tool of discourse for understanding rational, objective reality. The idea of logos represents the corroboration of perfect insight with the universal laws of nature. Logos is the language through which nature communicates rather than a language that emanates from our conventional thoughts.

With the idea of logos, the bedrock of Heraclitus's philosophical pondering lay in this conception: the visible order of the world masks the hidden processes of nature, whose harmonious transformation is driven by the processes of heat or fire.[14] The flow of the 'river' of existence is possible through unity and correlation of opposite forces[15] (Fr. 111).[16] The opposite forces of hot-cold, upward-downward, fresh-old, and other contrasting dualities cause the changing, moving, and transmutation involved in the process of becoming. This endless stream of flux represents a non-dual stream of reality, although shrouded in opposite forces. The stream constantly changes, but it is the sameness of the change without an instant of rest or discontinuity.

History of Political Thought 6/3 (Winter 1985), pp. 381-404. See also Virginia Lyle Jennings Howard, *Nietzsche and Heraclitus*, Master Thesis, Louisiana State University, Department of Philosophy Spring 4-13-1992. Louisiana State University LSU Digital Commons.

[12] Seibt, Johanna, "Process Philosophy", *The Stanford Encyclopedia of Philosophy* (Summer 2020 Edition), Edward N. Zalta (ed.), https://plato.stanford.edu/archives/sum2020/entries/process-philosophy. (Accessed April 18, 2020).

[13] Kirk, *The Cosmic Fragments*, 33. This fragment is extracted from the work of Sextus Empiricus.

[14] Diogenes Laertius, *Lives of Eminent Philosophers*, trans. by R. D. Hicks, (London: William Heinemann and New York: G. P. Putnam's Sons, 1925), Book IX, 415, 417.

[15] For a more succinct discussion of Heraclitus' major points see, Oliver Meschnig, *Der indische Heraklit: Die moderne Rezeptionsgeschichte der Vorsokratiker im Lichte interkultureller Betrachtung*, https://www.academia.edu/12176599/Der_indische_Heraklit. (Accessed February 6, 2020).

[16] Kirk, *The Cosmic Fragments*, 130-33. This fragment is extracted from Stobaeus.

Heraclitus extends his poetic conception of the phenomenon of "changing sameness" for all things of the world, not just the natural state of a river: "The sun is not only new every day," Heraclitus says, "but always new at every moment." (Fr. 6). Nothing stays still in life.[17] But there is a sort of "recurrence of the same," or "eternal recurrence of the same," as Friedrich Nietzsche referred to it in *Die fröhliche Wissenschaft* in 1882. The world seems static to our sensory system, but it is a sort of optical illusion that leads many to cling to misleading beliefs of permanence rather than the logic of change and sameness. Thus, the world is in a perpetual state of flow and transformation, but due to the illusion of 'temporary permanence,' this regularity of change cannot be grasped in a snapshot view of the world of being.[18]

Despite the seemingly ethereal nature of Logos, the apparent world has a hidden harmony which may not actually be that difficult to detect and understand. In fact, in order to understand the fleeting days of life, only 'one' day is needed to know the bigger picture: "One day is equal to every other." (Fr. 106)[19]

Logos thus meant understanding the language of the true nature of the 'changing sameness' of the world. It described the understanding of what is really being mirrored in the lawful cosmos.[20] It was designed to strongly discourage personal or relative logic used by people to manipulate the interpretation of reality in order to favor their own biases rather than actually understanding it as the reality it represents. Heraclitus said that the language of the hidden structure which matches the nature of reality has been partially or completely lost in everyday speech and existence due to the many filters that humans invented, such as religion and culture. Those who are not in possession of logos, entangled in their personal, subjective beliefs, are the "sleep-walkers" who do not understand the flow, fire, and flux of reality.

In contrast to the human filters of invention, one could say that the dynamic world always existed in its own logical "language". But with the dawn of conventional human language, a subjective reality came into conflict with the lawful "language" of nature. This clash and cognitive dissonance have alienated humans from the mechanism of the natural world ever since, causing much confusion simply due to the influence of a 'wrong personal language':

---

[17] Ibid., 264, 14. This fragment is extracted from Aristotle.
[18] Being is the basis of Parmenides philosophy whereas becoming is that of Heraclitus.
[19] *Fragments by Heraclitus* Translated by John Burnet, 14.
[20] Enrique Hülsz, "Heraclitus on Logos: Language, Rationality and the Real." In *Doctrine and Doxography: Studies on Heraclitus and Pythagoras,* edited by David Sider and Dirk Obbink, (Berlin: De Gruyter, 2013), 285-7, 290. https://www.academia.edu/6138708/Heraclitus_on_Logos. (Accessed February 5, 2020).

"The Logos: though men associate with it most closely, yet they are separated from it; and those things which they encounter daily seem to them strange."

(Fr. 72)[21]

Apart from the power of reasoning, logos signifies intelligence, discourse, word, harmony, law, wisdom, fire and commotion.[22] It means there is an intelligent order of making and unmaking in a lawful nature and universe; it only takes a rational mind to perceive and understand it. The lack of understanding of nature and the function of things in the world would have to lead to alienation and personal turmoil.

In some ways, he defied using haughty and pretentious philosophical expressions and scolded other Greek philosophers for giving in to the words rather than the real understanding: "Much learning does not teach understanding."[23] He skillfully drew a line between listening to the Word (Logos), naturally out there ready to be perceived, and listening to *his* words—this way, understanding life is common to all instead of subjective interpretation of one person or another:

"Listen not to me but to the Logos."

(Fr. 50)[24]

"Those who speak with sense must rely on what is common to all, as a city must rely on its laws…"

(Fr. 114)[25]

Logos is the language of a rational and unceasing world which speaks to those whose inclination of mind reflects the universal principles and captures the spirit of reality.[26] So there are those who tune in to the universal principles as well as to the flow of life as if they had already lived through it once before and have not been as conditioned by their own biographical limitations.

Einstein seems to embody Heraclitus's Logos: In generating his theory of general relativity in 1915, Einstein deciphered the remote laws of outer space that had nothing to do with his own earthly, horizontal life. When Einstein accessed

---

[21] *Fragments By Heraclitus* Translated by John Burnet, Arthur Fairbanks, and Kathleen Freeman, 10. https://antilogicalism.files.wordpress.com/2016/12/heraclitus_fragments_final.pdf. This fragment is extracted from Marcus Aurelius. See also Kirk, *The Cosmic Fragments*, 44, 47.
[22] Michel Fattal, "Le logos d'Héraclite: un essai de traduction," *Revue des Études Grecques*, tome 99, fascicule 470-71 (Janvier-Juin 1986), 142.
[23] Laertius, *Lives of Eminent Philosophers*, Book IX, 409.
[24] Kirk, *The Cosmic Fragments*, 65. This fragment is extracted from Hippolytus.
[25] Ibid., 48. This fragment is extracted from Stobaeus.
[26] Kahn, *The Art and Thought of Heraclitus*, 22.

something so out of reach, the 'logos' of his mind was accessing the 'Logos' of the universe—like a perfect lock-and-key. This and similar scientific discoveries represent the vibration and resonance of another realm of logos emanating from a well-reasoned mind, which accords to the reality of the world.

As for the origin of the order of the world, Heraclitus sees no duality between the orderer and ordered: the world is self-made and self-organized. "The ordering, the same for all, no god nor man has made, but it ever was and is and will be... insofar as it is generated, it is identical with its own eternal source, everliving fire."[27] This image of fire matches Heraclitus's microcosmic attributes of human and natural life—self-generating, self-organized, fluctuating between moisture, earth, and fire, and back again.

Heraclitus also connected resonance and dissonance in the picture of human life. Resonance exists when the workings of nature coherently corroborate and couple perfectly with human existence. At the same time, dissonance is also present because the human psyche, conditioned by its mortality, has yet to fully perceive a complex world.[28] This is where Logos represents a resonance with the language of the rational structure of the world. But more importantly, it is a way for those who seek a clearer perspective to live a more far-seeing, gentle life in an outwardly confusing world. Heraclitus wants to make sure that humans do not fall under the influence of their own illusions and their view of the world as a static entity.

Khayyam's language pairs off with the flow

In a tone similar to Heraclitus, Khayyam as a mathematically-minded, rational poet, mapped out the relentless process of the becoming of the world and while poeticizing it in the context of human experience. Through the fluid and symbolic language of the quatrain, Khayyam described the true nature of the rational universe and what could be expected of the world: nothing more, nothing less. This bare regularity of the processes of the world has often been tangled with, its straightforward understanding derailed by convoluted religious or personal beliefs.

Khayyam decries parochial beliefs and personal wishful thinking when reality is so naked and repeatable. Although expressed in a style more literary than the Heraclitan "logos," Khayyam's language is also an invitation to rational thinking since he considers all other assertions to be lacking empirical and verifiable evidence. The misperception of reality is directly correlated with the human

---

[27] Ibid., 45, 132-34.
[28] See Kahn, *The Art and Thought of Heraclitus*, 23, quoting Laertius, *Lives of Eminent Philosophers* (XXXV, D 45).

cognitive system. Heraclitus also referred to this problem when he said the eyes and ears are often bad witnesses for people since their cognitive faculty lacks understanding. (Fr. 107)[29]

Khayyam uses allegory and imagery, inviting everyone to public reasoning and an examination in a common public realm. He calls on people to note, time and again, that caravans of humans ceaselessly and repeatedly arrive in this old 'lodge' for a while and then depart. In this visible existential design, there is no one who comes back after death. As an astute scientist, he was quite clear that the process of birth and death is irreversible, self-organized, and without an anthropomorphized and personalized organizer such as a god.

In aiming to wake people up from their illusion of resurrection or reincarnation, he reaffirms Heraclitus's point that "one cannot step twice into the same river":

> Dear Heart, the reality of the world is fleeting and illusive
> And you won't benefit by complaining about this long and taxing ride.
> Instead, allow your body to sail freely with the flow, and dodge trouble.
> The direction of your destiny cannot be reversed and there is no point of return.
>
> *(rubai 32)*

Things do not happen twice and identically: the flow of existence is neither reversible nor relapses to undo itself, as Khayyam poeticizes: "Be mindful, do not share this veiled clue with anyone: A withered tulip will never blossom again." *(rubai 47)* All the fluctuating forms of the physical universe arise due to cause and effect; forms are in place impermanently before they are demolished and replaced by others. Refusing to believe in religious stories, Khayyam attributes this process of flux not to the malicious intentions of a god, but to the objective waves of change and sameness that are the underlying nature of reality. In some of his poems, Khayyam parodies those who anthropomorphize the work of this gigantic universe. In order to deconstruct this anthropomorphizing of such massive chains of cause and effect, Khayyam sarcastically inquires, what kind of drunk person (in other words, which god?) makes something so elegant only to destroy it over and over? Who in their right mind destroys one's own property the way things are destroyed in the universe on a daily basis?

The phenomena of making and unmaking that keep the flow harmonious demands another kind of logic that does not correspond to the human behavior of craving and the psychology of clinging. Universal laws function not in monotony and constancy but by maintaining opposite forces at the same time; the dual and unchangeable laws of birth and death, construction and

---

[29] *Fragments by Heraclitus* Translated by John Burnet, 14. Kirk, *The Cosmic Fragments*, 61, 281. This fragment is extracted from Sextus Empiricus.

demolition. As stated by Heraclitus, flow without the opposite forces would not be possible. If this tacit universal logic is not recognized and de-personalized, it clashes with the ineffectual human psychic wish for permanence—a clash that causes despair and sadness. Khayyam tries to rescue humans from their futile struggle to swim against the already determined flow of the stream:

> On the tablet of existence, what must be has been shown.
> The world's pen has been worn down from constantly writing 'good and bad'.
> From the dawning day all the [opposite] forces were laid down.
> Our grief and exhausting struggle are pointless.
>
> *(rubai 26)*

Khayyam's metaphorical version of a flowing river of life instead likens human existence to a production cycle of clay pots formed and then broken and the clay recycled into a new pot. An identical pot could never be recreated in this unidirectional cycle. Such cycle or flow for Khayyam and Heraclitus is self-ordered and has no orderer.

In denying the existence of an orderer and a maker for the world, Khayyam, more than Heraclitus, faced threats from the religious establishment for his heresy. His heresy did not go unnoticed or unchallenged. The medieval Muslim chroniclers reported Khayyam's clashes with the conformism of his time when he was accused of apostasy.[30] His rejection of an orderer of the world is the rejection of theism/monotheism and can be considered Khayyam's first heresy:

> I passed by the pottery shop last night,
> Noticed two thousand jugs, some sitting silently, some speaking;
> Each began to ask me in their tone of voice:
> Where is the potter, the pot-seller and pot-buyer?"
>
> *(rubai 73)*

Much like Khayyam, Heraclitus's rejection of a god as the orderer as well as his message of the impossibility of a second return to life ("stepping twice in the same river") led to the suppression of his ideas and the disappearance of his writings during the repressive religious era in Christian Europe—an indication of heresy.[31] While we have no definitive words from Heraclitus on heaven and hell, based on his philosophy and worldview, we can imagine how he might have felt about the ideas of an afterlife. He probably felt much as Khayyam did, rejecting such counterintuitive beliefs. Such rejection of Islamic tenets led Khayyam to be accused of a second heresy: the rejection of heaven and hell and an afterlife.

---

[30] See Mehdi Aminrazavi, *The Wine of Wisdom: The Life, Poetry and Philosophy of Omar Khayyam*, (Oxford: OneWorld, 2007), 55-7.
[31] Kahn, *The Art and Thought of Heraclitus*, 136.

The promises of heaven and hell were actually the reward and punishment that one wished for one's friends and enemies—a totally anthropocentric temperament projected onto the world's natural habit of life and death, which are not punishment per se, but are simply the laws of cause and effect. Khayyam debunks their rationality of heaven and hell yet again in line with the Heraclitan theory of "never-twice," in a number of quatrains:

> How long should I continue to lay bricks, trying to build a stable anchor on an unstable ocean of existence
> I abominate the outward worshipping and am bored with temples.
> Khayyam, ask who is the originator of the belief of hell?
> And ask who indeed went to hell and who returned back from heaven?
> *(rubai 6)*

> How much longer, the chandelier of the Mosques and the sacrificial smoke of the Synagogues?
> How long shall we obsess about the fires of hell and the delights of heaven?
> Go and verify for yourself: the unfaltering laws of nature and certainties
> From the beginning of time were laid down, and they remain unchanged.
> *(rubai 31)*

Like Heraclitus, Khayyam reaffirms the present reality as the only and single reality we know, flowing like a stream. Consequently, Khayyam and Heraclitus exhort people to savor their free will before they fall prey to the unbreachable law of death. False hope, postponement of pleasure, and illusive beliefs would rob people of their greatest human life quality in the world. In laying out the process of the fleeting river of life, Khayyam encourages floating, enjoying the natural hedonism effortlessly provided by life before the capricious river speeds up and capsizes their raft. He warns that opportunities to enjoy the flow should not be considered year by year but rather day to day and moment to moment:

> Oh, cup-bearer, the flowers and meadows have become lush and moist,
> Grab the moment because by next week, they will be turned into dust;
> Drink wine and pluck a flower, since before you even realize it
> The flower has withered and the grass has turned into straw.
> *(rubai 121)*

Ultimately, Khayyam and his predecessor of process philosophy Heraclitus were not big enthusiasts of human emotionalism and sensorial delusion, which could easily forge self-deceit about death and a second return. Heraclitus viewed death as the opposite force of life, and it is this continual cycle that synchronizes the flow of the river of life. The dialectic of recurrent life and death which makes this flow possible was contradicted when Plato and similar thinkers introduced the immortality of the soul in subsequent Western philosophy.[32]

To both Khayyam and Heraclitus, the inexorable stream of existence will never cease. In this non-stop surge of existence, all seemingly differentiated things, whether humans and all other beings, will become undifferentiated in the universal flow. The time from birth to death is a time to be spent in awareness. This awareness helps us counter our self-made anguishes. Our paradise and purgatory are the very choices we make in this swerving world, according to Khayyam:

> The Cosmos in commotion is an echo of our decaying body,
> The Oxus River is an expression of our untainted tears,
> Purgatory is but a flare of our futile anguishes,
> Paradise is a moment of our tranquility.
>
> (*rubai* 142)

Khayyam is not so happy about the cruel predicament of the human end, but he sees no better alternative than training the mind to stay tranquil by floating and flowing on the surface of life without entanglement with the past or future. He encouraged each caravan of humans who arrive in this old and disloyal inn not to defraud themselves with future plans, but instead stay on top of their affairs before their turn to vacate the inn for the next caravan's arrival.

How can it be heretical to believe that life, like a river, never returns in the opposite direction? Doesn't this approximation correspond to the core of human logic? No religion should take this logic as an offense, and no precepts are violated by such significant observation of life. The constant flow of the river of life takes all generations for a short ride to navigate and enjoy. This educative imagery directs humans to locate themselves in a river of life that can only be sailed once, not twice, just because the first time, they did not get enough out of it. Thus, the river of life remains the same river, yet each time its sailors are different.

Philanthropic philosophy despite the hurdles of public thinking

Both philosophers were astonished by people who live in the same world subject to the same laws and yet lag behind in thinking, speaking and acting in accordance with the common principles of natural and rational reality. The misanthropic attitude of these two thinkers toward an illogical public is not a secret. Among other disapproving things about the public, Heraclitus had this

---

[32] Graham Parkes, "Death and Detachment: Montaigne, Zen, Heidegger and the Rest," in *Death and Philosophy*, 75-87, edited by Jeff Malpas and Robert C. Solomon, (London & New York: Routledge, 1998), 76.

to say: "Men are deceived over the recognition of visible things in the same way as Homer, who was the wisest of all Hellenes..." (Fr. 56)[33] "Those who hear without the power to understand are like deaf men; the proverb holds true of them -- 'Present, they are absent.'" (Fr. 34)[34] Heraclitus believed that such unaware people would not necessarily benefit from face-to-face teachings because after they leave the teachings, they revert back to their opinions.[35]

> "They that are awake have one world in common, but of the sleeping each turns aside into a world of his own."
>
> (Fr. 89)[36]

Khayyam was aware of the same problem and the obliviousness of the masses. The public's propensity to cling to its beliefs and opinions rather than living with the rational mathematics of life prompted Khayyam also to label such people as 'sleepwalkers'.

> On the face of the earth, I only see sleep-walkers,
> Under it, I see those consumed and sealed off,
> When I visualize the landscape of nothingness,
> I see the unborn and the expired ones!
>
> (*rubai* 52)

Heraclitus and Khayyam were aware that there seems to be something cognitively and obscurely wrong which prevents large numbers of people from assimilating and dealing with the rational world around them. At some point in their lives, both moved away from public appearances. Nevertheless, despite the majority who were not aware, these two heroic philosophers never gave up on people and the potential to 'wake up,' so they continued with their philanthropic philosophy. Despite their sociological frustrations, both philosophers shared their most profound realizations of the universe with the public up to the end of their lives. As much as their stances seem 'arrogant,' in fact their erudite approach was down-to-earth and accessible, and perhaps most importantly, they saw themselves in the same river of life with others whose rafts were either going astray or capsized, and who needed to be thrown a rope so they would not drown. Khayyam and Heraclitus threw out philosophical ropes for any who wished to save themselves.

---

[33] *Fragments by Heraclitus* Translated by John Burnet, 8. Kirk, *The Cosmic Fragments*, 203-4. This fragment is extracted from Hippolyte.
[34] *Fragments by Heraclitus* Translated by John Burnet, 5, Kirk, *The Cosmic Fragments*, 47, 203.
[35] Vitthiyes Shan, Introduction of Heraclitus https://www.academia.edu/29801328/INTRODUCTION_OF_HERACLITUS. (Accessed February 5, 2020).
[36] *Fragments by Heraclitus* Translated by John Burnet, 12. Kirk, *The Cosmic Fragments*, 63-4. This fragment is extracted from Plutarch.

Chapter 3
The Liberated Drunkard: Daoism and Wine in the *Rubaiyat*

The metaphors of 'wine' and a 'drunken man' have often been associated with the name and poetry of Omar Khayyam. So it is startling to see that Zhuangzi (Chuang Tzu), the great Daoist (Taoist) thinker of the fourth century B.C.E., applied the same metaphors in almost the exact same philosophical and psychological manner as did Khayyam. It seems that these two very different writers employed such metaphors in a similar way, aiming to orient the minds of their audience towards having a view of life from a more relaxed angle than the usual angst-ridden state of mind:

> "When a drunken man falls from a cart, he may be hurt but he will not be killed. His bones and joints are no different from those of other men, but the degree of harm done by the fall differs radically... Having been unaware that he was riding, he is now unaware that he is falling."
> (Zhuangzi, Chapter 19, *Fathoming Life*)[1]

Zhuangzi refers to someone who does not have a stiff attitude towards life, who allows the natural flow of things to take shape, who is free of worry, like someone drunk on wine. This person is a sage, and nothing can harm him in life:

> "The frights and shocks of life and death have no way to enter his breast, so he is unflinching no matter how things may clash with him. Finding wholeness in liquor [wine], he reaches such a state—imagine then someone who finds his wholeness in the Heavenly [Dao - Nature]."
> (Zhuangzi, Chapter 19, *Fathoming Life*)

Zhuangzi's drunkard and his wine remind us of Khayyam's invitation to 'drink wine.' Both are prodding us to loosen mental tension. Wine loosens the stiff mind, loosens the ego and loosens the constant attempt to gain control over

---

[1] Brook Ziporyn (Translation and Introduction), *Zhuangzi: The Essential Writings, With Selections from Traditional Commentaries*, (Indianapolis: Hackett Publishing Company, Inc., 2009), 239.

matters of nature and circumstances that cannot be swayed or controlled, whether in the present or in the future. Khayyam writes:

> I am acquainted with the appearance of the world of existence and non-existence;
> I know the interior of the highs and lows.
> Despite this bank of knowledge, I am humbled,
> Because I know of no state better than that of drunkenness.
>
> (*rubai* 99)

> My existence will be in jeopardy without precious wine;
> Without wine it is hard to bear the burden of physical existence.
> I adore the moment when the *Sāqi* whispers:
> 'Take another cup,' and I am satiated, unable to do so.
>
> (*rubai* 76)

To gain some insight into the meaning behind these metaphors and the relationship between Zhuangzi's philosophy and Khayyam's perception of living an unfettered life, we can explore the ageless philosophy of Daoism in ancient China. Zhuangzi is considered one of the key systematizers of Daoist philosophy in China, but Laozi (Lao Tzu), the founder and great master of classical Daoism, also communicated about drunkenness. To him, the drunken mind is in a state near to the Dao, a state in which everything is itself and at ease. The drunken person is not ambitious; the heart is empty and hollow, which means nothing is lacking.[2] The drunken man or woman corresponds to a sage who forgets himself, and through this forgetfulness, he or she is preserved.[3]

The Dao spoken of by Laozi is the Way of nature, the expression of the natural laws that operate everything harmoniously ("the 10,000 things"), humans included. But despite the Dao and natural harmony, human suffering continues. Over much time, many insightful sages puzzled over the reasons for and the way out of human suffering. As one of these insightful thinkers, Zhuangzi observed a rift between the workings of nature and the cognitive and behavioral workings of humans. The way humans impose themselves on nature and how they try to construct their own mental reality while forgetting about nature has caused this problematic rift, throwing humans out of their natural harmony and disaffecting them in odd and obscure ways.

---

[2] Lao Tzu, *Tao Te Ching*, translated by Ch'u Ta-Kao, (New York: Samuel Weiser, 1973), Chapters III, IV, V, XV.
[3] Ibid., VII.

Human harmony can be divided into *existential* and *circumstantial* perspectives. According to Zhuangzi (and Khayyam), existential harmony is when one's understanding of nature and natural flow matches one's behavior, corroborating with the reality of things. Existential harmony, in Daoism, requires perseverance on the part of the human practitioner through wise engagement or 'non-disruptive activity' (*wu wei*)—non-action at the right time—letting life take its natural course rather than controlling, manipulating or even simply worrying about it. Despite the ups and downs through time, natural or existential harmony repairs itself and brings its forces together without shortcuts or manipulative actions. Processes such as the healing of a wound or absorption of food in the body require no effort. Coexistence with others, following the law of interdependence, understanding the non-anthropocentric mechanism of existence, living with awareness of time-space and the flow of energy, and the experience and acceptance of aging and dying are examples of mastering existential harmony.

Circumstantial harmony, on the other hand, is a personal attitude toward harmony. Although it is fluid and unpredictable time-place dependent, the circumstantial harmony lies in the nature of a non-impulsive and non-emotional mind, which paves the uncomplicated and graceful flow of things. It is a drunkard state of mind. It includes vital acts such as practicing patience in the face of crises, subduing the anxious mind, avoiding harmful imagination and mental proliferation, and preventing a reactive life—all for the sake of harmonizing with one's surroundings. In the Daoistic perspective, it can be said that if one has already become skillful at observing the harmony of nature and existential matters, then circumstantial matters can also be managed through practical insightfulness, as well as non-disruptive activity.

The general problem arises when deviating from the Way (Dao) that nature has assigned to living beings. Nature and humans, despite being of the same prototypal derivation, look as if they are following two different paths. Nature is itself. It follows its own intrinsic laws, which remain stable, and flows forward. All other species follow nature; they corroborate with natural harmony. Meanwhile, humans are not typically representative of nature; they follow their minds; they pursue their own projects, which are variable, unpredictable and often divergent from the natural emanation of things. It is the compulsion of the human thought process that drives humans to follow their ego, ambitions and beliefs on the one hand, and yet they feel the contrast with their longing for natural living on the other. This dichotomous stance has often blurred the vision; it has caused confusion and has fueled fear and anxieties. By resorting to the power of clever individuals or interpretations based on culture, masses of people at large have depended on their intellectuality, piety, wealth, fame, cleverness and domination in order to ignore and even defy the natural processes and natural laws that govern the existentially harmonious world. Counterintuitive beliefs such as defying death and promoting immortality have been part of this exhausting dichotomous living.

> "Developing the Heavenly [natural Way] empowers life; developing the Human [ego], plunders it."
>
> (Chapter 19, *Fathoming Life*)[4]

Zhuangzi decided to address the fine-tuning of this very human anomaly. As a naturalist and Daoist analyst, Zhuangzi discerned that the problem lay in a perpetuating and exhausting self-absorption. Zhuangzi reverses the situation by turning to nature for guidance and noting that nature has no ego, no fear, no anxiety, and flows through time; in the meantime, things get done effortlessly. Returning then to the metaphor of drunkenness, we can see why Zhuangzi approvingly alludes to the drunkard who does not toil and harbors no anxiety about the pointless details in life. The drunkard who drinks wine abandons the exhausting struggle of constantly doing, wanting, and thinking. He gets on and off the carriage of life without hyper reflection—and even when he falls off the carriage, he is not hurt because of his loosened attitudes.

> "Those who fathom the real character of the life in us do not labor themselves over the aspects of life that deliberate activity can do nothing about. Those who fathom the real character of fate do not labor themselves over what understanding cannot alter."
>
> (Chapter 19, *Fathoming Life*)[5]

For Zhuangzi, the key principle lies in assessing life circumstances, deciding what things need to be dealt with, and what things need to be left to the flow of time and nature. To move away from an artificial social and mental construction of nature ("loosening the mental inclinations"), Graham Parkes expresses a Daoist technique: "The Daoists recommend a technique they call 'fasting the heart' or 'emptying the mind', which involves waiting patiently until all ideas, opinions, and presuppositions about the way the world is, fade away. Free of mental clutter, the mind can then respond to the situation as it is, rather than as we would prefer it to be."[6] One responds then to a situation with a lucid mind, not with an impulsive snap.

---

[4] Ziporyn, *Zhuangzi*, 240.
[5] Ibid., 236.
[6] Graham Parkes, "Confucian and Daoist, Stoic and Epicurean. Some Parallels in Ways of Living," in *Confucius and Cicero: Old Ideas for a New World, New Ideas for an Old World*, 43-58, edited by Andrea Balbo and Jaewon Ahn, (Leck: De Gruyter, 2019), 51.

This understanding of the discretion of how nature handles things is the understanding of Dao or the Way, and the aim is to follow it, coalescing one's mind with it. For Zhuangzi, being a drunkard is to let go of one's constant agendas and manipulation by simply giving in to the process and participating with it in order to improve the flow of things, both circumstantially as well as existentially. Through this practice, one's mind slowly comes closer and closer to the natural mechanisms of the life to which we all belong. It is as if the knowledge of nature and life becomes one's own knowledge.

We can easily imagine Khayyam and Zhuangzi sitting and talking together, perhaps sharing a pot of tea, nodding their heads in strong agreement with each other when exchanging ideas about the natural harmony. Like Zhuangzi, Khayyam's realism also centered around a knowledge of the world with clear-cut, natural limits which are unchangeable. The lows and highs of human destiny also have their limits; all come to an end at some point. So the nondual flow of the world should teach humans how low and high points coalesce by themselves without any interference, like the fierce turmoil of a storm and the quiet calm afterwards. The non-interventionist mind of a drunkard does not bother with what cannot be changed or manipulated:

> The good and evil in human life,
> The low and high moments in our mood which create our destiny—
> Don't ask the world to resolve them: sound reason should know better.
> The world is a thousand times less intrusive than you.

(rubai 34)

Both Zhuangzi and Khayyam encourage getting drunk on the wine of wisdom. Khayyam prescribes his wine for two ailments. The first is for the existential tension of worrying about impermanency and death. The second is to address the personal entanglement with desire, happiness, fame, wealth, and above all, grief. To a drunken person with his altered state of mind, they cannot ponder birth and death, especially when the joy of here and now is at hand—future for a drunkard is more of an illusion than reality. This drunken state is a state of being one with life without the usual personality inhibitions. Khayyam shares:

> Since coming to the world was not my own choice,
> Then the choice of departure is surely also out of my hands.
> Get on your feet and make a firm decision, oh *Sāqi*
> That I shall wash down worldly despair with wine.

(rubai 94)

The going away of winter and the coming of spring
Is like turning the pages of our existence.
"Drink wine, don't be sad," said the wise sage:
All the griefs of the world are poison, and wine is the antidote.

(rubai 128)

According to Zhuangzi (and Laozi), life and death are interdependent opposites and are one single strand, like morning and evening.[7] Life and death, day and night, are the inner transformations of this single entity; nothing should disturb you.[8] Death is a trivial episode, like going to rest in a modest fashion.[9]

The usual trauma of dying has as much to do with the conditioning of the human mind as it has to do with the gradual human transition from nature to culture. The loss of connection to naturalness gradually became an embedded anomaly that prompted Zhuangzi's and Khayyam's reflections and remedies. Zhuangzi has absolutely no hesitation in saying that if humans wish to have equanimity, they will have to accept reality the way beasts do:

> "Beasts that feed on grass do not fret over a change of pasture; creatures that live in water do not fret over a change of stream. They accept the minor shift as long as the all-important constant is not lost. [Be like them] and joy, anger, grief, and happiness can never enter your breast."
>
> <div align="right">(Section 21, <i>Tian Zifang</i>)[10]</div>

To Khayyam as well, the joy of living is in naturalness, whereas fickleness is a curse, giving rise to capricious behavior and distorted expectations.

In this wheel of existence with impenetrable frontiers,
Drink wine with a joyful heart, because the circle around you is just right.
And when it's your turn, don't sigh in despair.
It is a cup that everyone is given a chance to taste in their turn.

(rubai 125)

---

[7] Graham Parkes, "Death and Detachment: Montaigne, Zen, Heidegger and the Rest," in *Death and Philosophy*, 75-87, edited by Jeff Malpas and Robert C. Solomon, (London & New York: Routledge, 1998), 76.

[8] A. C. Graham, *Chuang-Tzu: The Inner Chapters*, (London: Unwin Hayman Limited, 1989; 1981), 23, 131, 177.

[9] Ibid., 177.

[10] Burton Watson, translator and editor, *The Complete Works of Zhuangzi*, (New York: Columbia University Press, 2013; 1968), 326. https://archive.org/details/thecompleteworksof zhuangzi/page/n5/mode/2up.

The stress of living is countered by a "drunken state." A drunken state means that the past with its bitter-sweet memories, the future, death, and other preoccupying thoughts are unshackled, and the path of *here and now* is tread. A drunken state also means flowing like a fish in the water: "As fish go on setting directions for each other in the water, men go on setting directions for each other in the Way."[11]

Zhuangzi considers delighting in life to be a real, authentic state. In not hating or fearing death, the destination becomes clear, and in a drunken state, the dream (the flow of natural energy) and reality (physical life) rejoin.[12] The words of Zhuangzi about being drunk in life are echoed again: The time of getting on and falling off the carriage is not noticed; life and death are nothing to he who is drunk by wine.[13] Along the same lines, Wang Fuzhi, the seventeenth-century philosopher with a Confucianist tone, articulates that the drunken state removes the anxiety of consciousness and replaces it with a naturalness that sits in the unconscious:

> "We delight in life because of the consciousness that comes with life. But consciousness has no support as soon as life ends—not to speak of ten thousand years later. When conscious of the pleasure of drinking wine, we are unconscious of the sorrow of weeping."[14]

Here Khayyam is also precise in insisting that delight comes with life moment to moment; it is neither about tomorrow nor about thousands of years later, when we will have no consciousness; it's clearly and only about now:

> Oh friend, let us not grieve the tomorrow that has not arrived.
> Let us treasure the life at hand now,
> For when we depart from this ancient lodge
> We shall join those who departed seven thousand years ago.
>
> (*rubai*, 130)

In Zhuangzi's preoccupation with making Daoism a non-creationist, non-interventionist philosophy, he emphasized the importance of awareness of 'self so' (*ziran*) and 'forgetting self' (*zouwang*). Both states are for mastering the self.[15] *Ziran*, is a *self* who is *so*, a self without mental exertion (*wu wei*), who

---

[11] Graham, *Chuang-Tzu*, 138.
[12] Ziporyn, *Zhuangzi*, 76-77. (Chapter 2, *Equalizing Assessments of Things*).
[13] Thomas Merton, *The Way of Chuang Tzu*, (New York: New Directions Publishing Corporation, 2010; 1965), 106.
[14] Ziporyn, *Zhuangzi*, 449 ("Selections from Traditional Commentaries on the Inner Chapters".)
[15] Ibid., 624-5.

continuously *forgets* the past and forgets his self-importance in fleeting reality. These states may not misguide a person by undermining the ideal values of persevering in life while being prepared to take responsibility for one's own faults.[16] *Ziran, zouwang* and *wu wei* are psychological and personality tools in order to attain freedom from the chains of reaction and mental tension. They are the states of mind to loosen the self until the self gradually becomes its natural self—a self that is 'so.' Then, "sitting in forgetfulness," in Zhuangzi's description, is a form of meditation that is the nucleus of a deeper understanding of things.[17] Thus, in a drunken state, with freedom and the inclination to flow like water, all these states manifest themselves in the mind.

Zhuangzi's notion of a happy heart is found in the deeply embedded, quintessential Daoist concept of *wu wei*, meaning the ability to choose inaction at the time of inaction, and choosing action when it matches the flow of things. In order to attain a state of *wu wei* or equanimity, or a state of suchness without any extra effort, one's psychological state requires maturity in accepting the contrasting forces of life: low-high, day-night, good-bad, pain-pleasure, life-death as they come. *Wu wei* is the state of nature that is by no means monotonous—it is a state produced by opposite forces (*yin-yang*), which give rise to an equilibrium. To exercise this equanimity, one must understand and process the contrasting effects in the mind rather than being passive or taking a non-judgmental position solely out of moral naiveté. A Daoist certainly makes judgments and takes actions, but only if they contribute to the natural and constructive flow of things. Nonaction out of desperation, naiveté or detachment fails to detect the benefits and harms of such nonaction.

According to Laozi, Zhuangzi, and Khayyam, a state of drunkenness represents possessing a broader understanding of the nature of life, about birth and death, of greedy and frugal living, and the harm and benefits of our thoughts. Such an outlook aims to uproot the busy and reckless mind by bringing it back to a platform from which the soothing panorama of coming and going can be seen without taking any particular action. Humans can, in fact, be similar to nature, acting as bridges between and harmonizers of the opposite impulses of life. This is existence in a state of non-disruptive flow, being at ease and yet living life in harmony with others and nature. Fusing one's mind with the flow of nature results in a poise, humble life, as Zhuangzi divulges:

---

[16] Ibid., 625, 298, 158, 366.
[17] Mathias Obert, "Rückzug und Freiheit im Zhuangzi: Ansätze zu einer komparativen Ethik," *Perspektiven der Philosophie, Neues Jahrbuch Online*, Band 28 (2002), 378.

"I received life because the time had come; I will lose it because the order of things passes on. Be content with this time and dwell in this order and then neither sorrow nor joy can touch you. In ancient times this was called the 'freeing of the bound.' ... that's the way it's always been. What would I have to resent?"

(Section 6, *The Great and Venerable Teacher*)[18]

This attitude of 'freeing the bound' as we grow old and naturalism in order to experience contentment is elevated to its peak in the Khayyamian perspective as well. Nonstop thinking and worrying, sometimes even without an objective reason, often leads people to unhappiness and troubled emotions, despite their might and wealth. Khayyam's contentment with an attitude of loosening the ties represents living in simplicity, not merely with modest surroundings, but also transporting a tranquil and wishless mind to everyday living.

I want a jug of precious wine and a book of poetry,
Strength to breathe, and a half loaf of bread to eat.
This way you and I find ourselves together seemingly destitute-
But actually, happier than the wealthiest king of the land.

(*rubai* 98)

It can be assumed that the mind of 'the wealthiest king of the land' is not quiet and probably vacillates between indulgence and anguish, victory and defeat, a desire for living longer in the face of an inevitable death. A quiet mind in Khayyamian outlook is, therefore, happier than a wealthy king's.

The first step to attain this quietude is to let go of the duality of joy and sorrow. Perfect joy is to be without joy[19] Zhuangzi says: "Resting content in the time and finding his place in the flow, joy and sorrow had no way to seep in."[20] The floating drunken mind releases the rigidity of joy-sorrow. In fact, this mind can turn the sorrow of the death of loved ones and friends into a 'pleasant sorrow.' This is to say, not only is one able to recover gently from the sorrow but one is also able to understand joy as a simple fact of being in the natural world. Transient emotions would no longer have the power to fluster one's state of being. In a remarkable description of inspired equanimity, Zhuangzi says that even if nine out of ten of your old friends have now passed away, the joy of life still should flow uninhibitedly in you.[21]

---

[18] Watson, *The Complete Works of Zhuangzi*, 127. See also, Ziporyn, *Zhuangzi*, 148-9.
[19] Merton, *The Way of Chuang Tzu*, 145, section 18.
[20] Ziporyn, *Zhuangzi*, 93, 148 (Chapter 3, *The Primacy of Nourishing Life*).
[21] Ibid., 316 (Chapter 25, *Zeyang*).

Khayyam's words are very similar when he speaks of aiming to reach an imperturbable state of understanding nature and natural processes as our friends expire one after another:

> The cordial friends all expired.
> The agent of death took them down one by one.
> We were in the celebration of life sharing wine,
> Whilst those before us had already gotten drunk on the same wine.
>
> (*rubai* 38)

> Dear friends, when you meet in congenial companionship,
> Toast to the memory of friends who are absent among you.
> Clink your wine cups together,
> And when the next one's turn comes, turn over his cup.
>
> (*rubai* 83)

The deepest awareness comes with the highest level of equanimity. Such awareness de-personalizes the field around it. It follows the nonjudgmental course of things: "Things should be allowed to follow their own course, and men should not value one situation over another."[22] Such equanimity lies in contentment, which is already there in the core of life. In judiciousness of *wu wei* and simplicity, human contentment manifests itself and contentment is linked with simplicity. Laozi explains that the virtue of simplicity is superior to all other virtues; however inactive it seems from the outside, it lacks nothing, it is self-reliant, and its practitioners rule the world.[23] The wealth of simplicity will never be finished, nor will it capitulate to the command of the world (because there is nothing to be capitulated), as Laozi puts it.[24] "He who knows contentment is rich."[25]

The Dao practitioners were not suggesting that people acquire knowledge, but rather they tried to restore them to simplicity.[26] Similarly, Khayyam also takes no interest in verbal knowledge. Words can fill the mind, but the quiet nature of life is the ultimate frontier of existence. Being aware of the confoundedness of human theories, Khayyam firmly stood by the harmony of a largely wordless human experience with life and the splendor of joy in simplicity:

---

[22] Roger T. Ames, James Hamilton Ware, "Zhuangzi," https://www.britannica.com/biography/Zhuangzi. (Accessed May 12, 2020).
[23] Lao Tzu, *Tao Te Ching*, XXXVIII, XLIX.
[24] Ibid., XXXVII, LVII.
[25] Ibid., XXXIII.
[26] Ibid., LXV.

Tomorrow, I'll take down the flag of hypocrisy.
Despite my grey hair, I intend to make the most out of wine.
The years of my life have added up to be seventy;
If I don't live delightfully now, then when?

(rubai 141)

It seems 'happy heart' are just words, echoing over and over,
But a mature companion exists in reality: the pure wine of true happiness.
Do not let go of the cheerful state that your wine jug generates.
The only thing that remains today is your wine cup!

(rubai 21)

For two convincing reasons, Khayyam declares anxiety over worldly matters to be futile: first, all personal good and bad will pass down the corridor of impermanency; secondly, the end of everything and the final human destination is death, dust and oblivion. This panoramic projection can relieve a person from petty, hollow, or short-term anxieties. Although a person without anxieties in societies might be seen as silly, lazy, imprudent, or rebellious, Khayyam regards it as one's prerogative to relish an existential freedom and subsequently experience the irrevocable joy of living—returning once again to a drunken state. It is an act of unattachment, seen through the beauty of a passing life:

Today is my turn to feel happy and young;
I drink wine to let joy inhabit my life.
Do not slander me for my rebellious choice, which brings pleasure to my life.
Although an adventurist choice, it's my way of rewriting life.

(rubai 16)

Death is nothing: a frivolous funeral

From their bird's-eye view, Zhuangzi and Khayyam viewed the work of nature without individual distinctiveness and abandoned anticipation of life after death. In one instance, Zhuangzi's disciples wondered what would happen to his corpse after their master's death! The disciples feared that crows and vultures would eat the master's corpse if they left it abandoned outside. The response of Zhuangzi to such a concern was a parody about his own funeral. He said the paraphernalia of his funeral is fully prepared, nothing more and nothing less to worry about. "Above ground I'll be eaten by crows and vultures, below ground by ants and crickets. Now you want to rob one to feed the other.

Why such favoritism?"[27] Here, the naturalism of Zhuangzi and his insightful and benevolent considerations view of natural processes is clear. He made a funeral, and the corpus of rituals seem like a frivolous ceremony.

In remarkably the same vein, Khayyam opens the gate to deemotionalize and depersonalize our own death and the way we view natural processes. The funeral is simply a cultural and religious convention for those who have been left behind, not for the deceased whose body shall be consumed and scattered in nature. Khayyam encourages people to witness for themselves that no one is exempt from the reprocessing laboratory of nature, whether wise or foolish, whether we believe in astrology or not, whether we are given a magnificent funeral or dreadfully consumed by a wolf in the wild or ants underground:

> Since this spinning wheel did not even give priority to the wise ones,
> Why should it matter whether there are seven or eight planets in our astrology?
> Since death and the suspension of all desires is the final destiny,
> It doesn't matter if we are consumed by ants in the grave or a wolf in the wild.
> (*rubai* 40)

On a grand existential level, all sentient beings die and are forgotten by nature. Why should the death of humans be special? Does nature care who dies and who doesn't, or how they die, or what happens to their corpses? Zhuangzi and Khayyam were very clear about seeing death as part of natural processes rather than some sort of prearranged divine plan of how people should die and whether they arise again. They both viewed death as an indiscriminate, impersonal and egalitarian act of nature on a daily basis. One ends up as the prey of a predator, another dies of old age, while another dies prematurely. Death is nothing to nature, given the countless deaths constantly and daily happening in nature.

Gloom is an unknown emotion to nature. But humans, due to psychological, cultural and societal reasons, personalize death, thinking about it differently than the way nature actually handles it. No matter which entities die, nature turns them all into dust, and minerals, and food for the vultures, worms and ants. In this way, all entities vanish permanently without a trace. It can be affirmed that nature engages in the trade of oblivion– all entities are forgotten and gradually erased from memory. In Daoism, all things become empty of

---

[27] Ziporyn, *Zhuangzi*, 340 (Chapter 32, *Lie Yukou*). Another noteworthy translation is: "Well, above ground I shall be eaten by crows and kites, below it by ants and worms. In either case I shall be eaten. Why are you so partial to birds?" See Merton, *The Way of Chuang Tzu*, 156.

what they once were. Here, emptiness or nothingness is not a metaphysical concept pointing to the absence of life, but rather is considered to be the very nature of existence—nothing is the root of existence.[28]

Zhuangzi taught that great people never dread death and have no great lust for life either; they exit without resistance. "Easy come, easy go;" they never ask where they go to![29] Zhuangzi triumphs over death by removing the person who thinks of death from the middle; this way, there is neither pessimism nor optimism, neither joy nor sorrow, no horror of decomposition by accepting the process of transformation.[30] The wise ones do not think being alive is delightful and death repulsive. They emerge and submerge without struggle.[31]

Khayyam also presents existence-annihilation as the greatest drama in the universal amphitheater. The artists appear on the stage to play their magnificent role and are then replaced by another group time and again. This remarkable performance has certain clarity to it, which the performers must discern; they are commissioned for a temporary appearance on the stage.

> We are the marionettes and the world is the puppeteer:
> Even though it seems real, it is transitory and ephemeral.
> We each play a protagonist role for a brief time and
> Then go back into the booth of oblivion, one by one.
>
> (*rubai* 50)

In the theatre of existence, the birth and death of all beasts and all humans are identical, with no advantages. The birth and death of a scholar, a villain, and a fly are equal; as Khayyam said, we appear and disappear in the same fashion. Not only would the hard labor of nature have involved in making a human or a fly dissolve equally in the death of the organism, but in human communities, the aging and death of a scoundrel are equal to that of a saint. This certainly defeats the argument that humans are biologically superior over other living beings or that pious ones are more privileged over non-pious ones. The laws of biology and the irreversible process of death, according to Khayyam, are not there to be manipulated by cultural jargon.

Yet, the dramatic interpretation of death by humans in their respective cultures can destabilize emotions for a long time. Cultures feed these dramatic

---

[28] Zhihua Yao, "Typology of Nothing: Heidegger, Daoism and Buddhism," *Comparative Philosophy* 1, no. 1 (2010), 83.
[29] Merton, *The Way of Chuang Tzu*, 61.
[30] Graham, *Chuang-Tzu*, 23-4.
[31] Ziporyn, *Zhuangzi*, 139 (Chapter 6, *The Great Source as Teacher*).

interpretations of death, which can be difficult to extricate oneself from.[32] It's important to realize that the aim is not to feel *nothing* at the idea of death (i.e., no emotions), but is instead to come to peace with it, to acquire a feeling of acceptance with the idea. Zhuangzi says death is no damage to life; the damage comes from one's own attitude.[33] He adds, "Know that all things in the world are equal and the same."[34] Laozi also joins in, pointing out that when the sage gives himself to life and forgets himself, he is well looked after.[35] There is no funeral in nature. Nature is relentlessly in the state of becoming, transmuting, and turning the dust of one's corpse into another thing. There is thus no sadness in the domain of natural life—the sadness is in the domain of human life.

Khayyam came from an Islamic culture, a culture that has embellished the narrative of death and after-death to the extent that humans feel special, enjoying a heavenly status in nature. In order to *disempower* this special status based on religious justifications, Khayyam composed a number of quatrains to do away with the special treatment of humans, including the Muslims, after death. Khayyam's unambiguous position was to confront popular cultural superstitions—the 'cult of the dead.' To him, human culture and religion are nothing but conventions, and human beliefs in them are often counterintuitive vis-à-vis the immutable laws of nature. What is clear to Khayyam is that the process of death is irreversible, and there is no reappearance in this or another life for another chance.

Khayyam also believed that people of different cultures are often so enwrapped with their ancestral religious traditions, sacred laws and truth-seeking inclinations that they truly forget they are biologically equal to the people of other cultures. Following ancestral beliefs and truth-seeking are sometimes lifetime projects of people based on their culture. In Daoism and Khayyamian thought, liberated minds are free from the constructed labels of their cultural environments. That is to say, human existence is the work of interdependent and nondiscriminatory laws of nature, not the work of native gods or a capricious arbitrator.

Easy come, easy go, like a breeze, says Zhuangzi! Nature forgets those who passed away, and it is oblivious to their pain and pleasure, even though humans with their memories don't wish to lose themselves forever. Zhuangzi taught a

---

[32] See Parkes, "Death and Detachment," 76-8.
[33] Merton, *The Way of Chuang Tzu*, 137.
[34] Watson, *The Complete Works of Zhuangzi*, section 19.
[35] Lao Tzu, *Tao Te Ching*, VII, XIX.

philosophy that advocates a state of mind that has a perfect fit in life, like a foot that fits in a comfortable shoe without being aware of or troubled by it. "The forgetting of the foot means the shoe fits comfortably." [36]

The drunkard is unobstructed by life and is not concerned with boredom, impermanency or death. The naturalness is when the human project and nature's project connect, come close, and coalesce. The joining of the two projects becomes a necessity, especially when humans confront sensitive and existential issues. Zhuangzi assures us that when joy and sorrow come and go, they cannot be stopped from flowing in human emotions; we just need to remind ourselves that we are a temporary assembly to process these emotions in the world.[37]

The picturesque surroundings of nature are our reminder to take in joy before our turn comes to an end. Khayyam inspires us:

> Take your cup and jug, oh seeker of pleasure,
> Walk in joy around the meadows near a stream,
> Knowing that this spinning wheel has given birth to many beautiful darlings
> But then turned them into cups and jugs hundreds of times.
>
> *(rubai 66)*

***

In conclusion, the resonance between Zhuangzi's ideas and Khayyam's is strikingly evident, despite belonging to different generations and geography. Perhaps it was just a coincidence. Or perhaps, since Khayyam's hometown of Nishapur lay on the Silk Road where the ideas of Daoism could have reached there as easily as the Manichaeism of Nishapur and Central Asia reached China, he was directly inspired by reading or hearing of some of Zhuangzi's ideas. Or maybe, the existential ideas of Khayyam and Zhuangzi are so fundamental that they arise on archetypal and atemporal levels. Their overlapping narratives of admiration for a drunkard's tranquility, the joy of flowing with the rhythm of nature, and refusal to worry about death address universal existential human struggles using the same approach with the same imagery.

This psychological guidance makes sense to those who realize the foolishness of trying to control the uncontrollable in life and who wish to shift from living in a panicked and controlling state to living in harmony with the natural flow of things. With such a leap, nothing has actually changed in regards to the circumstances of life and death; only one's perception has changed, flipping

---

[36] Ziporyn, *Zhuangzi*, 251 (Chapter 19, *Fathoming Life*).
[37] Ibid., 298-99 (Chapter 22, *Knowinghood Journeyed North*).

over obstructive beliefs to an inner gaze, becoming a happy witness and celebrator of life. In a drunken state, one is not a controller nor a driver but rather an easy rider who understands that despite the bumps and the curves in the road, the journey through the beautiful scenery matters more than the destination.

Chapter 4
Self-Rule, Joy and Emptiness: The Bedrock of the Buddhist and Khayyamian Paths

"All things lack entitihood, since change is perceived. There is nothing without entity because all things have emptiness."[1]
(Nagarjuna's *Mūlamadhyamakakārikā*)

Oh oblivious ones, physical appearance is nothing but emptiness,
And this nine-sphered cosmos is also empty.
Just cultivate a delightful heart now in the midst of a decaying existence.
We live precariously dependent on the next breath, and even that may soon be empty!

(*rubai* 101)

Despite their outwardly contrasting lives, the third-century Buddhist monk-scholar Nagarjuna (ca. 150-250 C.E.) and the twelfth-century poet-scholar Omar Khayyam put forth approaches that are fundamentally more alike than different. It is intriguing to ponder how two great thinkers, living almost nine hundred years apart and with entirely different cultures and personal backgrounds, could have ended up with such similar philosophical outlooks. But both Nagarjuna and Khayyam were ultimately seeking an existential solution to the same philosophical problem.

Their ideas connected on two fundamental levels. On the one hand, because of the constant change and resulting impermanence of nature, the world is "empty" of any true and lasting identity. On the other hand, liberation from this confusion can occur when that "emptiness" of the world is recognized and present moments of life are savored. Both Nagarjuna and Khayyam invite their readers to harness the awareness of change and impermanence in order to appreciate each moment. Let us explore their deep and breathtaking contemplations further to discover how these two thinkers' approaches complemented each other, to our great benefit hundreds of years later.

---

[1] *The Fundamental Wisdom of the Middle Way*, Nagarjuna's *Mūlamadhyamakakārikā*, translation and commentary by Jay L. Garfield, (Oxford: Oxford University Press, 1995), chapter 13 (Examination of Compounded Phenomena), 35, verse 3.

The impetus behind the philosophy initially dispensed by the Buddha and later expanded upon by Nagarjuna was the conundrum associated with the conjunction between human life and the world, a conjoining that often ended in a clash, needing a solution. Nagarjuna's solution lay in seeing the world's impermanence, leading to liberation. Like the Buddha, Nagarjuna emphasized the three perennial principles of existence: non-self, impermanency and confusion. Non-self is expressed in different ways such as transient phenomenon, non-substantiality, emptiness, no true identity/nature, and other similar euphemisms. Impermanence is the mechanism of time delineated by the nature of relentless change from one stage of existence to the next, and as a result, everything exists in an intermediate stage. Confusion, which leads to the pain of existence, refers to the state of a deluded mind that ignores the reality of impermanence with endless change and the ultimate emptiness of all phenomena. Within these three principles, Nagarjuna found the key to unraveling the conundrum of existence.

According to Nagarjuna, the relentless shifting of the world of phenomena finds its deeper roots in an empty, indistinct and indefinite course of action in the inner structure of the world. He argued that despite the misleading impression of entities being solid with a fixed beginning and end, all things are always in an intermediate state. Humans fall victim to their own biographical entanglements and illusions about linearity, whereas they themselves, in fact, embody the universal shifting of all things in the pulsating apparatus of impermanence.

In Nagarjunian Buddhism, whatever phenomena rise, exist, and cease in the world do so interdependently, based on the laws of cause and effect. Things do not come into existence nor go out of existence solely due to their own self-nature. This is to say nothing exists for itself, by itself, and out of itself. There is no known origination nor complete cessation or the end station of things. Things exist due to previous causes, not from themselves—no self-causation.[2] By drawing upon this mechanism of interdependence, also called 'dependent arising,' Nagarjuna argued that phenomena are constantly shifting and thus ultimately empty of their own nature—but this is *not* a literal emptiness.[3] Instead, it refers to an *emptiness of permanent identity*, and the mechanism of change is the instrument of this emptiness.[4] This ontological approach assumes that all identities are temporary and remain fluid. Given this astute

---

[2] Ibid., chapter 1 (Examination of Conditions), 3, verse 1.
[3] Ludovic Viévard, "La vacuité et sa valeur instrumentale," *Journal Asiatique*, 288.2 (July 2000), 422.
[4] Ibid., 415-16.

view of the physical world, Nagarjuna can retrospectively be seen as much like Heraclitus, a precursor of Process Philosophy, which ultimately was corroborated with science (physics and biology in particular) as well as with the modern philosophy heralded by Alfred N. Whitehead.[5]

Passing from a state of confusion to liberation is called 'nirvana' in Buddhism. 'Nirvana' is a compound Sanskrit word built from *ni* ('out') and *vana* ('blown'), referring to blowing out the flame of the confused and unknowing mind for the sake of living a heedful life. Nagarjuna, as an astute Buddhist thinker, believed that the liberation of nirvana meant living in this everchanging world while truly knowing, being aware of the nature of impermanency and the emptiness of all things. It meant being saved from one's own ignorance as well as freed from the burning flame of impulses. Despite the profundity of such a state, to Nagarjuna, nirvana is in fact nothing extraordinary. It represents a clear and sudden paradigm shift toward liberation and the joy of life—like flipping the coin to its other side!

The same cognitive understanding and its resulting emancipation was the goal of Khayyam. As we will see, he fostered a very similar concept of emptiness. Khayyam's deductive interpretation of existence matched that of Nagarjuna's view of emptiness: all things eventually turn into dust, losing their form and name and becoming traceless and forgotten. That is to say, everything is 'empty' of an inherent identity. Those in existence not only decay and reduce to nothingness, but also become the cause for the rise of a new "caravan" of life. And it is this very nature of existence that keeps the 'samsaric' wheel of impersonal laws of causality turning. Khayyam, similar to the Buddha and Nagarjuna, believed that erroneous opinions about this cyclical process lead to disillusionment and displeasure. The Khayyamian idea of "pleasure" requires being fully aware of and accepting of this cosmic and natural process. Before we draw some obvious parallels between Nagarjuna and Khayyam, let us put the Buddhism of Nagarjuna in a more methodical perspective and understand why he loomed so large in his dialectical philosophy that he was given the title of the 'second Buddha.'

---

[5] Christian Thomas Kohl, *Denkweisen aus Asien und Europa: Nagarjuna, Albert Einstein, Niels Bohr, Roger Penrose, Ein Bilderbuch*, (Saarbrücken: Akademiker Verlag, 2012). See pages 31-47. Another version is published as an article titled: *"Denkweisen aus Asien und Europa: Nagarjuna und Whitehead,"* (2016). https://philpapers.org/rec/KOHDAA. By the same author, an interesting article of images, philosophy and modern physics can be found in: https://philpapers.org/archive/KOHPIE.

Nagarjuna, the 'Second Buddha'

Nagarjuna was no ordinary Buddhist philosopher. It was the historical Buddha the first who "turned the Wheel of the Law (*Dharma*)," initiating the path to understanding the activities of existence and human psychology, but Nagarjuna is seen as the one who put this cognitive wheel in gear again.[6] Thus, as a master philosopher, Nagarjuna is often called the 'second Buddha.'[7] He changed the course of Buddhist philosophy consequentially.

It was almost seven hundred fifty years after the Buddha's death that Nagarjuna undertook the interpretation of the Buddhist scriptures and systematized a fresher intellectual understanding of the Buddha's teachings, perhaps reasserting a return to original Buddhism.[8] Nagarjuna actually did not invent any new ideas, but rather he innovatively expanded upon the older Buddhist idea of dependent origination.[9] He borrowed material from the older Buddhist canons, and especially the very important first-century scripture known as *Prajnaparamita Sutra* (Perfecting Wisdom Sutra). This sutra is known for the expansion of penetrative wisdom, bringing it to its climax, and going beyond any limit.[10] Through Nagarjuna's expansion on such ideas, the core of his discourse on emptiness, as we will see momentarily, goes beyond the borders of Buddhism by opening a new universal philosophical avenue.[11] He consolidated Buddhism on these philosophical grounds and consequently founded the Madhyamika (Middle Way) sub-school within the Mahayana School of Buddhism.

Along the way, Nagarjuna overturned superstitious beliefs about the world, which were prevalent among the masses and even among certain Buddhists of the time. His intention was to rescue those "caught in the weeds" of details of rituals and scriptures. This created a schism from the doctrinaire Buddhism, and in so doing, Nagarjuna is perceived to have the same soteriological intention as the Buddha, who also broke away from the old existing schools of

---

[6] Manish Meshram, "The Significance of Heart Sutra in Mahayana Buddhism," *Shabd Braham - International Research Journal of Indian languages* 2, no. 12 (2014), 77.

[7] See Douglas Berger, "Nagarjuna (c. 150—c. 250)," *Internet Encyclopedia of Philosophy*. https://www.iep.utm.edu/nagarjun/. (Accessed April 25, 2020).

[8] See Gary Donnelly, "To What Extent is Madhyamaka a Reassertion of Original Buddhism?" *British Journal of Undergraduate Philosophy*, 6, no. 1 (Heythrop Spring Conference 2013): 70-81.

[9] Ibid.

[10] Meshram, "The Significance of Heart Sutra in Mahayana Buddhism," 75.

[11] Jean-Marc Vivenza, *Nâgârjuna et la doctrine de la vacuité,* (Paris: Albin Michel, 2001), 9.

Self-Rule, Joy and Emptiness 71

his time.[12] Nagarjuna's intention was to expand the intellectual capacity of people to understand the end product of the Buddha's teachings rather than succumb to social and moral conventions by performing rituals and pleading to monks for liberation. Both the Buddha and Nagarjuna encouraged a deeper understanding of the world as a means of one's liberation.

Nagarjuna's work was, on the one hand, designed to reform the pedantic monopoly of the lengthy, difficult Scriptures, and on the other, to open the channel of Buddhist conversations among common people so that the whole society could participate. The Mahayana approach, with its shorter and less rule-oriented scriptures, allowed non-monks to learn the teachings of the Buddha, interpret them according to their own understanding, and have the possibility of attaining nirvana. This rebellious, populist stance aimed to make the teachings of the Buddha more accessible in a way that had previously been prevented by the monastic culture. The Mahayana tolerance galvanized the rise of philosophically rebellious pioneer thinkers and sub-schools[13] hardly encountered in the other branches. And since the popularity of the accessible Buddhist method founded by Nagarjuna led to the vast translation of *Prajnaparamita Sutra* into different languages from Central Asia, China, Tibet and beyond, perhaps Khayyam himself at some point even became aware of the work of Nagarjuna.

This iconoclast and altruistic stance sounds quite similar to Khayyam's stance as a freethinker in the face of a restrictive religious establishment. In fact, one of the essential elements of Mahayana Buddhism is the idea of a 'bodhisattva', one who lives a virtuous life like a buddha, dedicated to helping other living beings attain liberation. Although Nagarjuna's masterwork, the *Mula-madhyamika-karika* (Fundamental Discourse of Middle Way [Madhyamika]), is one of the most prodigious and intellectually intensive pieces of Buddhist literature, his goal remained sound and simple because he was a bodhisattva—a people's liberator. Echoes of such an intellectual-social task can be detected in Khayyam's iconoclastic position and work as well, centuries later. From the Buddhist perspective, one could consider Khayyam also to be a bodhisattva, a lending-hand buddha offering his *Rubaiyat* as a text for people's liberation, much as

---

[12] Viévard, "La vacuité et sa valeur instrumentale," 411-13, 427. Nagarjuna is fulfilling the role of a bodhisattva who helps others to attain liberation from confusion and despair.
[13] Mahayana gave rise to two main sub-schools: Madhyamika and Yogacara. Out of Madhyamika two other schools of thought emerged, namely: Prasangika and Svatantrika. Zen school was another revolutionary Mahayana schism which emerged by synthesizing Madhyamika, Yogacara as well as Daoism. The Tibetan Buddhism, on the other hand is a complex synthesis of Mahayana-Madhyamika-Prasangika combined with tantra and various elements extracted from the ancient religion of Bön and shamanism in Tibet.

Nagarjuna offered people an understanding of the Middle Way as a path to liberation. In this context, it is essential to briefly shed some light on how Nagarjuna's discourse of the Middle Way paved the path to attain nirvana or emancipation from one's own deluded mind.

Emptiness, always intermediate state, and nirvana

What does it mean to see the world as 'empty'? One can imagine Nagarjuna sitting, with his eyes closed in meditation, seeing the world exist in an implicit state of movements occurring at different speeds. With this awareness, one *never* sees things as complete, static, done or absolute, no matter the illusion of immovability and stability. Such illusions arise simply due to the variations of the speed of change. For example, movement from state to state can be observed in a blossoming flower much more easily than in larger, more complex objects like mountains. And yet, all things rise, move, change, fall, and this is the Middle Way of Nagarjuna. The Middle Way refers to the constantly changing, intermediate states—a never-ending process.

Nagarjuna embarked on the position of defending the Middle Way, the conception that things are always in the state of becoming, by challenging the essentialists who believed the world is real and everything has its own intrinsic nature with certain fixed characteristics.[14] Nagarjuna found the essentialists' and absolutists' worldviews contradictory and incompatible with his own dependent origination conception[15] That is to say, that phenomena exist but are dependent on other phenomena and are subject to cause and effect.[16] Nagarjuna avoided extreme views. He simply said that things are between being and nonbeing, the middle way.[17] The middle way view clearly points to the emptiness of any concrete or lasting identity of all objects throughout the history of their existence.

As introduced earlier, it is important to understand that connotations of "empty" and "emptiness" in this context are not negative, nor do they mean nonbeing or 'nothing.' It does not mean things are empty or nonexistent, but instead connotes not having a fixed identity—a thought without a thought.[18] Not having one's own nature is not a conscious decision or choice that entities such as humans make; it is a mechanism imposed upon existence. According to

---

[14] See Donnelly, "To What Extent is Madhyamaka a Reassertion of Original Buddhism?" 71-81.
[15] Zhihua Yao, "Typology of Nothing: Heidegger, Daoism and Buddhism," *Comparative Philosophy* 1, no. 1 (2010), 84.
[16] Donnelly, "To What Extent Is Madhyamaka a Reassertion of Original Buddhism?" 78.
[17] Yao, "Typology of Nothing," 85.
[18] Vivenza, *Nâgârjuna et la doctrine de la vacuité*, 12-13.

Nagarjuna, nothing can last forever, nor is everything (raw material) destroyed forever; things cause the appearance and disappearance of one another.[19] In its application by Nagarjuna, emptiness is a process and a mechanism rather than a concept to be framed.[20] He extrapolated the Buddha's *suñña* or 'empty' or 'no-self'[21] from the individual to the universal, providing a dependable linguistic way to articulate reality beyond limited cognitive experiences.

The Mahayana Zen Buddhists realized that the intermediate state is the only viable state to be aware of, and this awareness is the never-changing and never-ending *Now*. Knowing that movement and change are happening in all objects and in ourselves means that this intermediate event is always taking place here-and-now! The *intermediate state* and *nowness* are bound together—that is to say, Real Existence means confirming the state of things in the present time. The Zen masters realized we always live in the state of nowness no matter when and where. The dichotomy between the experience of now and the linearity of time is a cognitive error linked to the human experience of a linear biography from birth to death since the 'movement' of time conventionally feels rectilinear rather than constantly now. Time seems demonstrative of things shifting, but in fact, time itself is in an intermediate state as well. This means we incessantly inhabit our own intermediate state in nowness. Each generation perceives time to be fresh in its lifespan; with every new birth of a person, time seems to be refreshed. But in fact, time is neutral; only the inhabitants and the interpreters of time have changed.[22]

Humans through the historical ages have consistently pondered the meaning of the endless cycles of birth and death. In Buddhism, the repetitive, infinite process of generation and degeneration is referred to as *sam-sara* in Sanskrit, 'same-flow' ('same-serum [sara]'). Samsara is beginningless and is intertwined with the past (like the 'river' of Heraclitus, the same interconnected flow but different waters each time). In the Nagarjunian sense, understanding samsara and the cycle of birth and death means understanding the impermanency of all births and deaths and the empty nature of all selves. In other words, samsara

---

[19] Ibid., 30.
[20] See Viévard, "La vacuité et sa valeur instrumentale," 411-429.
[21] *Majjhima Nikaya*: Cula-sunnata Sutta, Maha-sunnata Sutta (MN 121, 122). The Buddha, according to two sūtras in *Majjhima Nikaya*, recommended contemplation on emptiness (*suññata*).
[22] For a broader treatment of 'time' and its different dimensions according to the mystics and Sufis, see Mostafa Vaziri, "Das Zeitverständnis im Sufismus," in *Chronos - Kairos - Aion, alles eine Frage der Zeit?* Paul Danler Hrsg., (Würzburg: Königshausen & Neumann, 2019), 71-80.

is the flow of phenomena in the material world and nirvana is the eye that sees the flow.

Nirvana then means gazing at the unambiguous and repetition of samsara and life processes. From this vista, nirvana is nothing spectacular or difficult to attain. In fact, in a surprising twist, Nagarjuna says clearly that samsara and nirvana are one and the same thing. This means nirvana is a worldly experience and understanding of samsara without a solid and permanent anchor.[23] Nagarjuna"s own words testify to this simple step: "There is not the slightest difference between cyclic existence [samsara] and nirvana." Thus, there is no gap between samsara and nirvana.[24]

In this way, Nagarjuna follows in the footsteps of the author(s) of *Prajnaparamita Sutra*, who considered samsara (the world) as nirvana and nirvana as samsara. Form is empty (no-self), and emptiness is not different from form; form is not different from emptiness.[25] Emptiness is the basis of all principles (*dharmas*) of existence—true existence is a redundant, empty process.[26] This means a fully-grown human being carries death and emptiness within itself, although this fact is not instantly apparent. But in light of nirvana and samsara being one, human is only one step away from realizing nirvana. In a simpler approach, one could say that nirvana is the non-attainment of anything in particular. It is the state of suchness of the world which one realizes. On the level of mental wellbeing, nirvana frames the impermanency of life as the footing to be gained in order to methodically generate an antidote against any recurrent greed, fury and illusions that one may develop in the course of years of life—samsaric life.

In applying this logic, nirvana becomes the clarity of mind that arises by relinquishing all deceptive personal and cultural-religious views about the world in which we live. Nirvana is when the curtain of obscurity is lifted, and one can with a clear view perceive the cycle of coming and going without branding it, judging it, fearing it. Nirvana also involves grasping beneath,

---

[23] *Mūlamadhyamakakārikā*, chapter 25 (Examination of Nirvana).
[24] In Prajnaparamita Sutra, a similar claim is made: "whatever form there is, that is emptiness; whatever emptiness there is, that is form." See *Prajñāpāramitā-Hṛdayam The Heart of the Perfection of Wisdom*, edited by Edward Conze, translated by Ānandajoti Bhikkhu. https://www.ancient-buddhist-texts.net/Texts-and-Translations/Short-Pieces-in-Sanskrit/Prajnaparamita-Hrdaya.pdf.
[25] *Prajna Paramita Heart Sutra*, translated from Sanskrit into Chinese by Tripitaka Master Hsuan Tsang. Commentary by Grand Master T'an Hsu. Translated into English by Venerable Dharma Master Lok To. Edited by K'un Li, Shih and Dr. Frank G. French. (New York, San Francisco, Toronto: Sutra Translation Committee, 1995; 2000), 71-3.
[26] Ibid., 92-3.

above, and beyond samsara to be empty of any substantial existence—a vast land of nothingness and void. This mental panorama can free the person from all false expectations and cut the strings of anxiety and fear of death. The *Prajnaparamita Sutra* calls this the True Mind, not deluded by or immersed in the confusing events of samsara. Cultivation of this Empty Mind is nirvana.

As a consequence of this reasoning, any hope of locating a supreme and permanent deity is abandoned. There is no separate mover from the moved. The infinite movement and change of the objects, the mover and moving are one and the same thing.[27] By pushing away all metaphysical speculations, Nagarjuna leaves the matter to be worked out between the observing mind and the ever-changing world. Consequently, nirvanic or existential freedom does not take place in some euphoric or otherworldly state, but means living fully in the world of suchness without misreading it as something stable and substantial.

How Nagarjuna's logic may lead to a deeper understanding

Nagarjuna's paradigm shift means embracing a revolutionary logic that rejects any absolute assertions about the world. It challenges the assertion of the world being totally real because the entities constantly change. Consequently, as much as the world *is* real, it *is not* real for a very long time, so entities are *both* real and unreal, and *neither* real nor unreal. This tetralemma is how Nagarjuna rationalized the reality of things without being bound by the inflexible structure of language. He does not support the theory of complete annihilationism, in which things are destroyed and exterminated eternally. Instead, he subscribed to the notion that all things shift from being what they *were* becoming into what they *are* now and what they *will become* and so on. So the chain of cause and effect continues without the previous raw material permanently disappearing. In this way, he made a case that challenged both annihilationism and eternalism.

He also neutralized any authoritarian knowledge coming from priests or incredulous beliefs, instead putting responsibility back into the hands of thinking individuals, an endeavor initiated by the Buddha himself. As an original thinker, Nagarjuna even overturned a number of doctrinal Buddhist beliefs such as karma, reincarnation,[28] and the otherworldly understanding of nirvana. His far-reaching and persuasive corrective lens addressed the human error of perceiving reality as substantial and nonchanging, arguing instead for the non-absoluteness and non-self of all existing phenomena. Not surprisingly,

---

[27] Jan Christoph Westerhoff, "Nāgārjuna", *The Stanford Encyclopedia of Philosophy* (Spring 2019 Edition), Edward N. Zalta (ed.), https://plato.stanford.edu/archives/spr2019/entries/nagarjuna/. (Accessed April 27, 2020).

[28] *Mūlamadhyamakakārikā*, chapter 27 (Examination of Views), 79-83.

his logical arguments ran up against metaphysical and religious Buddhist dogmas, which were all well hidden under the disguise of the Buddha and Buddhism. Nagarjuna boosted the status of Buddha's Dharma as a *philosophy* of life and rejected the propensity of the monks and the masses to turn it into a *religion*. His tetralemma logic is a logic of the dynamic process of reality, the intermediate state, non-self, and emptiness; a logic whose constellation of imageries awaken the mind to reality as it presents itself, not a reality we tend to privately construct for ourselves.

Commonalities between Khayyam and Nagarjuna

There are clear commonalities between the way Nagarjuna portrayed the human experience of reality and the way Khayyam expressed it. Both Nagarjuna and Khayyam deftly bridged the existing reality of here-and-now with the empty nature of the world. Their common goal can be surmised from their explanations, which was to awaken their readers to a life that is real yet impermanent, joyful yet without attachment, and which closes with demolition leaving no trace of identity except to cause the rise of the next thing.

Nagarjuna and Khayyam extrapolated their readings of existence into non-anthropocentric as well as anthropocentric orders. The non-anthropocentric order is the process of things that emerge from emptiness and operate for a period of time and return to emptiness (as per Nagarjuna), or to nothingness (according to Khayyam)—'from dust to dust.' The anthropocentric order, however, explores the human psychological process of making a choice to live caught up in emotions, trepidation, and dogma, or to live with awareness, free from bondage. They empowered a life-embracing and fearless self-reliance. Their clarity is reflected in their words.

Let us evaluate the Nagarjunian and Khayyamian perspectives of the knowledge of life from two important perspectives:

1. Knowing the nature of the world
2. Letting go of anxiety-greed and cultivating pleasure

1. Knowing the nature of the world

Khayyam and Nagarjuna both perceived the process of the world as encapsulated in an endless process of rise and demise, with birth and death as the most irreversible of these processes. This understanding prompted Khayyam to categorically reject the immortality of the soul, and Nagarjuna to stand his ground: there was no self to begin with, let alone immortality of a self after death or even reincarnation.

The nature of the world is best depicted by Khayyam's poetical metaphor when he says the process begins with dust and ends in dust. This is a reflection of his mathematical and rational approach to the physical processes, where from dust to dust can be equated with the mathematical value of zero or nothingness. In the Khayyamian conception of addition and subtraction, birth and growth are addition, and decline and demise are subtraction. In considering human life as a mathematical equation, for example, before birth is zero. At birth, we can assume the value of 1 is added to life. In growing up to adulthood, another 1 is added, which makes an adult human life equal to 2. After adulthood, humans enter a subtraction period. In old age and decline of life, 1 is subtracted from life. In death, the remaining 1 is finally subtracted. So at death, the value is back to zero again—from zero to zero, from dust to dust (*rubai* 131)—from nothingness to nothingness. Khayyam, the poet-mathematician, ponders this mathematical equation of life:

> What is the use of my addition to and subtraction from this world?
> Where is the trace of our existence stored or seen?
> In this spinning wheel of existence, at every turn, through the lives of all,
> Burned and turned into ash - any trace of smoke anywhere?
>
> (rubai 18)

Khayyam, like other rationalist thinkers, had wondered about this unchangeable mathematical process that had no apparent alternative. He was quite forthright about cosmological and biological mathematics and determinism. Yet, he was also aware that the non-determinist aspects of life purely lie in the individual's personality, attitude and behavior. He established the coupling of determinism and non-determinism that make the human passage in the world a unique odyssey. The confusion in this empty odyssey has been so rampant that many people and communities fabricate explanations about the world, death and immortality. This is when Nagarjuna and Khayyam intervene.

The helpful argument advanced by Nagarjuna and Khayyam begins by disavowing knowledge of the world's fixed beginning and a fixed end, let alone a pre-beginning or post-end. Inferentially and carefully, they propose that empirical processes appear to be infinitely beginningless and endless. Nagarjuna shares:

> "When asked about the beginning, the Great Sage said that nothing is known of it.
> Cyclic existence is without end and beginning. There is no beginning or end."[29]

Nagarjuna suggests that the fallacy in misperceiving the age of the world may lie in the general human faculty, with the problem of the conception of past and

---

[29] *Mūlamadhyamakakārikā*, chapter 11 (Examination of the Initial and Final Limits), 31, verse 1.

future.[30] Nagarjuna was aware that many hastened to give the world a linear or even cyclical age that was compatible with the human measurement of time, but which was in fact a misreading of the complex processes and interdependency of this spinning and ever-creative juggernaut.

Khayyam captures the same insight by encouraging people to relinquish the persistent search for an archetypal beginning and end. In agreement with Nagarjuna, Khayyam says it is a fallacy to think in terms of a fixed beginning and a fixed end; the past and future:

> The harmony in which all are born and die, time and again,
> Seems an endless parade without a beginning or end.
> No one has a clue whether this has any hidden message or not,
> Or why we come into being and then disappear into a void.
>
> (*rubai* 10)

In describing the nature of the world, Nagarjuna and Khayyam emphatically moved away from metaphysical speculations or faith-based beliefs. Nagarjuna had to confront those Indian spiritualists and philosophers who believed the world is substantial and made out of solid stuff, created by the gods, and Khayyam had to counter the claims of the Islamic creationist theologians and philosophers who thought the world is created and has a precise beginning and is finite. Khayyam was aware that the religious people pushed faith in establishing the beginning and the end, while the logicians employed certainty. He maintained the middle path like Nagarjuna, subscribing neither to eternalism nor to annihilationism. He composed a number of quatrains addressing such questions, proposing that in the absence of any evidence, the speculations about the fleeting nature of life are, at the least, distracting and useless. He rebuked shortsighted philosophers who delivered self-convincing interpretations about this massive spinning wheel of the universe and yet could produce no proof for their theories before themselves becoming numb and muted by death (*rubai* 14).

> This sea of existence emerged out of its own shrouded source;
> No one person can know the true nature of life.
> Every person justifies it according to their ability
> But no one really knows the story of reality.
>
> (*rubai* 8)

Nagarjuna's approach to the same theme is perhaps less poetic than Khayyam's, but pledges the same commitment to staying clear of haphazard speculations about the making and the direction of the world. He even rejects

---

[30] Ibid., chapter 19 (Examination of Time), 50, verses 1-3.

those who support his theory of emptiness when they framed it as an ultimate concept, sensing that such minds seem to be veering towards obsession rather than a deeper understanding. Nagarjuna states that emptiness has to be understood the way it is, not the way some misperceive in the same way someone might misperceive a snake in a dark room to be a rope. Any belief in or obsession with emptiness derails the understanding of it.[31] He berates those who maintain the concept of emptiness with an absolutist and a metaphysical view. Instead, those who understand emptiness relinquish all views.[32]

In his turn, in alluding to emptiness, Khayyam proposes that the appearance and disappearance of phenomena at micro and macrocosmic levels are like the intrinsic tides of an ocean; they rise and drop on their own. He uses the imagery of an "ocean" to hint at the movement of the phenomena in the universe. While the "ebbing tides" are real, their reality is at the same time impermanent and even in some sense illusive. The fleeting reality, according to Khayyam, "is a pattern that has emerged from the tides of an ocean, And the ebbing tides shall return it to the seafloor." (*rubai* 42)

When it comes to the state of the human condition after death, both Khayyam and Nagarjuna (and the Buddha as well) refuse to entertain imaginary and concocted claims about the storage of the identity of an individual after death. They could not accept the arguments of metaphysicians and theologians that the bodies or the minds of humans are somehow 'mummified' and kept somewhere in a parallel reality. The existence of an entity when long gone seems as if it were never born, never dead, not real, and not eternal, as Nagarjuna argues in order to liberate his readers.[33] This approach qualifies the Buddha's pari-nirvana, a term that means a complete extinction of the flame of existence, exiting the cycle of being born a second time, as some may have expected it. Pari-nirvana was applied to mean irreversible death—the Buddha shall not return after death. It meant an end to any belief in reincarnation, an end to any eschatological aspiration,[34] and an end to the notion of resurrection.

Nagarjuna, taking a stance against reincarnation or any form of return, argues that it is not viable to claim that people have always lived uninterruptedly and continue to live permanently in some form. The human species evolves and changes, and an identical person can never exist in different times. Nagarjuna

---

[31] Ibid., chapter 25 (Examination of Nirvana), 68, 322-334.
[32] Ibid., chapter 13 (Examination of Compounded Phenomena), 36, verse 8.
[33] Vivenza, *Nâgârjuna et la doctrine de la vacuité*, 35-6.
[34] The Mahayana Buddhists eventually developed some eschatological culture and belief which points to the last Buddha, *Maitreya* who is awaiting in heaven to come to eradicate the last traces of ignorance.

declares "To say 'I was in the past' is not tenable." The agents and causes of rise and demise are unarguably offered in the past, present and future, but conceiving of an identical self in the past and future is not tenable.[35] Certainly, the idea of our atoms being reconfigured and reused by nature is totally conceivable; that is to say, we are not really 'disappearing without a trace' in a literal sense. But one's corpse is re-integrated into the cycle of regeneration and reconfiguration, not re-integrated into an identical psyche through reincarnation.

Nagarjuna and Khayyam, the two protagonists of no return after death, no next life, ask their audiences to explain how anyone can ever come back to life in any form? Death is the disintegration of physical and psychological elements. Humans cannot have a dual existence, one physical and the other psychological, where only the physical one dies and the psychological one survives. Nagarjuna expresses great doubt, wondering if such thinking is even sound.[36] This was a direct challenge against the belief in reincarnation.

Partial death of an individual sounded like ambiguous logic, and Nagarjuna remained disdainful and skeptical of such reasoning. One cannot be half-divine and half-human, or half permanent and half impermanent, half having lived in the past, and half still living in the future. The body and mind live together and die together. If a human being were a divine being, he would not even be born; he would remain divine and immortal. And if a human is not divine, he is therefore not eternal. Nagarjuna stood his ground and was outspoken in his generation against such irrationality.[37]

Nagarjuna relies further on logic to make his case, using the concept of the five aggregates. The Buddhist discourse on non-self describes five psychophysical aggregates that comprise every individual: body, feeling, consciousness, mental activities and perception. These aggregates are never constant throughout life and therefore cannot be permanent in any sense, especially after the collapse of the body and consciousness; these aggregates disappear completely. So any return, whether by resurrection or reincarnation, simply is not possible. Nagarjuna does not hesitate to also bring the Buddha into his analysis by maintaining that the Buddha himself had no inherent, permanent self or essence. Even the Buddha (as both a human and as an awakened psyche) should be counted as an impermanent physical entity with the five aggregates, not a

---

[35] *Mūlamadhyamakakārikā*, chapter 27 (Examination of Views), 79-81, verses 3, 6, 9, 13, 14.
[36] Ibid., chapter 27 (Examination of Views), 81.
[37] Ibid., chapter 27 (Examination of Views), 81, verses 16-17.

Self-Rule, Joy and Emptiness

metaphysical or immortal one.[38] Nagarjuna finds reincarnation problematic in regards to the obliteration of the psychophysical aggregates:

> "If they are impermanent, they do not transmigrate.... If someone transmigrates, then if, when sought in fivefold way in the aggregates...he is not there, what transmigrates?"[39]

Khayyam's reasoning is aligned with Nagarjuna's. He refutes any coming back to life and the second return of an individual in any form. Despite the cultural pressure on Khayyam to uphold the Islamic belief of survival of personhood-soul through the agency of god, he directly addressed the subject of death as a final phenomenon in a number of quatrains:

> I have journeyed and wandered in distant lands,
> Almost covered horizon to horizon,
> And I never heard a single person
> Say whether anyone had returned on this one-way path.
>
> (*rubai* 49)

In conjunction with the finality of biological death, he also refutes the promise-and-threat of *heaven* and *hell,* which directly suggest the idea of the rise and return of the dead ones. Khayyam is fearless in tackling and debunking all the imagined superstitions of an afterlife; the realms of heaven and hell are nothing but abstract fabrications, and the hope of return is illusory:

> Nobody has seen heaven and hell, oh heart.
> Tell me, has anyone come back from the other world, oh heart?
> Our hopes and fears are aimed at things which
> Are nothing but invented words, oh heart!
>
> (*rubai* 91)

The instructive aim of Khayyam is to have his audience be better equipped emotionally to accept the impermanency of life and death. Even our enlightening moments are impermanent. Through this straightforward lens, the mind is better groomed with less fear. Khayyam is blunt in addressing those who take life and death so seriously and harbor remarkable anxieties in their psyche. All things shall come to an end; it is frivolous to turn the body and mind into a storehouse of good and bad memories. He advises not to take a future that ends in death too seriously: "In disillusionment and discontentment, in the blink of an eye, we will crumble away and all our delights will disintegrate." (*rubai* 19). All our travels from one horizon to another, whatever experienced,

---

[38] Ibid., chapter 22 (Examination of Tathagata), 60, verse 2.
[39] Ibid., chapter 16 (Examination of Bondage), 41, verses 1-2.

heard, recounted, shall turn into nothing (*rubai* 102). None of the worldly gains can be transported into the realm of nothingness, like a joyful candlelight that slowly wanes and ends as nothing (*rubai* 107).

While such an irrefutable realism may sound uninviting and bleak, it defeats wishful, unrealistic idealism and instead encourages the acceptance of reality maturely and stoically. His advice is to engage with the world but remain nonattached. Such nonattachment is required because of the unceasing commotion of life circumstances and the human emotional vulnerability to the resulting ups and downs. Human biology follows the laws of change and is subject to commotion, decay, disfiguration and permanent disintegration of its elements like anything else in the universe. So Khayyam, like his atomist predecessors,[40] views our present configuration of the four elements in the here-and-now as a unique opportunity, even a token of delight (*rubai* 29).

In the Nagarjunian and Khayyamian view, loosening up, cultivating pleasure and enjoying liberation cannot happen unless the nature of the world is fully grasped. Both thinkers emphasize this because the nature of existence is transient. The five aggregates make up birth, old age, and death and then are freed into existence. Thus, agitation and grief arise as the consequence of birth.[41] In other words, the disposition of suffering is the unsettled feeling produced as a consequence of constant change. Nagarjuna also points out that suffering comes from the unwise agent, not the world.[42] Nirvana is thus to understand and embrace cyclic existence, not to evasively contradict or deny it. A vibrant nirvana is the comprehension of samsara—the coming into and going out of existence without being captive to the world.[43]

Khayyam's presentation of nothingness (*hich*) is in a similar way an attempt to liberate people from subjective falsities or irrational expectations in regards to the nature of the material world. The nothingness of Khayyam is made up of several layers: 1. an inexorable process of decay without any particularly obvious reason; 2. a life without a particular purpose: existential nothingness at its most radical level; 3. death with a complete disintegration of the individual's body and mind without any possibility of return whatsoever; 4. an impersonal process of existence: no maker, no destroyer, no judge, no compiler of individual actions; and 5. no heaven or hell in another reality. To the puzzling

---

[40] In his philosophical pondering, Khayyam may have easily had familiarity and access to both Hellenic Atomism of Leucippus, Democritus, Epicurus, and Lucretius as well as to the Indian Atomism of Nastika school (Carvaka, Ajivika, Jainism and Buddhism) including Nyaya-Vaisesika school. See Vaziri, *Liberation Philosophy: From the Buddha to Omar Khayyam*, 218.
[41] *Mūlamadhyamakakārikā*, chapter 26 (Examination of the Twelve Links), 78, verse 8.
[42] Ibid., chapter 26 (Examination of the Twelve Links), 78, verses 10-11.
[43] Ibid., chapter 25 (Examination of Nirvana), 73-6.

question of why human experiences and memories are all rendered into nothing at the end, Khayyam has no answer! The dismantling of one's life is an unsolvable and irreversible riddle. And yet, it is an inescapable reality that includes all sentient beings and all phenomena.

Nagarjuna keeps the human mind anchored and humble by not claiming too many unwarranted theories about the nature of existence. He explains that by maintaining a 'don't-know' mind, one is able to keep an empty mind and come closer to the nature of reality. "There are no words, no speech. So there is no one, no god, no nothing, no mind, no emptiness. ... This is your true self. Always keep a 'don't-know' mind."[44] Khayyam, by the same token, expressed his doubts about those who speak too soon, too fast, and with too much certainty about the world. The riddle of existence is not known to anyone. He reasoned that the goal of being in the world is not to constantly speculate about such worldly riddles, but to live an awake and joyful life. Khayyam would have wholeheartedly agreed with Nagarjuna's preference for a 'don't know' mind. Khayyam considers it ridiculous when people fabricate extravagant stories about the conundrum of existence from the point of view of a chattering mind rather than an empty, speechless mind (*rubai* 7).

In expounding on the nature of the world, according to the *Rubaiyat*, Khayyam doubts whether there is any known entity called 'god' who makes and unmakes things, all the while storing the deceased humans along with their actions in some other reality. The religious ontological perception is that an anthropomorphized god, the 'potter,' is single-handedly considered responsible for the details of sculpting and demolishing the objects of the universe. And yet, Khayyam, like Nagarjuna, sees the world as a factory of cause and effect. Khayyam overturns the archaic cognitive misperception that there is always a more knowledgeable human-like being (god) who makes uninterrupted decisions about the world. Khayyam calls the world an impersonal pottery shop that has no known pot-maker. This mysterious potter makes and breaks pots while using the recycled raw material from the broken ones. Such an image illustrates the vital concept of interdependence and offers an explanation of the connectedness of existence. Khayyam is explicit about this principle, often drawing upon another allegory—that of grass growing from the "clay" recovered from human corpses—to demonstrate it. It is due to this interdependency and the laws of cause and effect that there is no epicenter or a particular agent for making and breaking the pots—it is a universal and anonymous pattern. Khayyam's imagery of 'no pot-maker, no

---

[44] Thomas McEvilley, *The Shape of Ancient Thought: Comparative Studies in Greek and Indian Philosophies*, (New York: Allworth Press, 2002), 483.

pot-seller, no pot-buyer' opens new gates for understanding the impersonal and non-theistic world (*rubai* 73).

Khayyam mocks those who believe this impersonal universe will be kind to them, will preserve them and will return them to the world in an identical form. He also disparages the nature of the universe itself for its injustices, for its cruel obliviousness to human longings and emotions and suffering, and for the cruelty of destroying human life at the end. Regardless of one's wishes and hopes for after death, the names, signs, and symbols of human life soar like a water fountain in the beginning and then will be blown away like the wind (*rubai* 37).

Due to the unintentional cruelty of the world, humans are encouraged to wake up to this reality and savor their short existence. Savoring means being well-equipped to deal with the real world, accepting its nature and not expecting something else. Savoring is a kind of maturity, having the awareness that after a short existence, one will disappear forever. This is not a tragedy; it is simply reality. Rather than bemoan this fact, Khayyam as a protagonist of pleasure, poeticized the simplicity of the world. Rather than make up stories to try to deny the reality of the end, Khayyam encourages embracing it all: the beginning, middle, as well as the end of our biographical life. He downplayed asking questions about *why* we are here in the world, which can lead to a spiral of confusion, and instead encouraged focusing on understanding *what* the world is and *how* it works in order to be able to play and enjoy life:

> Khayyam, if you have become a drunkard, savor it;
> If you spend your time with a tulip-faced lovely one, savor it.
> Since the terminus of this world is nonexistence
> Pretend you don't exist. But since you do exist, savor it.
>
> (*rubai* 140)

2. Letting go of anxiety-greed and cultivating pleasure

The restorative philosophy of Nagarjuna and Khayyam is designed to let everyone know that since living in the world is challenging, one must create a new perspective to remove the grief and ambiguity that so often accompanies life. Unmistakably, Khayyam is the philosopher of happiness whose words are the building blocks of a strong mind that speaks for meticulously distancing from one's own deceptive moods as well as staying clear of clinging to the world. He encourages cultivating joy: sit in a green garden and drink enlightening wine, knowing that the world is fully primed to demolish our corpse and feed it to the same grass we may be sitting on (*rubai* 64).

The version of happiness in the philosophy of Khayyam and his like-minded predecessors like the Buddha and Nagarjuna did not require doing anything special; it only required a vigilant awareness. Khayyam is quite specific about the importance of nowness, sighing with contentment and feeling at peace. He knew of the propensity of the mind to constantly jump to the future and get ahead of itself. This tendency compelled him to respond in several quatrains, giving guidance on how to: 1. relinquish anxiety from the mind since the world is indifferent to our pain and pleasure, and the last station is death anyway, 2. avoid seeking meaning for the empty existence we live through, 3. keep the mind tamed, maintaining its awareness of now in order to live in the present life conditions, not in some imaginary realms of a never-arriving 'tomorrow.' Khayyam finds a perpetual dwelling on tomorrow conspicuously perverse because it spoils the lightheartedness of nowness (*rubai* 135).

Nagarjuna took a slightly different approach towards happiness, but it is very complementary with Khayyam's approach. Nagarjuna followed the footsteps of the Buddha in addressing how to become insightful and attain delight, and considers individuals to be solely responsible for their own pain and pleasure. Pleasure in the Buddhist context is the absence of 'poisonous' thoughts and tendencies in the mind. The Buddha outlined three thought-poisons that gradually pollute and corrupt one's character: *greed* in all its dimensions, *aggression* in speech-thought-body, and *ignorance* about the nature of self and the world. According to him, these poisons are not suffering in themselves unless there is a mind harboring and acting upon them. By domesticating and rewiring the mind, these poisons subside, which translates to the absence of displeasure, therefore an absence of torment. For effortless equanimity, Nagarjuna says, only those enlightened ones who realize the beauty of non-self and impermanency would experience pleasure—and more importantly, those who are nonattached to the duality of pleasure and displeasure.[45]

In light of Nagarjuna's analysis, the philosophy of letting go and the resulting pleasurable living can be achieved through two levels of inner work very similar to Khayyam's guidance: 1. knowledge of emptiness of self and the world, 2. acceptance of the state of affairs of the world in its present condition: the state of suchness. This state in the Buddhist context is also called *tathagata*: "thus come and thus gone." In the state of tathagata, there are no poisons; that is to say, there is acceptance of fleeting, painful, even boring existence. Tathagata points to the process of life and its natural circumstances without it being labeled as good or bad. The opposite of tathagata is a strong sense of selfhood and an ongoing wish that the world would be favorable to one's personal interests, or wishing that the world were different than what it is. Thus, the emanation of poisons gives birth to a strong and clinging self; otherwise, a non-self in the state of suchness cannot grasp any poisons.[46]

---

[45] *Mūlamadhyamakakārikā*, chapter 23 (Examination of Errors), pages 63-6.
[46] Ibid., chapter 23 (Examination of Errors), 66, verses 21-25.

Nagarjuna treats the notion of tathagata not only as the state of isness-suchness of the world in every moment, but also as the personal experience of nowness free from any attributes and free from clinging to time. The Buddha's mind was seen as the mind of Tathagata, flowing with time but without clinging to objects or concepts. ("Tathagata" at some point became a 'nickname' and another title for the Buddha). Nagarjuna shares his articulation of tathagata as being outside of selfhood, compulsions, and obsessions, and therefore being one with nature instead of being in a state of constant fixation on self:

"Those who develop mental fabrications…, fail to see the Tathagata… Tathagata has no essence. The world is without essence."[47]

Tathagata, according to the teachings of the *Prajnaparamita*, is also described as the embryonic and most true nature of being. Once tathagata-suchness-emptiness is realized, the mind can see that the *true* mind itself is empty and non-attached, too. The non-tathagata mind suffers because of: 1. wrong views (shortsighted temptations and impulses) 2. clinging to form (which changes), 3. clinging to desire, 4. clinging to formless realms (afterlife, heaven and hell), 5. and misknowing or unknowing.[48] Enlightenment, happiness, nirvana, emptiness and tathagata in the Buddhist lexicon are but designations for the same state of being; a state of nonattachment, flowing with the world, contentment.

Ironically, one needs the changing body and its bewildered mind in order to seek and reach the tathagata state. In liberation, the difference lies in knowing the border between confusion and clarity. In clarity, one is no longer attached, greedy, or oblivious to the emptiness of reality. Attaining tranquility and experiencing tathagata take place in the presence of incoming, daily impulses of the body and mind, not existing in some euphoric state. Attainment of nirvana is to realize the state of tathagata, an experience when a person lives uninhibitedly in nowness by using the fuel of the physical body as well as the reasoning power of the mind. (The body-mind interwoven together to enjoy painlessness and joy of living is a Tantric-Buddhist approach and practice). Nagarjuna conjectures that tathagata is neither in physical existence nor different from it.[49] Samsara and nirvana necessitate each other.

Khayyam is certainly a philosopher of grasping the state of suchness in the present moment (Persian *hãl*, or *dam*). In his view, joy is experienced when living in the simplicity of suchness of life free from religion and irreligion (*rubai* 75). Towards this end, Khayyam idealizes the kingdom of the mind over hollow material ownership and power (*rubai* 98).

---

[47] Ibid., chapter 22 (Examination of Tathagata), 62, verses 15-16.
[48] *Prajna Paramita Heart Sutra*, 63-4.
[49] *Mūlamadhyamakakārikā*, chapter 22 (Examination of Tathagata), 60, verses 1-2.

Self-Rule, Joy and Emptiness

> It is morning, oh my brilliant sweetheart,
> Compose me a new melody and bring out wine.
> As for the world, it has thrown to the ground tens of thousands of kings,
> Like summer months thrown out by the winter.
> <div align="right">(<i>rubai</i> 116)</div>

Much like the Buddha, Khayyam brings to light the two sides of the same coin of life. As we have seen, Khayyam talks openly about old age, decay and death as the cruel facts of life—one side of the coin. Meanwhile, he celebrates the sweetness of life to be enjoyed in total freedom and nonattachment—the other side of the coin. Khayyam keeps revisiting both sides of the coin, warning of the precarious and transient human condition while extolling the joys of life at the same time.

And the Buddhist *Prajnaparamita*'s simplest description of nirvanic joy is when there is no pain and grief in the heart.[50] Yet this barely sounds human: how can grief and pain be absent in the face of incoming impulses, aging, and imminent death? It's not to say that grief and pain will be absent, but that such pain is underlain with an acceptance of reality in which the joy of life can co-exist with pain. Or, at a more advanced psychological maturity, the real joy is when the dichotomy of joy-suffering is removed from one's personal equation. An aware person must distinguish between the non-suffering of the objective reality and one's own suffering mind, with the goal of coming closer to the non-suffering reality. Succinctly put, it is as though in reality there is no suffering, no cause of suffering, or even no death ... they are all experienced by the suffering person.[51] For those who struggle with the dilemma of death, Nagarjuna puts the matter in perspective fairly and squarely: existence without decay and death is not possible, and nirvana is integrated in existence.[52] The fear of death will have to be abandoned as it is nothing injurious; it is a component of an inevitable process. So joy arises through a peaceful acceptance of this fact. Grief and anxiety about the end are not all that are experienced in life; they can co-exist with joy.

> Khayyam's mastery of imagery brings such ideals to life:
> Since no one has any clue about tomorrow,
> Cultivate joy here and now and transform your sad heart.
> Drink wine by honoring the moonlight, this moon that
> Shall appear many times but one day will not find us anymore.
> <div align="right">(<i>rubai</i> 112)</div>

---

[50] *Prajna Paramita Heart Sutra*, 118.
[51] Ibid., 107.
[52] *Mūlamadhyamakakārikā*, chapter 25 (Examination of Nirvana), 73-5.

> The moonlight slashes the darkness of the sky.
> Drink wine, for one cannot find a better moment than now.
> Live a delightful life and bear in mind that the moonlight
> Will glow on our graves, lying next to each other.
>
> (rubai 111)

The empirical Buddhism of Nagarjuna and the empirical philosophy of Khayyam focused on the existential and psychological questions of life and tried to provide rational perspectives. Neither of them believed in a predestined life so long as human faculties were awake and lived in tathagata and nowness. The two thinkers were humanists and existential therapists who exhorted humans to be prepared by living a life of a self-reliant rationalist without being too attached to this unsettling world.

Ultimately, it is important to realize that the position of both Nagarjuna and Khayyam was not merely about living perfectly and happily. It goes without saying that human imperfection, fallibility and emotionality are very much embedded in human psychology. Rather, the ideas of Nagarjuna and Khayyam embrace both the perfect and imperfect sides of humans, their happy and sorrowful sides together—samsara and nirvana side by side. The warnings are against elements that always cast a shadow over human wellbeing, such as a compulsive mind, reactive living-by-doing, the danger of heedless living, and a metaphysically-driven mindset.

To escape these shadows and move into the lightness of being requires disentangling from all obstructions of the mind and suspending the fear of losing possessions or recognition and not returning to life. A state of nirvanic joy is moving forward beyond any confused state or anxious mental imageries.[53] For a joyful state, there is nothing to do or to be attained; it is always there. Ubiquitous suchness without suffering is the message of the Lotus Sutra.[54] Nagarjuna calls on the Buddha who espoused Two Truths, the conventional (an exterior view of the world) and the ultimate (the inapparent intermediate state or emptiness), and who taught a profound truth of a joyful mind by stopping the rise of suffering.[55] From Nagarjuna and Khayyam both we can better understand that what is required of us and our minds is to accept the co-existence of joy and grief courageously, not giving in to the urge to cover over or deny the true nature of life. Instead, if we live with decisive composure as each moment changes, we have a chance of understanding the truth of tranquility.

---

[53] *Prajna Paramita Heart Sutra*, 115-16.
[54] Ibid., 122.
[55] *Mūlamadhyamakakārikā*, chapter 25 (Examination of Nirvana), 71-2, verses 31-40.

Chapter 5
The Immortal Clay: An Echo of the Chandogya Upanishad in Khayyam's Allegory

> "Just as by knowing a lump of clay, my son, all that is clay can be known, since any differences are only words and the reality is clay."
>
> *(Chandogya Upanishad 6.1)*[1]

This allegorical anecdote, found in the Chandogya Upanishad, one of the oldest Upanishads, is the story of a father giving counsel to his twelve-year-old son who is proud of his bookish learning. But the father challenges his son: "Have you asked for that knowledge whereby what is not heard is heard, what is not thought is thought, and what is not known is known?" The son, in his curiosity, asks, "What is that knowledge?" The father urges him to go further to learn the unheard, unthought and unknown knowledge. He explains to his son that the ultimate reality of things is unquantifiable and undetectable to the eye and to the superficial mind. But the truth is that the entire universe is made out of one kind of material. Although objects appear to look different from one another and have different names, all pots, although different in shape, are made out of clay, and no matter what, they remain clay in their true nature and turn back into clay again.[2]

In this allegory, 'clay' represents the elemental existence, and all entities (pots) arise from and return to the primordial clay. This points to the fundamental Upanishadic teaching that all forms and names are but passing phenomena (*maya*), and true existence is the immortal Brahman. Brahman is the highest principle—in this case, represented by the primordial clay- and its personification is Atman, a fraction of Brahman that could be called a pot made out of the primordial clay. This premise of the Upanishadic teachings became the foundation of Vedantic Philosophy. Every living person represents and

---

[1] *The Upanishads*, Translations from the Sanskrit with an introduction by Juan Mascaró, (Delhi: Penguin Books, 1965; reprinted 1994), 117.
[2] See "The Chhandogya Upanishad by Swami Krishnananda," Chapter Two: Uddalaka's Teaching Concerning the Oneness of the Self: https://www.swamikrishnananda.org/chhand/ch_2.html. (Accessed May 28, 2020).

carries an Atman, which, upon the death of the body, joins and becomes the universal Brahman. Clay is thus the rhetorical expression of Brahman. The clay remains immortal and unchanged despite all the different forms of the 'pots' in the Universe.

Clay is a foundational material in the Cosmos and the earth and in human history. It has played an important role in the development of human civilization, and it is also true that the best quality pots are from oil-based clay (perhaps derived from animal and human corpses). Like the thoughtful writers of the Upanishads, Omar Khayyam also drew upon the metaphorical richness of this multi-purpose material for developing his clay motif to represent all aspects of physical existence.

Khayyam's immortal clay refers to the substance from which all the pots are made in the universal pottery shop. These pots are made from the same clay that came from previously existing bodies- from the bodies of kings, and beggars, and sweethearts. From clay, we arise, and to clay we shall return. All the pots, after they are broken, turn into dust and clay again and again—the immortal and forever clay.

> When precious life has left our bodies
> Clay will be put in both our graves.
> And then in digging the graves of others,
> The dust of your body and mine will be tossed and made into new clay.
>
> (*rubai* 57)

An overview of the Upanishads

The earliest Upanishadic texts were written down around the eighth century B.C.E. in the areas of the Indus valley, northwest of India, and continued to be produced up to the sixteenth century (starting from a few to 108 Upanishads[3]). A number of key Upanishads offered the first challenges to some long-standing Vedic religious (Hindu) traditions, including polytheism, animal sacrifice, and person-to-person reincarnation. With the proposition of Brahman placed as the highest principle in Existence, the Upanishadic challenge aimed to eliminate animal worship sacrifice for and supplication to the gods. Instead, the Upanishads replaced Brahman as the ultimate foundation for recognizing self as god. In fact, all animate and inanimate objects, including all the gods, emanate from Brahman, and to which they all return. This was probably the first philosophical attempt to challenge the Vedic beliefs of the priests and the people.

---

[3] The number of minor Upanishads were written in later centuries which currently the total number of them has reached 200.

The Immortal Clay 91

With this formulation, three important and critically revolutionary issues can be identified in the Upanishads, which were later developed in the Vedanta school of philosophy. Firstly, the idea of multiple lives of reincarnation, from human to human, or human to animal, was rejected. Instead, upon death, humans and all other sentient beings shall instead return to or 'reincarnate' in *Brahman*, not back on earth. Their Atman (self) shall unite with Brahman and not reincarnate in its previous form.

The second issue in the earliest Upanishads is the mention of Brahman, not god per se. This is significant because Brahman is an impersonal principle of existence, not a personal God. It is to be recognized that only in later Upanishads and exegeses does the term *god* appear; otherwise, the term *Brahman* does not mean god (in Sanskrit, it means *expansion*).

Thirdly, the earlier yogic authors of the Upanishads held the nondual and egalitarian stance that all humans and sentient beings equally contain Atman regardless of their caste and category, and that all share the same substrate, which will be left behind and end up in the same destination. The Chandogya Upanishad refers to all as "You Are That," the one who carries the true spirit of reality.[4] The declaration of 'you are that' points to an important existential fact, which can be interpreted whether you become enlightened and know the true nature of reality or not; you are still that regardless. That is to say, no matter which race or caste you are, you are made out of and return to the universal source: Brahman. This substrate that all have in common is referred to as 'clay,' or 'atman,' or 'brahman.' It is somehow beautiful, and perhaps somehow significant, that it is the modest, lowly material of clay employed for this metaphor. Not copper, not glass. Not even gold. The impersonal 'clay' serves as a universal base for making different pots which break and become clay again to make more pots, over and over.[5] This became the Upanishadic model of an impersonal universe.

---

[4] *The Upanishads*, Chandogya Up. 117-118.
[5] Ibid., 117. See also, Swami Tejomayananda, *Ganapati Atharvashirsha Upanishad*, (Mumbai: Central Chinmaya Trust, digitized, no date), 35. For ubiquitous references on 'clay' and 'pot' see also, Swami Krishnananda, *The Chhandogya Upanishad*, https://www.swami-krishnananda.org/chhand/Chhandogya_Upanishad.pdf.

Khayyam's metaphor of the 'clay of the potter'

The universal clay analogy may have been borrowed from this apparently 2,700-year-old Upanishad by Khayyam in the most magnificent and literary way possible to lay out his similar perspective. With his use of the metaphors of 'dust' and 'clay,' Khayyam builds his unique imagery of the world as a 'pottery factory.' The clay comes from the universal bank of clay that is salvaged and reutilized. His imagery is also parallel to that in the Chandogya Upanishad in the sense of the egalitarianism and universalism of the indistinguishable clay from which everyone is fashioned continually, time and again. Khayyam's message is unambiguous. Clay is clay! There is no rich clay, king clay, holy clay or poor clay. There is a natural humility in this model. In this way, Khayyam, much like the Upanishadic yogis, sends a cautioning message to the religious and political elites of the society about their discriminatory and inequitable attitudes:

> As I passed by a pottery workplace,
> I witnessed the master's foot on the wheel,
> Meticulously fashioning the jug's lid and handle
> From a king's skull and a beggar's finger.
>
> (*rubai* 71)

> It was the day before yesterday that I passed by a pottery workshop.
> The potter in each moment curved a creative form.
> I saw for myself what non-discerning eyes could not see:
> The dust of my father's corpse in every turn of the wheel.
>
> (*rubai* 69)

Another captivating realization is found in both the quatrains and the Upanishads, that when a finite human life end, it's as if it never was. Today we could think of it as a movie on a screen. The film seems real, but in fact, it is unreal, like a fictitious reality, a dream-like event that has had a reality but has vanished. Once the movie is turned off, it leaves no trace of ever having been on the screen. So human life, as it is portrayed in the Upanishads and in Vedantic philosophy, is but an illusory, bewitching experience (*maya*), an impermanent occurrence to meditate on for awakening. [6] The only everlasting reality is Brahman. Human experience is the coupling of the unreal (the ever-changing phenomenal world) and the real (Atman-Brahman), like a fleeting film running on an immortal-steady screen. This seemingly dual, fleeting world and a steady screen, in an insightful contemplation, emerges as a nondual experience.

---

[6] *The Principal Upanishads*, translated and edited by Swami Nikhilananda, (New York: Dover Publications, Inc., 2003; originally published in 1963), 39-44.

The Immortal Clay

According to Khayyam, before one realizes it, life passes; one has aged and then dies and disappears forever. This impermanency causes the loss of connection with the past, as the bygone events are only memories and reminiscences in the living person's mind (not the deceased ones). In looking back at all the past generations, in Khayyamian terms, there is nothing left of them, neither forms nor mind, except for the dust which has been reabsorbed into the universal chemistry.

> Cultivate pleasure, because life only provides us this moment.
> Each floating atom comes from the disintegrated dust of kings like Jamshid and Kayqubad.
> The state of the world, with its fluid foundations for our impermanent life
> Is more like an imagination, a deception, a transitory moment, a dream.
> (*rubai* 109)

> Do as the spring tulip does: unfold like a cup in hand.
> Spend your time with a tulip-faced beauty in every turn;
> Drink wine felicitously since this violet-colored cosmic wheel
> Converts you into dust suddenly, before you realize it.
> (*rubai* 122)

Khayyam walks his readers through the impersonal process of making and unmaking. There is no personal god involved in this process nor a god to plead for swaying this process. And in the Upanishads, as mentioned before, Brahman is also not a personal god; in the Khayyamian sense, It is the hidden 'pot-maker' with its universal clay who governs the universal pottery workshops. This pot-maker is aloof and detached from all human pain and pleasure, as it is ready to break down any pots to turn them into clay again. The pots are impermanent, but the universal clay that the pot-maker uses is immortal. The clay pervades existence and temporarily takes on physical qualities, and yet it stays clear of any permanent qualities. Even human-made gods or deities are finite and come from and return to Brahman.

> "All objects, animate and inanimate, are included in It. Gods, men, subhuman beings are parts of It. As the unchanging Reality behind the universe, It is called Brahman."[7]

Brahman is infused in the world from which all things emerge, yet is the "unchanging Reality" outside of it. Thus, Brahman is the impersonal clay of the universe. The clay of Khayyam is also infused in the world out of which colorful flowers, humans, grass and all animate and inanimate objects are crafted.

---

[7] Ibid., 31.

Khayyam reviews the cycle of clay over and over, and he concludes that the beginning and end of all things are clay and dust—the ultimate principle:

> Since the clouds sprinkle rain on the petals of the tulip in the new day of spring,
> You also rise up confidently and grab your wine cup.
> Bear in mind, this grass that is staring at you
> Will one day be growing from the dust of your corpse.
>
> (*rubai* 62)

> Be cautious, since you live below some treacherous heavens.
> Drink your wine since you exist in the world of mishaps.
> Because your beginning and end is only dust,
> Visualize yourself not lying on the ground but under it.
>
> (*rubai* 131)

Enlightenment to Khayyam is the realization that the world and its processes are impersonal. This enlightenment corroborates with the Upanishads that everyone is one's own god, so to speak, and is responsible for one's own delight. Any tendency to personalize and emotionalize the natural processes lead to confusion and despair. Khayyam, in his turn, repeatedly reminds those who plead to their personal gods and are so attached to their emotions that neither gods nor human grief will change the universal course:

> Whoever laid the foundation of the earth and the spinning cosmos
> Didn't anticipate that hearts can be broken.
> Darlings with wine-colored lips and musk-scented hair
> Are buried in the hollow ground and the coffin of the dust.
>
> (*rubai* 24)

In dealing with transmutation, Khayyam is a master philosopher. He shows a two-stage way forward. The first is that while the clay of an individual or our existence experiences a vibrant life right now, it is like a clay cup that is filled with the wine of joy. In due course, the cup will be thrown to the ground and shattered again. This process is as clear as daylight in the mind of every realistic person. So why sorrow and confusion when joy is readily and ubiquitously accessible, Khayyam asks.

The second stage to remember is that if one's final destiny is to be turned into dust and clay, then one's clay is an immortal clay. This immortal clay has been passed down from time immemorial, and for humans for many millennia and many generations, and therefore one must be prepared to let go and contribute to the flow of this universal clay so that other entities can be crafted from it. In one sense, Khayyam's take on immortality is similar to the Upanishadic conception of Atman-Brahman, that the *clay* and the vibrant force of life (the *wine*) will be soaked together and live forever—only forms change and new identities will take conventional designations. Clay and wine themselves are immortal, even though the crafted cups made out of the same clay take different forms and names and the wine is absorbed into and exudes from these differently shaped clay cups. Khayyam sees his own figurative immortality through the clay cup and the wine he once enjoyed for a while, which are now passed down to make another body:

> On the day when my life is uprooted
> And its branches and splinters are dispersed,
> If a cup is crafted from my clay,
> It will come to life again once it is filled with wine.
>
> (*rubai* 81)

Summary

It is true that the biological configuration of human beings is different from other configurations of life, yet all share a common denominator that finds its roots in organic life. In modern scientific vernacular, we talk about the immortality of genes, the substratum make-up of all living beings. But as the Chandogya Upanishad states, "differences are only words and the reality is clay." This is to say, one must discern the immortality of clay from the belief in the immortality of the cup—an individual. In this connection, clay is the only substratum that is left behind after death. While the "existence" of the clay is certain, the immortality, or even the existence, of a soul remains ambiguous and unverifiable notions.

Khayyam's allegorical and poetical imagery upholds this Upanishadic prototype for a more perceptive examination. From a naturalist and a scientific point of view, he considered that once a pot is broken and shattered, it can never return to its individual and original figure—the decay and entropy are irreversible. A broken pot can never be repaired to its original state due to an inherent decay and entropy. He refuses to submit to the magical thinking of immortality which promoted the full return of a human being biologically and psychologically. To him, as well as to other rational-minded thinkers, the process of physics and chemistry is unidirectional and chronologically is irretrievable. Khayyam's idea of irreversibility is not limited to just physical existence alone but represents a complete departure of the body and psyche:

> From those who have disappeared from this long road,
> Who has re-entered to share with us the secret?
> Take heed of entering and exiting this road; don't let your craving obstruct it.
> Leave no trace behind, since you will not return.
>
> (*rubai* 46)

His compositions aim to discern between whatever subjectively emanates from the human mental faculty that is based on a generational, conditioned-emotional mind, and the objective laws of existence. As a philosopher-poet with scientific training, Khayyam reminded the population of his medieval times, and beyond that, the laws of conversion and transmutation are universal and timeless. Irrespective of time, culture and religious belief, all humans and creatures upon death undergo the process of rot, disintegration, and eventually conversion into dust, reuniting with the earth from which all life, food and living beings emerge. The entire constellation, including the earth, is composed of the primordial dust and rhetorical clay that the Upanishad and Khayyam described. Clay it was, clay it is, and clay it will be. Given this reality, Khayyam and the Upanishadic yogis offered one way to understand the human quandary, how to make sense out of the immutable universal clay we are entrusted with in order to manifest an awakened life without attachment to a body whose identity is transitory, let alone its ownership.

Part II:
Therapeutic Approach: Four Essays

Chapter 6
Poetry-Philosophy as Medicine:
A Historical Background

One rarely thinks of a 'prescription' of poetry as a treatment for an illness, but in fact, maybe poetry and philosophy can indeed serve as a form of medicine. In this essay, we will see how philosophical poetry had been and can be used as a means of therapy. This is, in fact, not a new idea. We will explore how, historically, both philosophy and poetry were highly esteemed by ancient and medieval physicians and philosophers as a kind of 'medicine' or treatment for mental and emotional conditions. Centuries later, modern research has demonstrated how stress, confusion and disturbance change the brain physiology and can lead to psychosomatic symptoms. One could say that the lack of a balancing philosophy translates into a lack of perspective on life and its circumstances which contributes to insecurity, anxiety and illness. Therefore, having a philosophy and drawing upon the power of poetry can both help balance perspectives, strengthen the power of interpretation, and contribute to wellness. Exploring the connection between the mind's wellness and illness and the power of words has long been a source of debate and inspiration.

*****

Throughout history, the human need for physical survival existed alongside the need to survive mentally and emotionally. Oftentimes, heartfelt words and spontaneous connection with others have helped meet these psychological needs, existentially rescuing humans. On a more significant level, the power of commonsensical words can direct the mind and feelings towards a deeper understanding of self, others and the panorama of life, and engaging ideas have always provided mental food for continuous reflection and contemplation. It was for these reasons and out of these needs that philosophy and poetry emerged, to remedy and rescue humans from their own void and misunderstandings. The poetry-philosophy platform may have been rooted in a desire to create an open forum and egalitarian access to free thinking—in other words, to 'free one's thinking' and thus free oneself from the existential tensions.

The quintessence of sharing views, whether through written or oral transmission, whether prose or poetry, has often meant orienting the disoriented, as well as healing the wounds of the mind—self and others.

Indispensable and timely words have always helped mitigate the unbearable pain of existence and prevent emotional collapse. The influential words of philosophy and poetry, at one time, have aimed to aesthetically portray the material environment of the world, at other times have aimed to heal and bolster the minds of those trapped in alienation and disconnection from self and the world.

In premodern societies, psychiatry or psychotherapy did not exist as we know them today. There were no clinical criteria for diagnoses of psychological instabilities or emotional turmoil; there were no pills to take or formal therapy sessions to attend. People simply improvised life in the ways they knew best. At the most, average people held dialogues on a one-to-one basis as a means of making sense out of life and the multitude of circumstances that they were experiencing. Such 'conversation therapy' may be the oldest style of psychotherapy, which of course, still continues quite spontaneously in social interactions throughout all cultures. This level of connection and communication is the most fundamental human necessity.

In many traditional societies even today, the art of quoting just the right proverb, poem or anecdote at just the right time has remained an important conduit of cognitive and social growth, a kind of wisdom counseling. In these societies, it starts in childhood, hearing older people quote a specific poem or symbolic story in order to expound upon it, and gradually internalizing such poems for oneself. In this way, one learns to tap into the wisdom of such poems to assist in developing character, understanding, and virtuosity in life. This skillful method of interpreting life was often taken for granted, but in reality, it helped individuals and communities throughout the ages to bear the broader journey of life without being mentally and emotionally displaced by ultimately inconsequential and fleeting circumstances.

The words-mind-body relationship

Ever since Ivan Pavlov's salivating dog experiment and his consequential work *Conditioned Reflexes: An Investigation of the Physiological Activity of the Cerebral Cortex*, modern medicine has been forced to pay attention to the physiological activities of the cerebral hemispheres. Through his experiments, Pavlov brought the discipline of psychology closer to the science of medicine. Pavlov won the 1904 Nobel Prize for medicine, and his remarks in his Nobel address are quite relevant here: "Essentially, only one thing in life is of real interest to us—our psychical experience. Its mechanism, however, was and still is shrouded in profound obscurity. All human resources—art, religion, literature, philosophy, and the historical sciences—all have joined in the attempt to throw light upon this darkness. But humanity has at its disposal yet another powerful resource—natural science with its strict, objective methods."[1]

Pavlov's discovery revealed that psychical factors trigger the highest nervous system and consequently have effects on the cellular level, such as secretions of enzymes, hormones, and adjustments in physiology that are quantitatively measurable. The mechanism of this intricate function between the brain and body is incredibly complex, and new areas of study are quite revealing.

First, in understanding the mind-body connection, it is important to distinguish between a psyche that is involuntarily governed by biological/physiological processes, hormones, and neurotransmitters (e.g., schizophrenia, manic-depression), and a psyche that itself voluntarily influences the physiological activities in the brain and eventually the body, leading either to health or illness. The former is related to the fields of psychiatry, biological psychology and behavioral neuroscience, whereas the latter is linked with the revolutionary field of psychoneuroimmunology (PNI). Keeping this in mind, there are certain areas of study between the two disciplines that overlap. Taking a more holistic model to study the human mind, we can say that at the center of a circular web is the psyche, and next comes the brain, and then the system branches outwards to include physiology, body, behavior and beyond. This web of systems has accordingly given rise to the disciplines of neuroscience-neuropsychology, cognitive psychology and social psychology.

With these concepts in mind, it can be said that humans are accumulations of psychological experiences, cognitive input, and memories, all of which affect behavior and consequently influence our destinies in life in our given environments. There are those individuals who allow their psyche to be a conduit for positive input and are tuned for optimistic emotive states, conditions that advance their physiology to retain its normalcy and even enhance body-repairing physiology. The opposite of this, of course, has more serious consequences, as we shall see in the next essay.

Obviously, humans are not strictly rational or black-and-white thinkers, and the emotional conduct that humans often exhibit can take the form of an overwhelming, irrational engagement with the self. This is a conditioning that has taken an unnecessary toll on people's health, taxing their states of being as well as their social behavior. In addition, non-object-based anxieties and fears that are generated in the human mind, not based on any immediate threats, seem to be among the many ambiguous behaviors that humans exhibit. These not only increase but also complicate the existential struggle. The human mind can easily dwell on self-induced hopeless attitudes, on an evocation of melancholic sentiments of the past, anxiety for the future, despair due to death,

---

[1] Michael Specter, "Drool: Ivan Pavlov's Real Quest," *New Yorker* (November 24, 2014).

the fear of loss, and, most heavily, the fear of one's own death. These internally processed emotional traumas in life may assail the brain's performance and perturb its normal cognitive function. Such disturbances can also have lasting effects which may deplete the body and its function.

In considering Pavlov's well-known work—which was not just about dogs and behavior—he extrapolated that undesirable psychic-biological conditions can be reversed. The mood can be reversed by creating conducive energizers such as listening to music, engaging in illuminating dialogues, reading uplifting poetry or philosophy, thinking about solutions rather than constantly focusing on problems, engaging in introspection, engaging in kind and altruistic acts, appreciating art, sitting and observing nature, and other such beneficial activities that transcend anxieties. And according to Democritus, it is principally wise and constructive to focus on what one has in life, not what one lacks. These actions and thoughts can change and soothe the chemical activities of the cerebral hemispheres, affecting the brain and ultimately the body through the peripheral nervous system. Microcirculation may be enhanced, and muscles in the body can begin to feel relaxed.

The constructive power of words in philosophy and inspirational poetry has the potential to steer the brain's activities toward deeper understanding, and can thus sway the physiology. A mind that experiences an instant understanding of new and delightful ideas is analogous to a tongue whose taste buds savor something fresh and delicious. The brain, with its sparkling synapses, can similarly enjoy relaxing thoughts and positive inspirations. Each little bit of such experience can go a long way towards advancing our physiology in the direction of health and joviality. Cultivating a poetical and philosophical mind while re-creating one's perspectives can change things around, orienting one towards a greater admiration of life.

In order to appreciate Khayyamian poetry in particular as a therapeutic and transformative philosophy, let us turn our attention to how classical physicians and philosophers believed poetry-like philosophies could help people improve health by gaining psychological, emotional, and cognitive stability.

Historical links between philosophy, poetry and medicine

The power of words on the inner workings of the mind, and consequently the health of the body, was recognized long ago. In ancient and medieval times, philosophy and its ideas about life and medicine were studied together, one necessitating the other: one treated the mind, and the other treated the body, but with a very small gap between the two. At the same time, poetry has often been a melodic method of conveying philosophy. A poem is a compact, intelligible and lucid reflection on angles of life for both the erudite and general public to absorb and enjoy. A number of ancient and medieval philosophers have addressed the general importance of poetry, including Aristotle, al-Farabi, Avicenna, and Averroes.[2] The creative and imaginative rhymed use of language, which includes commonsense facts of life as well as syllogistic or deductive reasoning, could often make the object of interest more intelligible either in simple or composite forms and was also easier to memorize—and thus more accessible to the mind. Metaphor, meaning, and reasoning power all come together as a compelling linguistic tool that generates new feelings.[3] Therefore, when we talk about philosophy and medicine, we can also extend those connections and effects to poetry.

Both medicine and philosophy were considered arts in ancient Hellenic culture. Hippocrates (460-377 B.C.E.), the ancient and celebrated physician of the classical age, considered medicine the art which heals the body and philosophy the art which heals the mind. The ancient Greeks used the term *iatrike*, which was later translated as 'medicine.' Medicine was, in fact, a *techne* 'art' rather than a science with all its rational (non-divine) explanation of disease and health.[4] To Hippocrates, while philosophy was not medicine that could heal diseases, medicine was not entirely independent from philosophy either.[5] Philosophy alone could not heal physical illnesses, nor could medicine heal existential and mental burdens, but they complemented each other.

Hippocrates became a pivotal thinker for his understanding of the nature of the human constitution and for establishing a common ground between medicine and philosophy. The two arts—medicine as a practical art and philosophy as a theoretical art—benefitted humans. Both disciplines came closer to each other, but each has had to offer more evidence to support their theories and claims.[6] It seems the work of philosophy was a boost to the work of medicine. It was presumably observed how philosophy improved the state of 'patients,' but the empirical evidence remained imprecise. However, the confluence of the 'healer of pain' and the 'lover of wisdom' and their relationship reached its climax at the time of Hippocrates. It gradually came to the attention of the philosophers that by following the rhythms of nature, humans could retain their health since the body and nature resemble each other, having the same elements.[7]

---

[2] See Salim Kemal, *The Philosophical Poetics of Alfarabi, Avicenna and Averroës: The Aristotelian Reception*, (New York: Routledge), 2003.
[3] Kemal, *The Philosophical Poetics*, 2-10.
[4] See Ilham Ibnou Zahir, "Hippocrates: Philosophy and Medicine," *European Scientific Journal* 12, no. 26 (September 2016): 199-210.
[5] Ibid., 201, 204, 206-7.
[6] Ibid., 203-4.
[7] Ibid., 207, 209.

The investigation of the body-nature relationship can be seen in ancient Chinese medicine, in which Daoistic philosophy described the body-mind constitution as mirroring nature: both the body and mind can get out of balance when they violate the principles of nature as well as their own intrinsic capacities. Normalcy can return only when the mind and body are aligned with their natural energy. While performing unceasingly, nature remains quiet and never overacts; it never exceeds its limits, and by the end of the day, it gets things done. Humans are advised to embody these industrious and yet stoic qualities of nature in order to stay attuned with nature. The ill body and mind, from this perspective, are those which ignore and deny their naturalness. So, the mind that knows the philosophy of nature also knows the philosophy of life. Together, Daoism and the evolution of Chinese medicine accomplished two tasks: demonstrating the link between philosophy and health and the link between nature and human psychophysical makeup.

On another front seeking a link between philosophy-poetry and medicine, Avicenna (980-1037) emerged as a skilled medieval physician, philosopher and medical author born and bred in Central Asia along the Silk Road.[8] In his time, students who studied to become physicians would first study philosophy. Avicenna himself set that example by deepening his philosophical quest during his own pursuit of medical knowledge. He believed that the body and mind are absolutely intertwined.[9] He noted that it was through this connection that if unfavorable life circumstances arise, psychopathologies and psychosomatic symptoms would surface. In such cases, inspirational and sagacious philosophy and poetry were the preferred therapy instead of drugs. For example, one of Avicenna's methods and recommendations for the treatment of depression was music therapy and aromatherapy in order to generate exhilaration. This treatment was not only for melancholy alone but also for anxiety, fear of death, and a range of psychosomatic conditions.[10] He and similarly perceptive physicians recognized that certain mental imbalances caused physical ailments that required a physician-philosopher's comprehensive intervention to treat the whole patient, not just the body or just the mind.

Interestingly, in a perspective that is reminiscent of the ancient Daoistic perspective, Avicenna viewed the quality and vibrancy of the mind, and

---

[8] See Zahide Özkan-Rashed, *Die Psychosomatische Medizin bei Abu Zaid al-Balhi*, (Düren: Shaker Verlag, 2019).

[9] Seyed Abbas Zahabi, "Avicenna's Approach to Health: A Reciprocal Interaction Between Medicine and Islamic Philosophy," *Journal of Religion and Health* 58 (2019): 1698-1712.

[10] Mostafa Araj Khodaie et al., "Avicenna (980-1037 C.E.): The Pioneer in Treatment of Depression," *Transylvanian Review* 25, no. 17 (May 2017): 4377-4389.

ultimately the body, as being similar to the personality of water.[11] Water attains its purity and vigor by flowing naturally; otherwise, in stagnation, it will become a swamp. Similarly, the mind, as well as the body, are governed by the dynamic principles of freshness and flow rather than stagnation. A mental blockage that causes somatic ailments can potentially be unblocked by conducive ideas or even by a philosophical jolt. The mind may then flow again, and so can the body's rhythms.

Apart from his prodigious work on medical and philosophical undertakings, Avicenna was also a literary poet and composed two categories of poetry. One category was his medical-poetical masterpiece, *al-Ur Juza fi al-Tibb* (*Didactic Poems of Medicine*), which conveyed didactic medical information in a poetic form that was easier to memorize and keep accessible rather than trying to memorize scientific prose. (In fact, in medieval Europe after Avicenna there was an increase in the trend to compose medical poems.[12])

In addition, it appears that Avicenna supported poetry therapy for patients[13] alongside evidenced-based didactic therapies of the time. The other category of poetry Avicenna composed was designed to evoke inspiration and euphoric feelings and release tension.[14] (In this category of poems by Avicenna, there are

---

[11] Regarding water and its nature in Taoism, see Lao Tzu, *Tao Te Ching*, translation by Ch'u Ta-Kao, (New York: Samuel Weiser, 1973), chapters 8 and 78.

[12] Rabie El-Said Abdel-Halim, "The role of Ibn Sina's (Avicenna) medical poem in the transmission of medical knowledge to medieval Europe," *Urology Annals* 6, no. 1 (Jan.-Mar. 2014): 1-12. https://www.ncbi.nlm.nih.gov/pmc/articles/PMC3963335/. Regarding the link between poetry and sciences, there has been a historical link when various medieval Persian and Arab poets turned multiple sciences such as; mathematics, astronomy, anthropology, psychology, sociology, anatomy, and certainly medicine into poetry. For example, Nasir Khosrow (d. 1088), the Persian poet, traveler and philosopher who put human anatomy with its body parts and the connecting vessels into poetical meters. His anthropological and the seven-year-traveling experiences, not only were incorporated into poetical verses but also, he produced a fascinating travelogue (*Safarnameh*) prose documenting his life experiences from Central Asia to Near Eastern lands, Mediterranean coasts all the way to Egypt, all around mid-eleventh century.

[13] Majid Nimrouzi et al., "Avicenna's Medical Didactic Poem: *Urjuzhe Tibbi*," Acta Med Hist Adriat 13, Supl. 2 (2015): 48-9.

[14] Nimrouzi et al., "Avicenna's Medical Didactic Poem: *Urjuzhe Tibbi*," 45-56. I can attest to the high level of sophistication in composing these medical poems by Avicenna. I personally have in my collection an out-of-print bilingual French-Arabic copy of *al-Ur Juza fi al-Tibb* or *Poème de la Médicine*, Texte Arabe, Traduction Française, Traduction Latine du XIIIe siècle, avec Introductions, notes, et index. Etabli et présenté par Henri Jahier et AbdulKader Noureddine, (Paris: Société d'édition "Les Belles Lettres", 1956). This medical poetry book of Avicenna was initially translated into Latin between twelfth

only a number of such poems left behind). On a different note, it has been claimed that a manuscript archived in Paris next to Khayyam's shows a few quatrains from Avicenna.[15] The suspicion has been raised that perhaps some of the *rubais* (quatrains) attributed to Khayyam were actually composed by Avicenna.[16] Although Avicenna was well-versed in poetry, this claim cannot be supported with evidence.[17] But then, it seems that Khayyam himself, although being a full-time astronomer and mathematician, may have, in fact, been influenced by the Avicennian school of medicine and composed his poetry aiming for psychological treatment.

Another outstanding medieval clinician, chemist, and philosopher was Muhammad ibn Zakariya al-Razi (854-925), who made remarkable contributions in the field of the science of medicine as well as rational philosophy. His wide-ranging accomplishments included mastering the distinction between smallpox and measles, discovering how to distill alcohol, establishing subdisciplines of psychosomatic medicine, psychiatry, neurology, pharmacology and pediatrics, playing the lute and using music for healing,[18] and being a vegetarian and animal rights activist.

For thinkers like Razi, the mind was a combination of psychology and physiology, subject to changes triggered by ideas of philosophy. As a philosopher, Razi was not convinced by what he read from Aristotle, Proclus and Galen.[19] He instead turned to pre-Aristotelian thought, engaging with the natural philosophy of Pythagoras.[20] Razi proposed that humans have a rational mind, a thinking and deductive mind (*al-natiqa*) located in the brain. The rational mind, being located in the brain, is capable of imagination, cognitive

---

- and thirteenth-century Europe which became an important medium for transmission of medical knowledge to the continent.

[15] Christian Rempis, *Beiträge Zur Hayyam-Forschung*, (Leipzig: Deutsche Morgenländische Gesellschaft, 1937), 14. The poetry of Avicenna seems to follow the style of his M'tazila mentor, Abdul Jabbār from Hamadān, see Frank Griffel, *Apostasie und Toleranz im Islam: Die Entwicklung zu al-Gazālīs Urteil gegen die Philosophie und die Reaktion der Philosophen*, (Leiden: Brill, 2000), 151-152.

[16] Soheil Afnan, *Avicenna: His Life and Work*, (London: George Allen & Unwin LTD, 1958), 82; Otto Rothfeld, *Umar Khayyam and His Age*, (Bombay: D.B. Taraporevala Sons & Co. 1922), 14.

[17] See Afnan, *Avicenna: His Life and Work*, 82.

[18] R. Shane Tubbs et al., "Abubakr Muhammad Ibn Zakaria Razi, Rhazes (865-925 AD)," *Child's Nervous System* 23, no. 11 (December 2007):1225-26.

[19] Thbrbse-Anne Druart, "Al-Razi's Conception of the Soul: Psychological Background to his Ethics," *Medieval Philosophy and Theology* 5 (1996), 246.

[20] A. S. Bazmee Ansari, "Philosophical and Religious Views of Muhammad Ibn Zakariyya al-Razi," *Islamic Studies* 16, no. 3 (Autumn 1977), 158.

authority and memory.[21] Rationality to Razi was the supreme principle that needed its own medicine, prompting him to write *Spiritual Medicine (al-tibb al-ruḥani)* and *The Philosophic Life (al-sira al-falsafiyya)*.[22] While animals do have a certain degree of rational mind capable of processing emotions, the rational human mind is designed to raise philosophical questions and explanations, as Razi points out.[23]

From Razi's point of view, therapy and healing of the mind meant removing various disturbances and distractions in order to better develop the rational mind capable of reasoning and thinking independently. In particular, according to Razi, reason is sufficient to maintain morality and to distinguish good from evil. Reasoning power was exalted as the ultimate authority, and no religious guide or prophet is needed to teach one what to do or what to think. Razi carried out his criticism against religion in general, and against prophecy in particular. Razi fundamentally supported autonomous thinking, choosing and resolving one's own existential matters without resorting to repressive religious authorities and sources. As Angela Straface states, Razi in *On the Tricks of the Prophets (Fī makhāriq al-anbiy'ā)* wrote that religions are among the main causes of conflict and wars among peoples. "Although al-Rāzī was not imprisoned or executed because of his ideas on religion and prophecy, he was censored for his opinions, resulting in his philosophical and theological works being destroyed."[24]

Razi was also wary of going to the opposite extreme and resorting to frivolous hedonism for solving one's existential turmoil. He warned about the role of pleasure and its limitations in supporting the well-being of the mind. In his books *Spiritual Medicine* and *The Philosophic Life,* Razi takes an Epicurean, and typically rational, position in regards to pleasure being neither positive nor negative, but rather defined pleasure as when pain and disturbance end.[25] For Razi, the drive for hedonistic pleasure—which is "purchased at the price of harm"—shall result in harm that is as great as the pleasure achieved, if not greater.[26] He also berates the naïve understanding of love by relaying the

---

[21] Alfred Ivry, "Arabic and Islamic Psychology and Philosophy of Mind," *The Stanford Encyclopedia of Philosophy* (Summer 2012 Edition), Edward N. Zalta (ed.), https://plato.stanford.edu/archives/sum2012/entries/arabic-islamic-mind. (Accessed July 29, 2020).
[22] Druart, "Al-Razi's Conception of the Soul," 247.
[23] Ibid., 252-3.
[24] Angela Straface, "Abū Bakr al-Rāzī, Muḥammad ibn Zakariyā' (Rhazes)," in Lagerlund H. (eds) *Encyclopedia of Medieval Philosophy*, (Springer, Dordrecht, 2011).
[25] In his approach to the science of the mind, Razi wrote a work entitled *The Book of Pleasure (Kitab al ladhdha)*, which has also gone missing.
[26] Ibid.

danger of it: "Love is an unfortunate condition that leads to subservience and surrender, madness and enervation."[27] The true pleasure and healing of the mind is when one avoids impulsive pleasure, irrational beliefs, and allows the pain-free nature of the mind to be restored.

Razi, the clinician and the musician, was also a poet. It is likely that due to his strong philosophical stances, his poetry would have been in the genre of philosophical healing, like that of Khayyam. Razi took a great interest in wisdom that could identify solutions to the elemental inclinations and deviations of the mind. Razi paved the philosophical road for future poets such as Khayyam, who also addressed challenges that derail the rational mind. By heightening the focus on the power of the brain, poets like Razi and Khayyam used their words to resolve the ongoing human emotional clash with the neutral and unemotional world. They realized that an abject condition of the mind is caused when it is caught between unstoppable life processes and self-absorbed ruminations. The goal in such philosophical healing was to shift the focus of the mind from self-involvement and create active interaction between the mind and the actuality of the transitory world, and hence salvage the cognitive equipoise.

Also playing a pivotal role in offering poetry that supported mental hygiene and clarity about life centuries later, Saadi (d. 1292) and Hafiz (d.1389) were Persian poets whose universal and wise messages have stood the test of time. They dedicated many poems to appeasing the existential tension that each person experiences in one way or another throughout a lifetime. They entertained themes such as joyful living in the face of the impermanency of life, and through the power of their linguistic eloquence, gave courage to their audience to remain aloof from the passage of time by lessening a sense of selfhood while aging and facing imminent death.

> Treasure the pearls of happiness found in the shells of physical existence;
> That the shells don't amass and hold pearls for long.
> Value the transient moment and drink wine in the garden of lush flowers;
> That the flowers' life lasts only a week. —Hafiz[28]

---

[27] Jalal Abd Alghani, "Medieval Arabic Love Theory Between Dissonance and Consonance: Abu Bakr Muhammad Ibn Zakariyya al-Razi and His Argument Against 'Ishq," *Acta Orientalia Academiae Scientiarum Hungaricae* 67, no. 3 (2014): 273-287.

[28] Hafiz, *Divan*, ghazal 162. https://ganjoor.net/hafez/ghazal/sh162/. (this poem and the following poems of Hafiz, Saadi and Rumi are translated by this author).

> At the end of the journey, you become clay for the potter's wheel,
> Seize and honor your own cup by filling it with wine. —Hafiz [29]
>
> I am a bird with wings tied down sitting in my cage,
> Once the cage is broken open, I will show how high I can soar. —Saadi [30]

Instead, Saadi and Hafiz offered engaging narratives that introduced a deeper existence steeped in 'love.' This non-sensual love has been interpreted on many levels, including Sufism, but has been fundamentally understood in an esoteric way to generate psychological energy (wine) so that the ephemeral nature of life is faced with courage and tranquil insight. The love that these poets communicated was a powerhouse found inside the self, which meant encouraging each person to be their own god, the solid and powerful master of one's own life, rather than to be tossed around by superficial and temporary happenings.

> Listen to the Love told by Hafiz, not the orator of the house of worship,
> Even if he is quite industrious and convincing with his rhetoric. —Hafiz [31]
>
> Like Hafiz, try to live a frugal life and journey through this ephemeral world,
> Selling out integrity to the villains even for bars of gold is bankrupt.
> The glory of the royal crown threatens the king's life with impermanency;
> A very seductive hat is not worth forsaking a wise head. —Hafiz [32]

Even though the works of Saadi and Hafiz are considered poetry, they have represented people's "psychotherapy" for centuries—reminders of how to live free-spiritedly. The socially and psychologically loaded poetry has served as a source of solace to pacify the capricious mind and as a conduit to live with confidence rather than with anxiety. For example, the *Divan* book of Hafiz's poetry is traditionally used as a guidebook for many people who continue to memorize the key tension-reducing verses. Traditionally, many in Iran hold the *Divan* in their hand, make a wish, and open to a page, believing that they will find wisdom in whatever words are given by Hafiz on that page. (This practice in Persian is called *faal.*)

Single-handedly, from medieval times all the way to the present, Saadi has provided Persian speakers with hundreds of educational anecdotes and exquisite poems that have transmitted social knowledge and rehabilitating an injured emotional self. The books of Saadi have been so significant in Persian culture that has made some say anyone who reads Saadi's book of poetry

---

[29] Ibid., ghazal 481. See https://ganjoor.net/hafez/ghazal/sh481/. This poem of Hafiz with its 'clay' and 'potter' metaphors seems to have come under Khayyam's literary influence.
[30] Saadi, *Divan,* ghazal 11. See https://ganjoor.net/saadi/divan/ghazals/sh11/.
[31] Ibid., ghazal 131. https://ganjoor.net/hafez/ghazal/sh131/.
[32] Hafiz, ghazal 151. https://ganjoor.net/hafez/ghazal/sh151.

(*Bustan* and *Ghazals*) and book of allegorical stories (*Golistan*) four times in their life will need no other books of wisdom, since both books cover the breadth of understanding of human activities on individual and social levels.

> One day I received from a dear friend
> An aromatic bag of dirt.
> I asked the dirt, 'Are you musk, or some perfume?
> For I am delighted by your scent!'
> It responded, 'I was just dirt.
> But I sat in the company of flowers.
> The scent you notice arises from their companionship,
> Otherwise, I am just the dirt I have always been.' —Saadi [33]

> The holder of insight in life has no apprehension of fortune or rank,
> Like the pure beauty of the moon, which has no color of yellow or red.
> A man with no proper clothes to wear,
> Is better than one elegantly clothed but void of manhood. —Saadi [34]

Apart from their mystical poems, Saadi and Hafiz devoted a branch of their poetry to the knowledge of human societies and people's inclinations based on their social classes—a sort of poetic "sociology." Both poets penned many poems dedicated to the topic of "social psychology." They forewarned their readership about fanatics, usurpers, theologians, hypocrites, narcissists, social braggers, the greedy, so on, and gave advice on how to deal with such negative influences.

> The world spins in favor of ignorant people who rise to the top;
> Pursuing wisdom and insight are your sin and punishment. —Hafiz [35]

> Take this news to the alley of the wine-sellers,
> That Hafiz has stopped practicing two things: religious abstinence and hypocrisy. —Hafiz [36]

Finally, throughout the last 750 years, the genius poetry of the great poet-philosopher, Rumi (d. 1273), has opened new gateways for the human mind.[37] Rumi's poetry symbolizes the union between the unconscious and consciousness, between words and the comprehensive reality of the world, and the union

---

[33] Saadi, *Golestan*. https://ganjoor.net/saadi/golestan/dibache.
[34] Ibid., *Mavaez*, ghete 2. https://ganjoor.net/saadi/mavaez/ghete2/sh37.
[35] Ibid., ghazal 269. https://ganjoor.net/hafez/ghazal/sh269/.
[36] Hafiz, *Divan*, ghazal 130 (see also ghazal 151). https://ganjoor.net/hafez/ghazal/sh130/.
[37] For an intercultural approach to Rumi's philosophy see, Mostafa Vaziri, *Rumi and Shams' Silent Rebellion: Parallels with Vedanta, Buddhism, and Shaivisim*, (New York & London: Palgrave Macmillan, 2015).

between a person and mundane everyday events. His poetry was intended for cognitive awakening.

In addition, Rumi's poetry combined with dance utilized the body and its sensory faculties to experience and naturally grasp the fullness of life. To Rumi, being fully developed in life was not always solely through reflection and theoretical knowledge of life but making use of the corporeal constitution as well. In the modern medical sense, we now understand how the secretion of dopamine and serotonin occurring through chanting poems and dancing leads to feelings of joy and release. The same system of poetry-dance of Rumi is used today by some for therapeutic purposes[38, 39] and could be considered a sort of a neuro-somatic approach.

> A sun arose not from the east nor the west but from the core of my existence,
> And like particles, the walls and the gates of my body commenced to dance.
> While we dance like the atoms in the light of the sun,
> Our days and nights become the means of our labor.
> By dancing, we accompany the lovers who seek Love,
> The way Shams Tabrizi[40] became our companion of Love. —Rumi[41]

***

In considering these brief historical examples, we come away with the realization that poet-philosophers in pre-modern times, in the absence of psychologists and psychiatrists, made worthwhile contributions to society by offering people practical words and self-help advice—poetry as medicine. Although many such poems and ideas were composed in the remote past, such as the poems of Khayyam, they still remain highly significant in understanding and remedying human psychology today and most probably in the future.

---

[38] See online paper by Parvin Naficy, "Poetry Therapy with Rumi in the Clinical Treatment of Frail Persian Immigrants in Late Adulthood," (January 2016).

[39] "Tanztherapie" is also gaining popularity and presenting credible results in its various settings. See Elke Willke, "Tanz in der Psychotherapie Entwicklung eines integrierenden Konzeptes zu einem kreativitätstherapeutischen Zugang in der Rehabilitation," Ph.D. Dissertation an der Universität Dortmund, (2005).

[40] Shams Tabrizi, a shrewd and rebellious thinkr, was Rumi's mentor and friend between 1244 and 1247 in Konya.

[41] Rumi, *Divan Shams Tabrizi*, ghazal 136. https://ganjoor.net/moulavi/shams/ghazalsh/sh136.

Chapter 7

The Entrapped Mind and Psychosomatic Alarms

After centuries of dormancy, a renewed interest in the impact of philosophy and poetry on the mind began to emerge in the nineteenth century. With the emancipation of 'rational psychology' as an independent discipline, the approach to the mind became part of the new philosophical establishment, breaking away from scholastic philosophy.[1] Physiologist, psychologist, and philosopher William James (d. 1910) pioneered the study of philosophy and religion in association with the human mind, as well as the question of the biological nature of a sick or healthy mind. James believed religion and philosophy are two disciplines inaccessible to scientific scrutiny, and instead are mental experiences whose usefulness and function connect humans to a greater reality. He was pragmatic about the role of personal and philosophical *experiences* of the mind and their impact on an individual's existence, rather than focusing just on what a mind *thinks*.[2] He certainly influenced the rise of phenomenology and laid the groundwork for modern philosophical psychology.[3]

The idea of directly associating the effects of mental and emotional experiences with illness or health can be traced back to the work of the almost-forgotten physician Georg Groddeck (d. 1934), who became known as the father of psychosomatic medicine. While remained undealt with for centuries, Groddeck empirically reestablished the relationship and the battle between mind and body. By proposing a scheme for psychosomatic investigation, he propelled to achieve a major result both in medicine and psychoanalysis. The battle between mind and body, he explained, pits the dark forces of the unconscious against the propensity for liberation by the rational consciousness. This intense bifurcation between the temptations of the unconscious and the rationality of consciousness is the split between illness (an obscure and dark mind) and health (clarity of mind).

---

[1] Reinhard Margreiter, *Erfahrung und Mystik: Grenzen der Symbolisierung*, (Berlin: Akademie Verlag, 1997), 126.
[2] Ibid., 128, 198-99, 341.
[3] Russell Goodman, "William James," *The Stanford Encyclopedia of Philosophy* (Winter 2017 Edition), Edward N. Zalta (ed.), https://plato.stanford.edu/archives/win2017/entries/james. (Accessed August 3, 2020).

The alterations in the biodynamics of the brain due to impulsive or obsessive thoughts led to curiosity about brain biology as a whole and how this dynamic manifests itself in the body. Groddeck's insights helped future generations of physicians and psychoanalysts understand the underlying reasons for many disorders and physical ailments that might be rooted in the negative forces of the unconscious. Groddeck coined the term "*Es*" ("Id", "It") for the inner workings of the unconscious, which Sigmund Freud picked up in his own work of psychoanalysis. (In fact, the cross-influences and exchanges between Groddeck and Freud in the field of psychoanalysis were groundbreaking but are beyond the scope of this chapter.[4])

Groddeck's realization of the connection between the unconscious and consciousness, and between mind and body, led him to theorize that the ill mind causes the ill body, while on the other hand, a healthy mind constantly repairs and heals the body. In treating psychosomatic illnesses, he had learned from his teacher Ernst Schweninger that "not illnesses themselves, but instead the ill *people* are the objects of medical treatment."[5] In some summaries of his work, it is also adduced that there are, in fact, no illnesses; there are only ill people. According to him, a volatile mind gives rise to many odd and obscure somatic problems, while a well-groomed mind can manifest natural self-healing and an unsullied and anxiety-free paradigm shift. Although some critics have expressed reservations about the approaches of some psychoanalysts and psychosomatists, it remains undeniable that many unwell people have suffered symptoms whose roots are deeply seated in their traumatized, and one could even say unphilosophical minds.

As for illnesses that do not have apparent psychosomatic explanations, Groddeck provided a realistic and constructive interpretation: a life without illness is not life, and a life with illness is not worthless but rather is another form of life that requires its own knowledge and values.[6] Thus, Groddeck played a large role in revitalizing awareness of the connection between the mind-body and philosophy-medicine. The forces of stress, fear and anxiety were recognized as

---

[4] Among a number of interesting articles, see, Steffen Häfner, "Georg Groddeck – Vater der Psychosomatik," *Zeitschrift für Psychosomatische Medizin und Psychoanalyse* 40, no. 3 (1994): 249-265. Also, Galina Hristeva and Mark F. Poster, "Georg Groddeck's Maternal Turn: Its Evolution and Influence on Early Psychoanalysts," *American Journal of Psychoanalysis* 73, no. 3 (September 2013): 228-53.

[5] "Nicht Krankheiten, sondern Kranke sind Gegenstand ärztlicher Behandlung." Christof Goddemeier, "Groddeck: 'Fanatiker der Heilkunst'," *Ärzteblatt* (Juni 2009), Seite 262. See also, Häfner, "Georg Groddeck Vater der Psychosomatik," 249-265.

[6] Elisabeth Vykoukal, *Georg Groddeck: Krankheit als Symbol - Schriften zur Psychosomatik*, (Frankfurt: Fischer Taschenbuch, 1983), 87-9.

destructive forces, which we now know are major causes of premature strokes, heart attacks and other serious conditions.

The efforts in medicine to understand the linkages between the psychic state, the activities of the brain, and the effects on health and disease have in the last half-century taken shape even more scientifically. The groundbreaking multidisciplinary field of psychoneuroimmunology (PNI) is opening up vast new areas of research in the mind-body connection. This field is demonstrating how cognitive states of stress, anxiety, fear and other non-homeostatic conditions trigger a cascade of unwanted amounts of hormones and neurotransmitters, and as a result, the physical body falls ill. In fact, PNI research actually offers more evidence about the imbalances of the physiology that cause illness than it can shed much light on what creates health and homeostasis. In an ironic twist, the mechanism by which a psychologically serene state of being, with no fear, stress, or threats sustains a steady physiology of health is not yet fully understood: it is actually harder to understand what is meant by 'healthy' than what is meant by 'sick.'

The physiologic responses to acute fear, stress, and threats, including the secretion of adrenaline and noradrenaline, neuroendocrine hormones (cortisol) and blood sugar increase, were and sometimes still are certainly needed in order to promote survival and motivate success.[7] But this survival mode has become more of a chronic state manifesting as anxiety in modern times when real physical threats are actually few—a sort of malfunction of the human mind-body. This ongoing disharmony can cause chronic pain, inflammation, infection and a consistently high level of blood sugar. For example, having high energy can sometimes be construed as a false signal of health. In fact, the extra energy may be coming from high blood sugar and or adrenaline, which are destructive over the long term.

Those who are chronically stress-bound in problematic circumstances of life are often unaware of the deviations in their neuroendocrine and immunological state in the early stages, aside from some minor signs and symptoms. Changes may occur in sleep-appetite patterns, or an amorphous disquiet may manifest within the body. The body is in a slow-motion process of a "fight-or-flight" state. This is the alarm stage of the body, according to Hans Selye[8] (d.1982), a physician

---

[7] Kara E. Hannibal and Mark D. Bishop, "Chronic Stress, Cortisol Dysfunction, and Pain: A Psychoneuroendocrine Rationale for Stress Management in Pain Rehabilitation," *Physical Therapy* 94, no. 12 (2014): 1816–1825. Published online July 17, 2014. https://www.ncbi.nlm.nih.gov/pmc/articles/PMC4263906/.

[8] Hans Selye published a number of books and articles about stress and disease, including his book: *The Stress of Life* (1956, republished several times).

who was the first to create a model called the General Adaptation Syndrome (GAS) explaining the biology of stress.

According to Selye, the alarm stage is the first stage and is still reversible. The second stage is when the body tries to repair itself. If one stays negligent to the prolongation of stressful or overemotional conditions, the body increases its glucose and cortisol levels. This persisting condition of the body consequently manifests more symptoms, and even though the body tries very hard to resist, disarray in its natural functioning begins to take over. Negligence at this stage will send the patient to the third stage of burnout and collapse. Alarm, resistance and exhaustion are thus the three interrelated psychobiological stages and physiological responses to a troubled and stressed mind. This model fundamentally emphasizes the significance of the *mind* and the role it plays in health-illness as well as in many cases of premature death.

*****

There are other emotive, philosophical and wide-ranging dilemmas in the human psyche that necessitate different and appropriate interventions. Positive Psychotherapy, developed by Nossrat Peseschkian, a modern psychiatrist and neurologist, is a hybrid of Oriental elements within a Western psychoanalytical framework. Within Peseschkian's books, one encounters numerous Persian poems, anecdotes, proverbs and more from Oriental poets and social philosophers.[9] Peseschkian quotes Ferdinand Sauerbruch in declaring that the impact of offering suitable poetry and anecdotal stories to patients often reduces the physician's need to prescribe sedating drugs.[10] Peseschkian realized that often a simple poem from Saadi and or the telling of a wise story from Nasreddin[11] could change a person's psychological state. The uniqueness of Peseschkian's seemingly simple method lies in knowing that some patients are, in fact, not medical patients at all. Rather than medication for the body, they need a specific adjustment of perspective on the greater reality of life so that they can tailor their view of reality based on the needs for their own existence.

---

[9] See Nossrat Peseschkian, *Der Kaufmann und der Papagei: Orientalische Geschichten in der Positiven Psychotherapie*, (Frankfurt: Fischer Verlag, 1979). See other books: Nossrat Peseschkian, *Positive Psychotherapie: Theorie und Praxis einer neuen Methode*, (1985), *Psychosomatik und Positive Psychotherapie*, (1993), *Angst und Depression im Alltag: Eine Anleitung zu Selbsthilfe und positiver Psychotherapie*, (1998).
[10] Peseschkian, *Der Kaufmann und der Papagei*, 7.
[11] The legacy of Nasreddin (Mulla Nasre-din), whether historically fictional or factual, is that he was a social philosopher who is famous in the Orient especially for his talent of capturing the spirit of social wisdom in short satirical tales.

Sometimes such modest and philosophical interventions can enhance reasoning power and liberate the suffering person by generating a shift of perspective which was previously lacking. The right symbolic anecdote or poem can provide a myopic individual with a pair of new glasses, so to speak, in order to better view the very same reality being lived in, but this time with clarity and far-sightedness. With this, peace and joy of living may touch one's heart and thus one's health. Peseschkian realized that there is, of course, no obvious or fixed solution for everything in life; each person needs a different level and type of support since the words may come from outside, but the apparatus to analyze the words is deeply buried in the mind.

The sounds of philosophy

In conclusion, the elements of life that *make* us and *keep* us healthy cannot be objectively or quantitatively measured and explained. Certainly, what keeps us fit are the basics: enough quality sleep, a nutritious and prudent diet, movement or sports, daily hydration by drinking water, and maintaining regular hygiene. But the qualitative factors for one's health are non-linear, random, complex and do not have clear borders. They could include quiet and conducive surroundings, fruitful dialogues and interactions with others, strong friendships, enjoying art and music, fostering emotional enrichment by caring for others and being cared for, being kind, having an altruistic attitude toward others, blocking anxiety-fear from nesting in one's psyche, all the way to virtuous practices in the society and cultivating a noble character. Many of these qualitative measures, in one way or another, are related to a wisdom-inclined and astute mind, which includes the development of a "parallel intelligence"; this will be explored further in the next essay.

The deeper health of the mind is interwoven with the art of philosophical thinking. Philosophers and poets, whether knowingly or unknowingly, continue to be the 'doctors' of the science of the mind, whose words inspire people to revamp misconstrued aspects of life. Such words are like music to the ears of those who yearn for them. Comprehending the meaning buried in the words of wise poets and philosophers can spark significant breakthroughs in reasoning power. From the earliest to later civilizations, humans have produced and enjoyed music, philosophy, poetry and literature, and inspiring conversations, and in bleak times, these beautified the minds of both the givers and the receivers.

Today, we know that any psychically exhilarating phenomenon such as music stimulates the mesolimbic or midbrain pathway circuit, and the listener experiences pleasure. The secretion of the neurotransmitter dopamine in this pathway increases the motivation for reward, and the incentive for joy is stimulated. The physiological impact of natural dopamine in the body boosts the immune cells and decreases pain as well as depression.[12] If music causes the release of dopamine, the resonating melodic words in poetry and inspirational ideas could also stimulate the mesolimbic pathway and produce beneficial sensations.

Despite uncertainties about the precise chemical changes in the body, the link between poetry and medicine in recent years is only beginning to be manifested, and poetry is gaining more attention in the clinical setting.[13] It seems highly likely that inspirational poetry with its melodic vernacular and persuasive messages could, like music, trigger the mesolimbic pathway to produce delight as well as a new horizon. The momentary delight that comes from a poem can effectively release dopamine and other chemicals in the brain and the body, enhancing a coziness of mind and a feeling of well-being.

It is, however, important to mention that dopamine as a neurotransmitter of momentary pleasure is no guarantee for establishing a long-lasting serene state or equanimity. In contrast, serotonin, mostly released in the gut (about 95% of peripheral serotonin is made in the digestive tract), has a more lasting effect on regulating and stabilizing emotions than dopamine. Serotonin enhances communication between the brain and other organs for improved metabolism and peaceful disposition. The deeper sense of cognition and satisfaction in life triggers the brain cells to release and re-uptake the serotonin, and therefore, the nexus of this biological process-and-cycle becomes conducive for a healthier sleep, digestion, memory and so on. But far more importantly, serotonin enhances a lasting and optimum sense of contentment and tranquility in life. Thus, by reading an invigorating poem and secretion of dopamine, the sense of pleasure is surely provided, but one cannot necessarily and relentlessly resort to repeating the addictive pleasure-dopamine cycle for a short-lived sensual delight. The foundational message of the poems would eventually have to be adopted in order to rescue oneself existentially from disorientation and pleasure-addiction.

---

[12] There are numerous publications in print and online regarding music therapy and increased levels of dopamine and reduction of pain, as well as alleviating depression in animals and people.

[13] See Dr. Rafael Campo as a contemporary physician who has composed poetry and pursued poetry as an alternative method of healing with his numerous books, TV presentations and interviews. https://www.rafaelcampo.com/. There is also "Hippocrates Society for Poetry and Medicine" which promotes inspirational poetry and annually awards a prize to the best health professionals. See http://hippocrates-poetry.org/index.html.

The interplay of tranquility in life (the work of serotonin) with certain conducive psychosocial stimuli such as music and poetry (dopamine) can galvanize one's physiology to generate more joy and vigor, and even healing.

Given this inseparable reality of mind-body and philosophy-medicine, the lines of Khayyam become more than just poetry. The intense clarity of his quatrains penetrates and invigorates the brain. Whether our judgment is based on taste or cognition,[14] whether our approach is logical or emotional, the straightforwardness and power of his poems lie in the unwavering philosophy of life presented and their insights into nature, all aiming to alleviate tension and cultivate tranquility. Khayyam's poetry has great potential to awaken the mind of two populations: those in pursuit of wisdom and those striving to appease and repair their mental tension. It can enlighten those who continue to forge erroneous and hasty views about the world, and reduce their attachment to the past and future.

The sounds of philosophy may come from different sources at different times in life, but in troubled times one can consciously turn to them in order to heal the traumatized brain and leave the ill-disposed and treacherous ego behind. This kind of philosophy cuts the invisible ropes that trap us as existential prey. Genuinely pondering the quatrains of Khayyam could fulfill the transformative and therapeutic needs of wayfarers along the often-confusing journey of self in life.

---

[14] Using the conception of Immanuel Kant. See Sartwell, Crispin, "Beauty", *The Stanford Encyclopedia of Philosophy* (Winter 2017 Edition), Edward N. Zalta (ed.), https://plato.stanford.edu/archives/win2017/entries/beauty.

Chapter 8

Wisdom Therapy and Khayyam's Poetry

The world may seem lavishly decorated for you,
But this surely would not distract the wise ones.
So many like you will come through, and so many will go.
Grab your rations before you are sacked.

(*rubai* 45)

In challenging culturally and psychologically embedded inclinations, Khayyam maximizes the idea of a 'self-project': to be heedful of the task of knowing the smart self while enjoying the world. By doing that, he minimized the unrelenting 'god-project,' so common in human cultures throughout the ages. Khayyam shifted the propensity from focusing on god to focusing on the self and on releasing the natural delight in life that is embedded in the human constitution. His poetry epitomizes a vibrant mind, inviting people to be more responsive toward life processes by viewing a broader horizon beyond the limitations of their own mental conditioning and beyond the confines of their cultural and religious beliefs. His stance was to increase the power of the mind by bringing humans closer to nature in a way that may have functioned coherently for humans before the advent of gods and religions. Khayyam's influential poetry is intended to uproot, or at least mitigate, recurrent existential and emotional anxieties by enlightening those caught in misinterpretations of life in general. Khayyam's eloquent, inquisitive, and uplifting poetry bridges the psychological distance between one's mind and nature. He reminds people that it is nature that governs our bodies, our making and unmaking, the chain of food, the coming and going of seasons, the expression of the forms and colors, and much more.

Khayyam noted the process of alienation from the natural world across cultures when people became obsessed with their own thoughts, constantly resorting to gods and miracles, hoping to sway unbending natural laws in order to attain immortality in heaven and fantasies of life after death and so on. Khayyam considered such fantasies to be illusory and ambiguous emanations of the mind within a given culture, projected onto an unambiguous world. By this projection, people continue to create certain dissonance with the predictable and empirical world. Oftentimes, the dissonant beliefs such as 'undying soul' or 'return after death' sound unremarkable in certain cultures because most people share the same belief, even though it fundamentally clashes with the objective world. However, the very same belief often sounds ridiculous to people outside of those cultures. This inconsistency between belief and objective reality required an intervention.

Khayyam, like many other brilliant thinkers (such as Epicureans, Pyrrhonians, Stoics, Carvaka, and Buddhists), focused on individual liberation[1] rather than theorizing about the riddles of existence. The most urgent riddle to be solved for him was the self, which he undoubtedly tried to solve by laying the foundation of self-project over the deflecting theories about the world and the gods.

His attempts to explain the physical processes of the world were in relation to their absolute utility in one's life. Having a bird's-eye view of existence, for Khayyam, meant fully recognizing the ongoing process of birth, growing up, aging, death, decay and disappearance, time and again, while also recognizing that one is personally part of a larger cycle of life. In yearning for the liberation of the self, Khayyam shed light on the depersonalization of the cycle of life. His attempt was to connect humans with the recurrency of the neutral recycling process in nature—all things arise, pass without clinging, and vanish in vacuity—like a breeze blowing by. Much like a Daoist thinker, Khayyam uses the metaphor of the 'wind' for a self that arises, blows, then settles with no possessions or attachments, and disappears in nothingness.

> When we were children, we attended the teachings of the masters.
> For a time, we took a delight in our high knowledge.
> But now, hear the end of the story:
> We soared like a water fountain and were blown away like the wind.
> <div align="right">(<i>rubai</i> 37)</div>

Khayyam was well aware of the difficulty the human mind with its intricate emotions, and embedded attachments would have in behaving like a breeze arising, blowing and disappearing without possession and without attachment. He was also conscious of how the existence and the hard facts of reality may weigh heavily and painfully for some. To ease this, Khayyam helps his readers learn the language of nature; a completely neutral nature, without any favorite friends or staunch enemies. Nature is indifferent to people's religious inclinations and status, whether a beggar or king, strong or weak. This natural egalitarianism presents a special beauty, something that is lacking in the unequal world of humans. Nature behaves neutrally when it comes to the demise and reutilization of the elements of corpses from all corners of the

---

[1] For detailed discussions of Hellenic and Indian schools in regards to personal liberation, see Mostafa Vaziri, *Liberation Philosophy: From the Buddha to Omar Khayyam*, (Wilmington: Vernon Press, 2019).

world. In teaching this language of nature, Khayyam aims to offer a kind of natural literacy to minds trapped in their own 'illiterate' thinking.

But how does 'natural literacy' lighten the load? In recognizing the neutrality of nature and its aloofness to our pain and pleasure, suddenly one learns to be self-reliant, realizing that by this logic, agonizing human scenarios stem not from the external world but in fact from the mind, because of the way human thoughts and beliefs are conditioned. This realization can lead to empowering the project of self and a potent paradigm shift. By freeing the mind from artificially conditioned thoughts and beliefs, one can live with the freedom of being a more connected part of nature.

Pondering on his poetry, one comes away with the awareness that the physical reality of our transient self is not governed by what we capriciously think, nor by the indoctrinating words in our cultural and religious surroundings. All physical entities are subject to universal laws regardless. Having accepted that the universal-physical laws cannot be swayed, Khayyam remains a proponent of psychological freewill outside of the physical laws, especially in choosing to have a delightful experience of the world. Attitude and the power of interpretation determine the quality of individuals' minds and, eventually, the quality of their lives. The goal of Khayyam is unbiased interpretation. It is to bring the inclinations of the mind, attitude and the body into a single harmony with the processes of life so that the mind does not drift away into thoughts of a depressing past or far-flung guarantees of an obscure future. It is to be present in the world of now.

Khayyam's position encourages joyfulness, a kind of self-therapy. The cultivation of this ability is possible when one takes into account the empirical conditions of reality while also recognizing the importance of one's philosophical outlook on life. *Thus,* Khayyam's ideas are therapeutic since his poetry creates both a platform for understanding an ephemeral reality and presenting a calming and yet insightful approach to a dynamic and unpredictable personal life.

In doing so, Khayyam was carrying on an ancient philosophical tradition. Philosophy has served as a source of emotional remedy for centuries, such as the Stoic philosophers who used philosophy to treat unsettled and unwell minds, and which even today, is being used as a therapeutic approach.[2] Khayyam's accessible and life-relevant poetry has been used in the past and can still be taken as a source of philosophical therapy. Khayyam's poetry offers a special quality of a deep knowing of self and the world. There is a wisdom in

---

[2] Donald Robertson, *The Philosophy of Cognitive-Behavioural Therapy (CBT): Stoic Philosophy as Rational and Cognitive Psychotherapy,* (London: Routledge, 2nd edition, 2019).

Khayyam's poetry that can profoundly touch the mind and heart, and when it does, it goes beyond philosophy and becomes a sort of 'wisdom therapy.' Wisdom therapy, or tapping into wisdom to develop oneself and strengthen one's life, encompasses having clarity about what wisdom means, how it operates and arises in the mind (or doesn't) through different kinds of intelligence, and exploring the distinction between individual and universal wisdom. Khayyam offers us a "master class" in how to use wisdom as a sort of therapy through the approach of carpe diem to transform one's life.

Wisdom: Understanding over knowing

In nearly every language, the word 'wisdom' refers to some form of insight or a deeper level of awareness. The etymological root of '*wisdom*' in modern English is linked with Old English, Old Saxon, and Old High German 'Weistum,' '*Weisheit*', which means 'sound judgment,' 'knowledge' and 'insight.' The Greek word '*sophy*' means wisdom (*phil-sophy*: affection for wisdom). Wisdom in Arabic is '*hikma*,' and in Middle and Modern Persian is '*khirad*,' both of which carry exactly the same linguistic and universal connotation and meaning: 'understanding with insight' 'deep sense of knowing,' or 'a mind which is reflective.'

'Wisdom' describes a world-familiar and judicious mind which manifests *understanding*, not *knowing* alone. Heraclitus, for example, expressed reservations about multiple Hellenic philosophers who "know, but don't understand." In other words, merely uttering impressive and erudite views should not be mistaken for wisdom.

Wisdom should also not be confused with three types of knowing: experience, skill and knowledge. None of these could promise a deeper understanding of the underlying aspects of life. In life, 'experience' alone does not inevitably lead to wisdom as some assume, nor does it equate with wisdom; hence Oscar Wilde's cynical remark: "Experience is merely the name men give to their mistakes." Unless these mistakes lead to a greater understanding, they are no guarantee of wisdom. Life experiences and narrations of the past as lessons for the future, especially by older people, are valuable, but such factual experiences may or may not carry a deeper scope of wisdom. Skill and knowledge are also valuable but are technical, and much skill can be gained with very little growth in wisdom. Pedantic knowledge of knowing things does not ensure a deeper understanding of one's own knowledge. Literacy and traditional education, needless to say, have essentially no correlation with wisdom, especially in modern times. Putting the matter another way: not all wise people are literate, and not all literate people are wise.

In keeping the premise of objective wisdom clear of another misleading assumption, it is also important to avoid connecting wisdom with spirituality and religion. By and large, those who have lived a positive life, or an austere and selfless life, have attained certain emotional stability and insightfulness in their own lives. But in serving gods or gurus or following doctrinaire precepts—while such individuals might be appreciated in their respective communities by others who follow such beliefs—they do not necessarily possess an all-encompassing and abiding wisdom. It can be presumed that they have created a self-serving wisdom, even though in many ways they lean toward positivity. And although through piety, religious practices have helped people manage stress, anxiety, fear of death and even past psychically embedded past abuses,[3] the influences of religion have also had adverse effects on mental health.[4] Nevertheless, on the question of religious wisdom, one may ask whether the same religious or spiritual people could untangle themselves from their own wisdom and relate to other kinds of wisdom as well, that is to say, the wisdom of other religions and spiritual communities, or ultimately even transcending all belief systems. Personal and spiritual inclinations do not necessarily result in espousing the deeper wisdom rooted in nature. From a broader anthropological point of view, universal wisdom demands a different mental and linguistic apparatus that can resolve the common psychological conundrum of life-and-death across cultures, for all of humanity without any particular personal or cultural dogma attached to it.

In premodern and preliterate communities, thinkers, poets and philosophers such as the Buddha and Khayyam intuitively tapped into a universal wisdom and thought of solutions that would work for everyone, beyond time and culture and "education." The latitude and the scope of a universal wisdom are based on a vision of an all-inclusive humanity with its collective archetypes (heart-to-heart), universal existential anxieties, confusion, fear, and processes of aging and dying. Wisdom means a sort of objective monitoring of life as it actually unfolds, not as one thinks or hopes it will unfold. Such archetypal wisdom manifests in different regions and times, with truly wise masters offering people powerful metaphors to aid their understanding. The general goal has always been to rescue people of various generations lost on the very same path of existence.

---

[3] For details, see Donald F. Walker et al., "Changes in Personal Religion/Spirituality During and After Childhood Abuse: A Review and Synthesis," *Psychological Trauma Theory Research Practice and Policy* 1, no. 2, (2009): 130-145.

[4] Christopher W. Dyslin and Cynthia Thomsen, "Religiosity of Young Adults: Does Childhood Maltreatment Make a Difference," *Mental Health Religion & Culture Religion & Culture* 7 (Sept. 2011): 625-631.

Parallel intelligence (emotional intelligence)

This brief discussion about parallel intelligence should serve as a prelude in appreciating the theme of 'wisdom therapy' that is inherent in Khayyam's poetry. Wisdom is the means of self-care in the face of incoming unsound and damaging impulses of the mind.

Humans as high primates have innate intelligence, and with it comes a different talent in each person in order to operate in the world. The question is whether or not everyone is equally equipped with a deeper awareness that observes, guards, assesses and corrects their regular everyday intelligence. It is not without reason that we often ask why it is that those with decent intelligence and high achievement experience distress and difficulties in their public and private lives: "They are so 'smart,' why do they have so many problems?" It is perhaps that they lack the ability to monitor their usual and ongoing intelligence and task performance while also living with wisdom. In other words, something is needed to step outside of oneself in order to reckon with the intelligence of achievement for a sort of damage control. We could call this other level "parallel intelligence." In some, such a complementary intelligence may already be either there and needs to be awakened, while in others, it perhaps needs to be cultivated and invigorated.

Parallel intelligence can be seen as how wisdom actually operates in the mind. It is almost as though there is a mysterious inner mechanism that overlays typical, everyday intelligence. Parallel intelligence goes beyond daily life, beyond circumstantial causes as the guarantor of wisdom, overseeing life affairs and processes beyond the immediate horizontal reality. It is another way of looking at intuition and the power of reasoning as they are contextualized and thematized in different philosophical traditions.

Parallel intelligence is like an internal observer with a feedback loop that self-corrects: it makes it possible to manage oneself, to adapt to new circumstances, to create more sophisticated cognitive tools to better cooperate with others and to be able to solve problems before they become ruinous. It is as if the dangerous self, or the self-defeating intelligence, is managed by a higher, intuitive intelligence. Otherwise, decisions that seem smart, shrewd, and clever can ultimately cause harm, and intelligence becomes self-destructive. This intuitive parallel intelligence would prevent one's own 'regular' intelligence from turning against itself like an autoimmune attack. Although it sounds odd, a person can easily become dangerous to oneself. An insightful cognitive system of oversight would carry out the task of self-protection.

The self-harm done at the hands of one's own conventional and mischievous intelligence may take two directions: failure or constant turmoil. The poor understanding of self, others and the impermanent nature of the world is some kind of *failing* of self which is due to too much self-focus. The *turmoil* is due to the disarray caused by constantly keeping oneself distracted under the banner of fun and being busy, but which may be either an addiction to recurrent pleasurable activities (physiological dopamine dependence) or escapism to avoid disturbing thoughts or feelings of emptiness and the cold reality of existence.

Parallel intelligence is the project of the self in order to master the mind. The end goal is self-repair, moving away from selfishness and too much focus on self, not just at one time, but in fact to remain agile and fluid, ready for self-inspection at all times. Parallel intelligence represents a diffuse sense of 'I.' This is the "master" 'I', not just a spontaneous reflexive and unreflective 'I.' Those who are 'victims' of their own intelligence could hardly imagine that they would be preyed upon by their own ego. Thus, this "second set" of brainpower, the parallel intelligence or wisdom, will have to be strengthened in order to anticipate problems or perform damage control on problems caused by the conventional intelligence or ego to fortify a serene and safe living.

An important aspect of parallel intelligence is its connection with emotional intelligence. Studies have been conducted on emotional intelligence and its direct constructive impact on well-being, even though it is subjective.[5] Other studies show the relationship between emotions and cognitive task performance, or how undesirable emotions can cause helplessness, frustration and difficulties in performing efficiently. So those with higher emotional intelligence have greater understanding and capacities to regulate their emotions and solve personal and life difficulties.[6] Emotionally intelligent people in their skillful dealing with life circumstances reveal that they know the world and its people so well. High emotional intelligence could have a strong correlation with intuition, which plays an important role in the insight and understanding of self, others and the world required in the role of parallel intelligence.

What is Khayyam's approach in connection with parallel intelligence? Khayyam, with his poems, perhaps prompts the highest cognitive abilities as a therapeutic method to curtail self-damaging intelligence, overexcited emotions, and counterintuitive beliefs emanating from the hot and relentless cognition. Parallel intelligence is a means of knowing and guiding the knower, and the formidable negotiation between parallel intelligence and the self can be called

---

[5] See Nicolás Sánchez-Álvarez, "The relation between emotional intelligence and subjective well-being: A meta-analytic investigation," The Journal of Positive Psychology 11, no. 3 (2016): 276-285.
[6] Nicola S. Schutte, Edward Schuettpelz, and John M. Malouff, "Emotional Intelligence and Task Performance," *Imagination, Cognition and Personality* (June 2001). https://journals.sagepub.com/doi/10.2190/J0X6-BHTG-KPV6-2UXX.

"wisdom." This wisdom, in Khayyamian reasoning, is the conduit for effortless living, resulting in less existential pain and more tranquility.

The approach to Khayyam's wisdom therapy

For a more concrete application of wisdom, Khayyam presented a universal wisdom, which serves everyone regardless of time and culture. By simplifying the interpretation of universal wisdom, progressive poets and philosophers like Khayyam made it accessible to people for down-to-earth utilization. This egalitarian and cross-cultural goal had a philanthropic intention behind it—to help ordinary people move past any doubt by reducing their fear of existence, viewing the panorama of reality, and finding joy in their hearts. Khayyam offered specific perspectives aimed at developing universal wisdom and understanding:

1. Wholeheartedly adoring and enjoying the life of the here-and-now
2. Accepting that life never stops flowing and constantly shifts: moments are the same, and yet never identical
3. Liberating oneself from self-made and culturally invented beliefs and anxieties
4. Realizing the risks ruminating about the past
5. Understanding that the fear of death is conditioning that can be deconditioned
6. Seeing that the longing for immortality is frivolous thinking
7. Reducing lamentation and veneration of the dead
8. Accepting that nothingness is the ontological foundation and destiny of all entities of the past, present and future: everything emerges in forms and names and then goes back to dust, to the immortal clay out of which new configurations are made.

Khayyam holds the deceptive mind responsible for misconstruing reality. It is this mind that over-emotionalizes, exaggerates aching life events and brings life into disarray, in which case common sense gives way to confusion. Consequently, it often seems that average people do not desperately seek wisdom until they are pushed to the corner of despair. Being either on the path of confusion or under the influence of 'the illusion of certainty' (using the words of D. Kahneman[7]) usually ends in a crisis of perspective and anticipation, thus failing on multiple cognitive and social levels. The aim is to bring the mind into balance in the face of this confusion, much like cognitive behavioral

---

[7] See Daniel Kahneman, *Thinking, Fast and Slow,* (New York: Farrar, Straus and Giroux, 2011).

therapy aims to rebalance the mind. Khayyam's poetry serves this purpose as well as wisdom therapy.

Poetry as remedy for existential anxiety

Even at just the first glance of the *Rubaiyat*, Khayyam's lines are liberating and powerful in their fresh outlook on existence. Going deeper, we can see that he detects the escapism of the mind and its repressive inclinations, specifically its attempts to deny and internalize the bigger picture of reality while outwardly trying to stay optimistic. Challenging this psychological escapism was intended to restore psychic hygiene.

Very directly, Khayyam laid out the competition between the dark mind and the joyful body, between the fear of living and the courage to die, between unclarity and enlightenment, and finally between despair and a true celebration of life. Within the haphazard impulses of the unconscious, Khayyam identifies the 'enemy' deep in one's mind that constantly agitates the consciousness. The surge of counterintuitive opinions and unattainable promises stems from the unconscious, such as the postponement of happiness to life after death.

> Today you have no access to tomorrow;
> Your perpetual dwelling on tomorrow is conspicuously perverse.
> Do not spoil the nowness of life if your heart is enlightened;
> There is no assurance how much longer we will keep on living!
>
> (*rubai* 135)

To pave the path for the victory of common sense, in his poetry Khayyam reminds us that all beings are vulnerable and mortal, and the body and mental faculty irreversibly die together. As much as humans do not feel comfortable with this law of biology, Khayyam's measuring stick is nature and its processes, not the unsubstantiated claims of the unconscious and religious optimists. He situates human life in the natural world, where the same rules apply to birds, flowers, humans, beasts and all of natural life. As mortal animals we come; as mortal animals we go. To counter this, he teaches the art of observation by using an intuitive analytical system and dropping the rhetoric of the conditioned mind. His poetry embraces simple empiricism, by which everyday life can be perceived realistically and verifiably.

Khayyam's cognitive treatment also entails recovery, for example, for those who are heartbroken because they have lost a friend or a loved one. He encourages us to use such an occasion to remember the past while celebrating life for as long as it is accessible to those who are left behind (see also chapter 3). Tranquility of the mind means being at peace with the "injustice" of impermanency.

> Oh, spinning wheel, demolition is your intrinsic nature.
> Injustice is your practice from time immemorial.
> Unfeeling earth, if we dig you open,
> There are deposits of precious mind buried in your coffers.
>
> (*rubai* 39)

This is where Khayyam makes his strong counsel about being wary of two dangers: busying oneself with too much self-importance while forgetting the reality of existence, as well as too much focus on culture while forgetting nature. Both phenomena restrict one from dealing directly with their own natural self and the actual event of death, something that animals deal with more daringly than humans. It is true that the fear and anxiety of death may be shaped in awareness from childhood onward, but 'death anxiety' corresponds to the progression of 'life anxiety' over the course of people's lives.[8] Therefore, his message clearly denounces succumbing to the fear of losing oneself into nothingness and death anxiety.[9] He invites his readership to ponder impermanency in a deeper fashion as well as actual death as a source of freedom (in the same way Nietzsche perceived it[10]) to encourage truly being alive now.

Death, on the deeper and larger scale of natural activities as well as in the simple Khayyamian philosophy of life, is not a defeat nor a negative event; it is part of the law of transmutation. In fact, in universal harmony there is no such thing as 'death' per se but rather a 'processing' of all things and converting them into new configurations, time and again. The universal dust is the basis for all things crafted and broken in the 'pottery shop' of nature. Wisdom in life in the Khayyamian sense means embracing and fully internalizing the process of change as well as the interdependency in nature—the cycle and recycle process.

Like many of the great philosophers, Khayyam's 'philosophy of death' treated death with dignity, not as a defeat associated with misery. Khayyam's wisdom also has an environmentalist style to it, resolving the issue of death by reminding us that the soil is nourished from the dust of our corpses; it becomes green again and the world revives, growing food and hosting a new caravan of

---

[8] For a great read on existential and death stress as well as therapy, see Irvin D. Yalom, *Existential Psychotherapy*, (New York: Basic Books, 1980), 29-217, Chapters 2-5
[9] See Graham Parkes, "Death and Detachment: Montaigne, Zen, Heidegger and the Rest," in *Death and Philosophy,* edited by Jeff Malpas and Robert C. Solomon, (London & New York: Routledge, 1998), 79, 83-4.
[10] Nietzsche "On Free Death" he says this about it: "My death I praise to you, the free death, which comes to me because *I* will it." See Friedrich Nietzsche, *Thus Spoke Zarathustra: A Book for Everyone and Nobody*, translated with an Introduction and Notes by Graham Parkes, (Oxford: Oxford University Press, 2005), 62-64.

beings. The vultures on the ground and the insects under it consume the leftovers of our corpses in order for life to flow uninterruptedly. The major things inclined to oppose this flow are the irrational mind, emotions and attachments, things that humans grapple with.

Khayyam believes unthinking people can easily become strangers to the world because of a lack of understanding of the natural principles that can be found in oneself and rejecting the fusion of the mind with nature. A self-absorbed mindset that views oneself as a separate entity from the rest of nature is inclined to view living as *success* and death as *failure*. Those who demonstrate such contempt for death by demonizing it, from Khayyam's point of view, need to recognize the grandeur of the universal vibrancy and innovation over their own emotional banalities.

While the mind's irrational tricks are the source of confusion, it is the fortitude of the mind that can become the principal liberator. The mind needs to be regularly doctored and to be given a jolt and inspiration in life. As a wise 'doctor' of the mind, Khayyam used poetry both to appease psychological tension and provide inspiration. His poetry has effectively heightened many minds during difficult times, times when one's wisdom has been 'ill.' The first-century Hellenic philosopher Plutarch said: "…there is but one remedy for the distempers and diseases of the mind, and that is philosophy."[11] Khayyam's poetical philosophy has certainly aimed to ease the "distempered and diseased" mind Plutarch referred to. It was a 'treatment' to curb the negative propensities and forgeries of the mind and help it return to its intrinsic, tranquil, and happy nature.

> I question the threshold of my torment whether I have enough or not,
> And whether to spend my life cheerfully or not.
> Pour wine in my cup, since I am not really confident
> Whether or not the breath I draw in will come out again.
>
> (*rubai* 137)

In contemplating the utility of philosophy in life, Nietzsche comes to mind as a prime example. Nietzsche faced great calamities due to poor health and personal defeats in life, and philosophy was his only tool. He used philosophy to rescue his mind from collapse. It was the power of ideas that kept Nietzsche going: "We must constantly give birth to our thoughts out of our pain, and nurture them with everything we have in us of blood, heart, fire, pleasure, passion, agony, conscience, fate, and catastrophe. Life to us—that means

---

[11] William W. Goodwin, *Plutarch's Morals*, vol. 1, with an Introduction by Ralph Waldo Emerson, (Boston: Little Brown and co., 1871), 17.

constantly transforming everything we are into light and flame, as well as everything that happens to us."[12]

The wisdom in carpe diem "therapy"

The concept of *carpe diem*, which is often used to describe the message of Khayyam's *Rubaiyat*, is a very old notion that can be traced back to Roman philosophers. The original "carpe diem" motif (Latin; 'seize the day' 'pluck the day') was used by the Roman poet of the first century B.C.E., Horace, who himself was influenced by Epicurean and Lucretian philosophy. The story goes that in a conversation with a girl named Leuconoe, Horace advised her not to seek an astrologer's prediction of how many more years one has left to live, but rather to savor the wine while time is flying by and we may not live to see next winter.[13]

Centuries later, the nineteenth-century imagery of carpe diem introduced by the translator of Khayyam's *Rubaiyat* FitzGerald gave the impression that Khayyam was somehow in denial of the realities of daily life. It is as if all that mattered was to enjoy one's short life by living just for the moment and drinking wine to relieve the pain of existence. However, those who associated Khayyamian life with just wine, feasting, and other indulgences were missing the structure of the holistic view of existence Khayyam was presenting. They misunderstood the broad-based depth of the "carpe diem" of Khayyam that was based on a clear-eyed understanding of the true nature of reality and life, not merely on superficial enjoyment.

It is interesting to compare the modern view of carpe diem with the richer perspective that Khayyam offers. Besides Fitzgerald's translation which promoted one narrow view of carpe diem, other modern manifestations of carpe diem today tend to fit four inconsequential categories: i. consumer culture, ii. a hyper-scheduled lifestyle to squeeze the most out of the day, iii. constant checking of the digitalized world instead of just simple living, and iv. a thriving spiritual culture of meditation[14] (Orientalized and New Age counterculture lifestyle). Also, the sense that doing as much as possible is the key to happiness has manifested as another modern anxiety disorder, namely,

---

[12] Nietzsche, *Thus Spoke Zarathustra*, ix, G. Parkes quoting Nietzsche's book of *Joyful Science*.
[13] R. E. Grimm, "Horace's "Carpe Diem"," *The Classical Journal* 58/7 (April 1963): 313-318.
[14] For an interesting, critical and psychological analysis of *carpe diem* in modern societies, see Roman Krznaric, *Carpe Diem Regained: The Vanishing Art of Seizing the Day*, (London: eBook, 2017).

the *Fear of Missing out* (FOMO),[15] the feeling of never doing enough or as much as others. It points to a never-ending sense of dissatisfaction with one's life. Aside from enthusiastic meditation, these practices have certainly derailed the earliest intention of carpe diem philosophy as laid out thoroughly by Epicurus and Lucretius and revived by Khayyam years later.

The hedonism of today, consisting of a constant urge to feel happy or being obsessed with pleasurable events and activities, is too volatile and capricious to anchor in. Given these modern behaviors and attitudes, it behooves us to unearth the concrete wisdom of carpe diem from the Khayyamian point of view. Khayyam certainly tapped into the wisdom of carpe diem, but with a depth that assumed understanding a much larger picture of life.

Like many intuitive thinkers, he was in favor of living in the present moment by relinquishing worrisome attitudes regarding the unpredictable life of tomorrow, including beliefs about an afterlife or heaven and hell. Khayyam's carpe diem represents equanimity in being heedful of the day without clinging to the result at the end of the day. To attain this mindset, he laid out a perspective that rejects dependence on the quantity of the content of the days of life. Instead, he asks whether, with the power of carpe diem, we are able to embrace the two sides of the days of life: the side that is soothing to human emotions with 'good' episodes and youthful days, as well as the side that is disturbing with turbulent, 'bad' events and difficult days of old age reminding one of looming death. Realizing carpe diem in the face of the variability of life circumstances requires a deeper perspective, going beyond a good or bad mood or attachment to outcomes.

As is reflected in his poetry, Khayyam's deeper savoring of carpe diem comes from a profound understanding of the fluid and impermanent nature of life. Khayyam's metaphor of 'a moving caravan of life' is relevant here, in that all the passengers in this caravan, including our family members, get on and off at different caravansary stops along the way—their births and deaths. With the awareness of this embarkation and disembarkation, one could master the common and well-identified itinerary, and for the sake of relishing the journey of life—carpe diem—*stop worrying* before it is one's own turn to get off. The journey has been real, but when it has already passed, it simulates a dream. As mentioned in the chapter of Zhuangzi, Khayyam allegorizes a "drunken mind," suggesting not to worry, while each day is to be delighted in before one's stop

---

[15] *Fear of Missing out* (FoMo) is an anxiety disorder that is intensified and exasperated by the constant news in the digital world and social media. FoMo is a mental and emotional condition that necessitates specific Cognitive Behavioral Therapy (CBT).

approaches. The same uninterrupted caravan of life carries on, just with different passengers along the way.

> There will come a time when we will not be, but the world shall continue,
> No name nor any trace of us will be left.
> Before our birth the world was not deficient,
> And after our departure, things will be the same as they were.
>
> (rubai 51)

What is central to understand in the Khayyamian approach about the days of life is the public realm of time, the non-private days which everyone shares. If the untrained mind tends to privatize life and time as 'my time' or 'my days', then the person is trapped in one's egotistic subjectivity. The realm of carpe diem is "public", held in common, available for all people and all other sentient beings. The present time is the only time in which everyone will have lived and shall continue to live—a time to be experienced and grasped by everyone whether one lives a short or long life, now or in the future. Perceiving the public time, which is shared by all people and all sentient beings of here-and-now, is one way of experiencing the carpe diem—a time whose ownership is nobody's.

Ironically, too much focus on carpe diem itself actually violates the natural flow of the day. Let the day flow without the fear of losing out. One should not try to 'seize' it as if it is material and storable—instead, live through it. The second-century Stoic practitioner, philosopher, and Roman emperor Marcus Aurelius, in his book *Meditations,* articulates this matter beautifully:

> "The present is the same for everyone; its loss is the same for everyone; and it should be clear that a brief instant is all that is lost. For you can't lose either the past or the future; how could you lose what you don't have? Remember two things:
> 1. that everything has always been the same, and keeps recurring, and it makes no difference whether you see the same things recur in a hundred years or two hundred, or in an infinite period;
> 2. that the longest-lived and those who will die soonest lose the same thing. The present is all that they can give up, since that is all you have, and what you do not have, you cannot lose." (Book II, 14)[16]

Khayyam also puts the attitude of appreciating time in perspective by saying the inclination of mediocre thinkers is more in favor of the quantity of time and its privatization for themselves. This greedy tendency for more quantity rather

---

[16] Marcus Aurelius, *Meditations,* A New Translation, with an Introduction, by Gregory Hays, (New York: The Modern Library). http://seinfeld.co/library/meditations.pdf.

than quality is a familiar behavior that prompts Khayyam to remind his readers that the true carpe diem means immersing in the quality and sameness of time for those living and those dead—it's all the same time. Khayyam also reminds his readers that the combination of impermanency and the here-and-now is sweet, while long-lasting frivolity is stultifying and creates an acrimonious dilemma in the mind:

> Pretend the world flowed according to your wishes- then what at the end?
> Pretend you lived your life story again- then what at the end?
> Let us imagine living to be a hundred years old just to fulfill the desires of the heart,
> And that you still had another hundred years to live- then what at the end?
> (*rubai*, 103)

In his deepest deliberation, Khayyam is not focused on carpe diem in a literal sense. He does not naïvely perceive life merely right now without a tomorrow beyond it. We must understand Khayyam in light of his phenomenological approach to carpe diem as experiencing existence in a body and mind in each moment of time.

He offers a sophisticated cognitive tool through his poetry that allows one to use present time as a token of impermanency and as a conduit to understanding the sameness of time despite its conceptualization as past and future. A mind primed in this way may remain unperturbed with the past and future, letting the traces of yesterday be washed away with the flow of time. That is why today is the only unit of universal time that is available to be perceived—the rest of time is a more dream-like perception. It is the capricious mind which clings to its own judgment of time. Meanwhile, this mind clings to dualities in labeling days of life as 'good' or 'bad,' or valuing the past and future over the present. Khayyam avoids such dichotomous labeling and prefers introspection for reconciling the duality of the conditioned mind.

Khayyam's carpe diem is freedom from living-by-doing. In effect, a good day is a day devoid of anxiety, free of the compulsion towards hyperactivity. Carpe diem is also linked with an array of other states of mind, such as celebrating life in its suchness and simplicity without wishing to change it and honoring this world as a gift without demanding more from it.

The concept of carpe diem is incompatible with ideas of an afterlife. Despite widespread existence in people's minds, the idea of heaven and hell to many naturalist thinkers, including Khayyam, is implausible. Khayyam cannot accept the validity of heaven and hell beyond the conditioned habit of belief in it. In addition, in contrast with carpe diem, the idea of heaven after death is an insinuation that this world is not good enough. This becomes the subject of his sarcasm and disparagement. Religious traditions report that after the mayhem of doomsday, some will be sent to hell and others to heaven to enjoy wine, milk and honey. But Khayyam, in his rejection of illusory and projected promises, shifts the focus on carpe diem to *this* world now, the world which has everything we need, as the real Paradise; a Paradise within reach:

> Paradise will have rivers and beauties, they say,
> And streams of wine and sugar, milk and honey.
> Pour the wine and put the cup in my hand today!
> Cash in the hand right now is a thousand times better than credit in the future.
>
> (*rubai*, 89)

The propagation of the belief that the faithful ones will be privileged for indulgence in hedonistic sensuality in heaven is also parodied by Khayyam:

> They promise that heaven is filled with angel-eyed beauties,
> And pure wine, and honey.
> But if I prefer my wine and a lover here - what's the problem?
> Wouldn't these be the final reward in heaven?
>
> (*rubai* 88)

In a completely rational approach, Khayyam dethrones god and divests himself of the imaginary planes. He explains that it is our state of being that define the real purgatory and paradise:

> Purgatory[17] is but a flare of our futile anguishes;
> And Paradise is made up of the moments of our tranquility.
>
> (*rubai* 142)

Carpe diem somehow becomes the casualty of the fear of death and the scenarios after death. Socrates once said that all philosophy is but a

---

[17] There is a historical link to construction of purgatory and hell in Islam, which of course goes back to its Judaic root. The name hell or *jihanam* in the Koran is mentioned close to eighty times; it is a development of the notion that comes from the Old Testament. Arabic *Jihanam* is derived from *Gehinnom* (*Gehenna*), which was a physical valley outside of Jerusalem with an ongoing fire, perhaps burning trash or other disposed material, and a place where children were sacrificed to god. See Kaufmann Kohler, Ludwig Blau, "Gehenna: Sin and Merit," *Jewish Encyclopedia* (1906). http://www.jewishencyclopedia.com/articles/6558-gehenna#345. It was a cursed and afflicted place where no one wished to end up. The fire of this valley was for the wicked and the purification of the dead. *Jihanam* in Islam evolved from the Jewish purgatory to be an otherworldly plane where the sinful and those who had turned their backs on Islam, at the end of time and the end of the world would appear.

preparation for death, 'practicing dying.'[18] Khayyam's carpe diem points to the same thing from a different angle. He likens human life to a house built on sand, and this moment is the only moment we have in our possession before the wind of impermanency blows away and obliterates this house. Thus, Khayyam's carpe diem is a practice of two things: learning joyful living in this impermanent house and developing a deeper awareness of death without a shred of nervousness. Death, according to Khayyam, is nothing to us, yet a joyful heart for every day means everything.

In an identical tone, when Horace[19] advised Leuconoe that we are uncertain whether we will get to see next winter, Khayyam makes his powerful point elegantly as well: "Do not spoil the nowness of life if your heart is enlightened; There is no assurance how much longer we keep on living!" (*rubai* 135). The past and future are fundamentally and psychologically illusive:

> The breeze of spring is soothing on the face of the flower,
> The open meadow and the face of heart-stirring ones is delightful.
> But what you say about the bygones of yesterday is not heartwarming.
> Be cheerful and put yesterday's chatter behind you. Today is pleasurable.
> (rubai 120)

A model of wisdom: always the same reality from top to bottom

In order to make a case for Khayyam's universalist wisdom and a universal framework for humanity, we can develop a visual model that conceptualizes the structural arc of his poems. One could think of it as Khayyam's cosmology. If we imagine a cone-shaped model, the broadest part of the cone is at the top and represents a perspective of the revolving heavens. The cone narrows downwards to become the spinning earth, then narrowing further to the shared biological life of human beings, and at the point of the cone at the narrowest angle is our psyche, seeking equilibrium. The magnificence of existence pointing to life is not just about us humans but is rather about a larger order of life. This complex structure proceeds from the largest objects to the smallest, and it is about their rise and demise and their complete obliteration without a

---

[18] Parkes, "Death and Detachment," 75.
[19] There is even a doubt that Khayyam meant carpe diem in an Horatian agenda. Khayyam's drinking wine is regarded to suppress the pain and sadness of life whereas Horace's drinking wine in moderation was to enjoy the moment. See Christine Kossaifi, "Bois du vin, cueille la rose et pense: Variation d'Omar Khayyam sur le Carpe Diem horatien," *Bulletin de l'Association Guillaume Budé* 2 (Juin 2001): 171-194. (see especially pages 175-7, 186, 189, 192-3.)

second return to existence. Similar to the Daoist and Epicurean thinkers, Khayyam believed we come from nature (*physis*), obey its laws, and return to nature.[20] In understanding nature, we understand its principles. The Epicurean poet Lucretius revealed that humans are not special and death is nothing to us and that upon death, the body and the mind as the epiphenomena of the body both die and their elements disintegrate and convert in nature.[21]

In spiraling down the cone from the universe to the earth, to humans and to the psyche, the last point is at the level of a dot: death. Khayyam chastises those who do not regard demise as the final point of all things and instead insist there is something else beyond this point. A number of important quatrains address the dissonance between what one wishes and what the natural laws actually dictate. In this connection, Khayyam reiterates that all things appear in this world only once. The cone only points in one direction; even galaxies are not allowed any reversal in course.

Underneath the dot of demise, there is an empty space—nothingness, a realm which Khayyam refers to on several occasions. This empty space reminds us that all traces of our animal body, cognitive properties such as memories, experiences, feelings of joy and pain will all vanish forever, dissipated and tossed out of existence. Khayyam is aware of how disturbed many may feel about this nothingness after death. He nevertheless encouraged his readership to relinquish wishful thinking of living beyond death—this way, the burden of existence is greatly lifted. As expressed in his poetry, his model of wisdom equips the inner workings of an individual's mind with the tools needed to extinguish the detrimental flames of emotionalism and subjectivism.

The quintessence of his philosophical therapy is to readjust the dislocated mental lens so that people could gaze in the sky and see all the stars, gaze at nature with its green leaves in the spring and fallen leaves in the fall, with its births and deaths, gaze at the incoming and outgoing thoughts and beliefs in our mind—our very psyche—and gaze at our own passing as just another impersonal event of nature. Khayyam's simplification of a greater philosophy of life is undeniably radiant in his groundbreaking poetry, all for one grand purpose: cultivating nonattachment and joy in this impermanent world.

---

[20] Graham Parkes, "Confucian and Daoist, Stoic and Epicurean. Some Parallels in Ways of Living," in *Confucius and Cicero: Old Ideas for a New World, New Ideas for an Old World*, edited by Andrea Balbo and Jaewon Ahn, (Leck: Degruyter, 2019), 44-47.

[21] Lucretius, *The Nature of Things*, trans. by A. E. Stallings, (London: Penguin Classics, 2007), Book III, 85; V, 157–159, 161–162, 165.

Rise up decisively and let go of the distresses of the impermanent world,
Be joyful and wonder about the moment spent in laughter.
If the nature of the world had a shred of trustworthiness,
You would not be next in line after so many before you.

(rubai 124)

Conclusion

Khayyam's poetical philosophy fills the gap between the three components of human life: our *personhood* with self-awareness, our *mind,* the power house which couples with personality, and our *animal* body with all its vital signs.[22]

He teaches us to coordinate the three together in life to enjoy and relinquish them altogether in death. He teaches dying as much as living. Khayyamian wisdom means keeping the impulsive thoughts and beliefs in balance without considering them as the basis of the ultimate reality. Often, many impulsive thoughts or learned opinions erode sound thinking and jeopardize a genuine delight and connectedness to nature. If we consider wisdom to be the bedrock for multidimensional psychological maturity,[23] Khayyam unambiguously encourages this psychological maturity. This is the point when everything begins to make sense, and the world is appreciated as a musical rhythm in which one note collapses and another note picks up the melody without the overall harmony being interrupted. This synchronization is only understood when one is *not* deeply immersed in disharmonic thoughts by perceiving the rise as 'good' and demise as 'bad.'

Why we come and we go from this world becomes an irrelevant question. The important fact for Khayyam is that we are here. His poetry teaches us a simple philosophy through which we come to discover ourselves as a simple yet delightful note in this world, to play our share, our part in the grand symphony of life on earth. In this work of art, we come to play our note only once and then must mute ourselves for the next note to pick up and continue the harmony of existence.

---

[22] Steven Luper, "Death", *The Stanford Encyclopedia of Philosophy* (Winter 2019 Edition), Edward N. Zalta (ed.), https://plato.stanford.edu/archives/win2019/entries/death.

[23] See Michael Linden, "Promoting Resilience and Well-being with Wisdom and Wisdom Therapy," in *Increasing Psychological Well-being in Clinical and Educational Settings,* Giovanni A. Fava and Chiara Ruini (eds), *Cross-Cultural Advancements in Positive Psychology,* vol. 8 (2014). Springer, Dordrecht. Https://doi.org/10.1007/978-94-017-8669-0_5.

Chapter 9
Khayyamian Thought as a Psychological Alternative

Khayyam's quatrains can be seen as a rebellion against psychosocial stagnation, raising people's awareness of alternatives to their own existential dilemma and transforming their attitudes toward their cultural environment. Khayyam's approach to life outlines *skepticism* towards rigid ancestral or religious beliefs, and *affirmation* of living joyfully here and now. Putting it differently, he supports independent thinking and experiencing the world in one's own innovative and evolutionary ways. Through this self-reliance, each person has the liberty to be skeptical about what is dictated by religion and culture, to exercise freethinking. Ultimately, the content of the *Rubaiyat* has shaken the minds of eager and often rebellious individuals, groups, underground societies, clubs, and celebrities over the last several hundred years to this very present moment.

Khayyam's work unquestionably impacted Persian-speaking society following his death, but his literary legacy didn't make a strong, concerted appearance until about 330 years later. In the year 1460 in Shiraz, an effort was undertaken to compile one hundred fifty-eight of his previously scattered quatrains, a collection considered one of the oldest comprehensive manuscripts of Khayyam's work. Centuries later, in 1844, this manuscript known as *Rubāʿīyāt-i Ḥakīm ʿUmar Khayyām* (رباعیات حکیم عمر خیام), would be purchased in Iran by a British Orientalist. This was destined to acquire great significance in the journey of the transmission of Khayyam's wisdom, as we will see later.

Let us first for a moment reflect on that motivation behind the effort, almost 600 years ago, in 1460, of a group of people in Shiraz to collect the scattered set of absolutely nonconformist poetry penned over 300 years earlier by an eccentric polymath. A deep and fearless drive to explore this poetry must have existed, which offered an alternative philosophy and represented a psychologically rational outlook outside of the mainstream religious and metaphysical realms. This intense interest arose despite Khayyam's heretical lines that disparaged many doctrinal Islamic beliefs. The vibrant and open intellectual life of Shiraz,[1]

---

[1] It is worthy to mention Shiraz and much of Iran during the 1400s were ruled by the Timurid dynasty and various Turco-Mongol confederates such as Qara Quyunlu (1406-

with its tradition of patronage of literature, took advantage of the competition between Sunni and Shi'i Islam, and embraced literary and artistic breakthroughs, and enjoyed flourishing trade and lifestyle.[2] It is likely that this undertaking in 1460 in Shiraz did not arise merely out of literary appeal; an embrace of such heretical poems probably also stemmed from underlying sociopolitical reasons, and this leaves us curious as to how the interest continued over the succeeding centuries, between 1460 and the 1800s.

Perhaps it is not surprising that evidence of Khayyam's ongoing influence was found in Central Asia centuries later. In a fascinating story from 1808, the statesman, spy, and chronicler Mountstuart Elphinstone of the East India Company describes being on a surveying mission in Kabul[3] when he encountered a heretical group known by the name of its founder, "Moollah Zukkee" (Mulla Zaki). This group, according to Elphinstone, believed that "all prophets were imposters, and all revelation an invention. They seem very doubtful of the truth of a future state [heaven, hell and end of world], and even of the being of a God …The followers of Moollah Zukkee are said to take full advantage of their release from the fear of hell and the awe of a Supreme Being." Elphinstone goes on to report what he had gathered from the group's Khayyamian stance: "Their tenets appear to be very ancient, and are precisely those of the old Persian poet Kheioom [Khayyam], whose works exhibit such specimens of impiety, as probably never equaled in any other language." Elphinstone adds that these impious ideas were seemingly prevalent among the nobility of the time as well. [4]

This chance encounter points to the enduring influence of Khayyamian skepticism and philosophy. In fact, the Afghan philosophical society described here was certainly in operation long before the arrival of Elphinstone and most likely was not the only group in Central Asia following the Khayyamian line of thinking. In the absence of powerful centralized authorities in Central Asia and the Eastern Iranian world, diverse and eccentric groups held meetings and

---

1469) and Aq Quyunlu (1469-1508).

[2] A. Shapur Shahbazi, "Shiraz i. History to 1940," *Encyclopædia Iranica*, online edition, 2016, available at http://www.iranicaonline.org/articles/shiraz-i-history-to-1940. (Accessed on March 31, 2021).

[3] Elphinstone was missioned to survey the situation before a potential Napoleonic invasion of the East.

[4] Mountstuart Elphinstone, *An Account of the Kingdom of Caboul, and Its Dependencies, in Persia, Tartary, and India*, new and revised edition, vol. 1 (two-volumes) (London, 1815;1842), 274. Originally, I first came across this account in Peter Avery and John Heath-Stubbs, *The Ruba'iyat of Omar Khayyam*, (London: Penguin Books, 1981), 120.

teachings, some of which may have conveniently created a cover under the banner of Sufism but actually had close ties to ideas of Khayyam.

Khayyam's work also resonated in nearby India. For almost 350 years (ca. 1500s-1850s), Persian had been the official language of India, and Khayyam's Persian *Rubaiyat* became very popular among the literati of that society during the 16th through the 19th centuries. A number of manuscripts of compilations of Khayyam's poems were produced during that time. These manuscripts carried Khayyam's words to many literati in the Indian subcontinent. The existence of nearly a dozen Hindi translations of the *Rubaiyat* between 1930 and 1958 in India,[5] and the attempt to compare the quintessence of Khayyam's thinking with certain Indian philosophical tenets (such as the Ajivika)[6] are a few instances of Khayyam's intellectual impact on the country.

One quite famous example of the influence of Khayyam in India is found in the interesting account of Paramahansa Yogananda, a renowned Indian yogi who emigrated from India to America in 1920 to teach yoga philosophy. During his career as a famous and highly sought-after yoga teacher, Yogananda focused on utilizing three texts as sources of wisdom: the *Bhagavad Gita*, the *Gospels (of Jesus)* - and the *Rubaiyat* of Khayyam. His first two choices of texts are logical and not surprising: the Indian *Bhagavad Gita* was a spiritual text from his homeland. And delving into the *Gospels (of Jesus)* for his American audience was a natural and expected choice. But why did he choose Omar Khayyam as his third vital source of wisdom rather than, say, texts from the Buddha, whose teachings were philosophically closer to Indian thought? Perhaps a rebellious, secular thinker such as Khayyam provided Yogananda the missing link in the psychology of yoga, with its goal of the union of consciousness with the body and with the world and nature, an essential subject Yogananda endeavored to convey to his audience. Khayyam's analogy of using the body to generate bliss (like using a candle to generate light) seems to have come very close to the approach of many yogis who aimed for the same thing (e.g., tantric practices).

---

[5] A. Castaing, "Vernacularizing Rubaiyat: The Politics of Madhushala in the Context of the Indian Nationalism," in *The Great 'Umar Khayyām: A Global Reception of the Rubáiyát*, A. A. Seyed Ghorab (editor), 215-232, (Leiden: Leiden University Press, 2012), 223.

[6] A. Rangarajan, "Attempts at Locating the *Rubáiyát* in Indian Philosophical Thought," in *The Great 'Umar Khayyām: A Global Reception of the Rubáiyát*, A. A. Seyed Ghorab (editor), 233-243, (Leiden: Leiden University Press, 2012), 236, 239, 241. For more details about the Ajivika school, which predates the Buddha and lasted until 14th century, see Arthur L. Basham, *History and Doctrines of the Ajīvikas: A Vanished Indian Religion*, (Delhi: Motilal Banarsidass, 2009; London 1951); and see also M. Vaziri, *Liberation Philosophy: From the Buddha to Omar Khayyam*, (Wilmington: Vernon Press, 2019), 113-117.

Khayyam's wisdom deeply resonated with Yogananda's teachings and would eventually engage Yogananda strongly later in his life.

Eventually, Khayyam's thought made it onto the Western literary scene. Half a century after the account of Elphinstone had circulated, an English writer named Edward FitzGerald learned Persian from his Orientalist friend Edward Cowell. He then encountered the manuscript from 1844, *Rubā'īyāt-i Ḥakīm 'Umar Khayyām*, which had been purchased in Iran by William Ouseley and brought to the Bodleian Library in Oxford University. FitzGerald used this manuscript to make a loose translation of a number of Khayyam's quatrains into English and first published the *Rubaiyat* in 1859 in London. (More quatrains were then translated and added in later editions).

FitzGerald's rendering of Khayyam's quatrains offered a kind of Epicurean ethos, a direct echo of the revival of the right for individual pleasure in line with the European Enlightenment movement that countered conservative Christian and Victorian ethics. The translation of such work proved to be a necessity at a time of social and intellectual transformation in the European continent. They complemented Epicurean and Lucretian philosophies of pleasure during ancient times in Europe,[7] and so on a more implicit level, Khayyam's psychological offerings of freedom suited a continent that had been under religious suppression for over a millennium.

FitzGerald's interpretation of the *Rubaiyat* ultimately became almost a household classic and was highly influential. It would heavily influence attitudes towards Khayyam in the West for decades to come. In the meantime, French[8] and German[9] translations quickly followed in the nineteenth century. With the translation of his quatrains into other languages, Khayyam slowly became a household name among Western and wider global literati.

Different interpretations of Khayyam's wisdom continued to inspire people globally as the years passed. We have seen that Yogananda was interested in Khayyam via FitzGerald's work as well, but from another angle. It seems that Yogananda had learned from a poet in India that Persian poetry often has two interpretations. In this regard, Yogananda decided to correct or add some themes in the *Rubaiyat* that he felt were perhaps missed by its English

---

[7] For more details of Epicurean, Lucretian notion of pleasure and their influence on European Enlightenment, as well a full chapter on Khayyamian notion of pleasure, see Vaziri, *Liberation Philosophy*, chapters 5 and 7.

[8] J. B. Nicholas, *Les Quatrains de Khèyam, traduit de Persan*, (Paris, 1867).

[9] Adolf Friedrich von Schack, *Strophen des Omar Chijam*, 1878, and Friedrich Bodenstedt, *Die Lieder und Sprüche des Omar Chajjam*, (Stuttgart, 1881).

translator Edward FitzGerald.[10] Yogananda consequently offered his own series of mystical commentaries on the quatrains of Khayyam in the 1930s and 40s, entitled *The Wine of the Mystic: The Rubaiyat of Omar Khayyam*.[11]

Perhaps one of the most intriguing people affected by Khayyam was Mark Twain, an American literary figure of the nineteenth century. Twain was so tremendously influenced by Khayyam's *Rubaiyat* that he composed his own quatrains and published his own *Rubaiyat* in 1898, containing 45 quatrains that echoed Khayyam's philosophy of life but were crafted in Twain's unique literary voice.[12] Like Khayyam, Twain's daring compositions confronted the themes of existence. Here is a quatrain composed by Twain with a style and content that remind us of Khayyam:

> Come leave the Cup, and on the Winter's Snow
> Your Summer Garment of Enjoyment throw:
> Your Tide of Life is ebbing fast, and it
> Exhausted once, for You no more shall flow.[13]

Although he was a man of exquisite satire, Twain disseminated social wisdom which addressed many existential issues such as death or fear of death. Twain's satirical prose echoed the Khayyamian position in plain and elemental words. Twain writes: "I do not fear death. I had been dead for billions and billions of years before I was born, and had not suffered the slightest inconvenience from it." Khayyam seems to refer to much the same empirical stance, speaking about the lack of memories from before birth and after death, expressing complete nothingness (non-existence): "When I visualize the landscape of nothingness, I see the unborn and the expired ones!" (*rubai* 52). Thus, Twain shared Khayyam's position by noting that we come from non-existence and go back to non-existence without a shred of consciousness remembering anything. Even though in parody, Twain directed his message at people who were misled and made fearful by the narratives of the afterlife.

Another famous modern literary figure experienced a profound impact on his first encounter with the words of Khayyam.[14] The American-British poet T. S.

---

[10] See Sri Sri Paramahansa Yogananda, *The Wine of the Mystic: The Rubaiyat of Omar Khayyam – A Spiritual Interpretation*, (Delhi: Macmillan Limited, 1997). See also, Aminrazavi, *The Wine of Wisdom*, 139.

[11] Rangarajan, "Attempts at Locating the *Rubáiyát* in Indian Philosophical Thought," 238.

[12] Aminrazavi, *The Wine of Wisdom*, 249-251.

[13] Aminrazavi, *The Wine of Wisdom*, 251.

[14] See Vinnie-Marie D'Ambroso, *Eliot Possessed: T. S. Eliot and Fitzgerald's "Rubaiyat"* (Gotham Library of the New York University Press), (New York: New York University Press, 1988, 1991).

Eliot describes what happened to him upon reading Khayyam when he was just fourteen years old: "It was like a sudden conversion; the world appeared anew, painted with bright, delicious and painful colours…"[15] Eliot, as we know, went on to become a highly influential poet himself. His depiction of the effect that Khayyam's philosophical power had on him is indicative of the ripple effect that both poets ultimately unleashed on the human mind and human societies.

The list of additional influential Western thinkers who were impacted by Khayyamian wisdom is impressive. For example, Mehdi Aminrazavi, in his most comprehensive book, *The Wine of Wisdom* (2005), notes that:

> Among other figures influenced by the *Rubʿāiyāt* of Umar Khayyam were certain members of the New England School of Transcendentalism, including Henry Wadsworth Longfellow, Ralph Waldo Emerson, and Henry David Thoreau.[16]

Khayyam's influence was, of course, not limited to famous literary figures in the West. The whole point of Khayyam's work was to make life-changing ideas accessible to the average reader. Over the years, people have sought solace in his writings. There have been those who were dismayed by the horrors of World War I who sought alternative hope in Khayyam's lines. And from the beginning of the twentieth century to today, the bohemian members of Omar Khayyam Clubs in England and America read Khayyam's poetry together as a source of a psychological alternative.[17]

At the beginning of a new era of secular thinking, the Iranian literati of the twentieth century also sought new social and intellectual alternatives. Khayyam's quatrains served as a long-standing piece of literature that could offer a modern way of rational reasoning. Thinkers such as Mohammad Ali Foroughi, Ali Dashti, and Sadiq Hedayat were pathbreakers among Iranian intelligentsia who analyzed and revisited Khayyam's poetry and Weltanschauung publishing books and articles related to Khayyam, which became the basis for much social, philosophical and religious critique.

In Iran, the popular practice of memorizing Khayyam's poetry still continues today among people everywhere. His poetry is seen as a neat 'package of wisdom.' Citing Khayyam's quatrains to generate the vigor and pleasure of living here-and-now often comes in handy in Iranian social conversations. Discussing

---

[15] Aminrazavi, *The Wine of Wisdom*, 255, 262.
[16] Aminrazavi, *The Wine of Wisdom*, 204-278, quoted in Mehdi Aminrazavi and Glen Van Brummelen, "Umar Khayyam", *The Stanford Encyclopedia of Philosophy* (Spring 2017 Edition), Edward N. Zalta (ed.), https://plato.stanford.edu/archives/spr2017/entries/umar-khayyam. (Accessed December 13, 2020).
[17] Aminrazavi, *The Wine of Wisdom*, 230-244.

his rebellious views also gives social cover for skeptics and secularists to rebel against religious dogmatism and even serves as a front for a new atheism, agnosticism, and skepticism in Iran. Meanwhile, Iran's music culture has arranged many of Khayyam's poems in beautiful traditional classical musical compositions, bringing his words and sentiments to a new level of artistry and accessibility. Some of the best-known artists who composed and performed pieces of music on the poetry of Khayyam in Iran include Fereydoun Shahbazian-Shamloo-Shajarian and the Kamkars Ensemble. Such homage to Khayyam keeps his legacy and thoughts fresh and alive in a music-loving country.

The social and psychological need for the poetry of Khayyam seems to have been inevitable and enduring, whether during his lifetime in the eleventh and twelfth centuries, in the year 1460 in Shiraz, in the 1800s in Kabul, England, and New England in America, or in the twentieth and twenty-first centuries in India and Iran and beyond. The translation of his quatrains has created a medium of collective awareness with the reminder that all humanity follows the same laws of nature and needs the same foundational knowledge for its own happiness, whether Western, Eastern, African, Hindu, Buddhist, Christian, Muslim, Jew, or any other world citizen around the globe. This foundation is inevitable since all humanity shares the same space, the same moments of life, and the same predicament: that at the end of our lives, our bodies will all convert into the same universal dust without national, linguistic or religious labels.

In seeking new alternatives to our human conditions, the inevitable cosmopolitan view makes others identical to oneself. The egalitarian outlook of Khayyam is an outwardly simple wisdom, and yet something that is perhaps challenging for many nationally-, ethnically-, and religiously-inclined people to internalize. And yet, in reinventing an intelligent self, we can no longer consider ourselves separate from or superior to others, nor separate from the rest of natural life, since our birth and our drive for a dignified and free life and our mortality are universal blueprints shared by all living creatures. This powerful wisdom transcends all invented identities, beliefs, theologies and mythologies, and reassures us that no one is exempt from the commands of the book of nature, even if, at our own peril, we take no notice of it.

Conclusion

The unique confluence of wisdom along the Silk Road, as manifested in the *Rubaiyat*, is a tour de force. The borrowings among the literati from ancient times to the time of Khayyam and beyond remind us of the universal search for solutions to the long-standing existential confusion of human life. Khayyam successfully synthesized various philosophical elements traced back to the Silk Road, and he elegantly fashioned them into a new poetical genre.

Khayyam was a prodigy of his time in sciences and philosophy. But he can also be considered a prodigy of modern times, with his teachings geared toward intellectual maturity and modern thinking. In the last nine centuries, he has remained a formidable people's philosopher who tried to liberate people from the flame of dogma, a kind of dogma which has remained dominant and has perpetuated itself in one way or another in the religious cultures of the last 5,000 years. In his well-reasoned poetry, Khayyam firmly encourages existential freedom and warns against allowing religious or political influences to control one's mind. The rational Khayyamian enlightenment requires transcending our animal natures, overcoming thoughtless obedience to an 'alpha male' and following impulses of territorialism. Such unenlightened living has led humans to despotism and ultimately ultranationalism and racism.

In his succinct interpretation of existential freedom, he also moved away from all kinds of metaphysical concepts and has in one way or another overturned the popular Platonic and Neoplatonic positions (which support the notion of the perfection of divinity in an imperfect cosmos whose commotion tries to come close and agree with the divine; the favorite themes of many religiously-minded philosophers and mystics, particularly in the Islamic Sufi tradition). Khayyam, as it can be construed in his quatrains, broke away even from the pedantic Avicennian and Aristotelian philosophies. He may be considered to have established a 'Khayyamian' school of thought so that whoever composed and continues to compose quatrains in the same line of thinking as Khayyam could be considered a Khayyamian, similar to those philosophers such as Lucretius who composed his poems in line with the Epicurean school of thought, and thus is considered an Epicurean thinker.

In every line of his poetry, Khayyam provides us tools for the art of living in this world day by day with an audacious pragmatic and naturalistic attitude. Concurring with his realistic outlook of life, his poetry is another reminder of the secular and unemotional nature of the universe. In complimenting Socratic advice of 'know thyself', Khayyam also suggests 'know nature' so that the mind would not find itself in the dissonance of the workings of natural processes. The hint behind the *Rubaiyat* is, the more we understand nature, the more we can enjoy it.

Khayyam, similar to many great Eastern and Western philosophers, emphasizes the radical confrontation with nothingness and purposelessness of the cycle of existence, at least from the platform of halting the propensity of the mental habit of generating anxiety, and instead of living freely and appreciatively without demanding more of it. His *Rubaiyat* is the story of nature and the story of our power to understand nature.

Part III:
The Quatrains

Chapter 10

The Flow of the *Rubaiyat*: New Translation and Classification

From perplexity to despair to joy, Khayyam expresses in poetic form the range of thoughts of a lifetime, drawing upon and building upon the many philosophical wisdoms he explored along the way. Like life itself, the *Rubaiyat* presents a complete and non-linear package of experiences and presents human wisdom and emotional instability. While some poems may seem dark and gloomy—leading to impressions of nihilism—, and others cheery and happy—contributing to a reputation of hedonism—all are of equal value, and we should try to read them without preference for one group of poems or another. The one hundred forty-three *rubaiyat* or quatrains translated afresh here represent the emotional and mental evolution of someone experiencing the world and puzzling over the nature of life with natural ebbs and flows.

In order to guide us along the path of his thoughts and recommendations, the *Rubaiyat* here is grouped into five categories. Each category brings to light a different angle of the human psyche. Within each category are sub-themes that Khayyam drew upon in his expression of these ideas. In his quatrains, he taps into variations on particular motifs, much like a symphony contains variations on a theme. Khayyam's variations on a theme give us new experiences and fresh angles from which to reflect on fundamental concepts.

Khayyam's poetry is a journey in stages, ranging from existential dilemmas and misgivings about the nature of the world to an acceptance of the nature of reality, culminating in the creation of a framework of liberation from anxiety, grounded in enjoying life as it comes.

The Five Categories:

I. Why? Doubts about life…
    Death… The law of the land
II. The riddles of the world
III. Wine…The change of perception… Pleasure of life…
    Enjoying impermanency
IV. The nature of the world…The potter recycles…
    No return … Jurists of religion… False hope of heaven and hell …
V. Nothingness

I. Why? Doubts about life… death… the law of the land

Khayyam comes face-to-face with actual human propensities of doubt, confusion, anxiety, and mixed feelings, feelings that arise when wondering about the meaning of life and death. This part of the *Rubaiyat* represents the sometimes-heavy whisperings of ordinary men and women facing their own life predicaments. He sympathizes with the pain of those who wonder whether being born to a life has any real purpose, particularly since it ends with a mind and heart full of memories that remind of losses of the past. The impersonal world remains aloof and does not discern between a king and a beggar, between rich and poor, between knowledgeable and unschooled, between the gloriously beautiful and unattractive, between young and old—we must all die.

In order to bring it out all into the open, he does not gloss over the misgivings that we all have about life. He doesn't repress the painful side of life, and at this stage, he doesn't sound like a wise master. In fact, his uncertainties are natural human curiosities, and exploring them is a constructive start when searching for a deeper solution to life. The themes of the *Rubaiyat* unfold like the onion skin, in which each layer shows a fresher level of the same life until one gets to the core of it. This first outer layer is about doubts and the feelings that come with feeling purposeless to the direction of existence. His lines guide the reader to acknowledge and reflect in order to eventually let go of enigmas that cannot be deciphered.

My body is well-sculpted,
Like a beautiful tulip or a sturdy cypress.
But it is still not clear to me why
The artist sculpted and embellished me. (1)[1]

The artist, in rushing to make me,
Deepened my confusion about the meaning behind this.
I will have to walk out of this world halfheartedly, without knowing for sure
The reason for this coming and departing. (2)

My arrival added no value to this world,
And my passing away will not decrease its grandeur or splendor.
I've not heard a sensible account
Of what is being accomplished by my coming and leaving. (3)

My heart can hardly guess what the meaning of life is.
It is said that only after death will I grasp the divine mysteries.

---

[1] Hedayat's Farsi version of the *Rubaiyat* is the classic reference source, so the numbers are for those who wish to read it in the original.

But beware: If, at this moment with a sound mind and body you can't perceive
   the mysteries,
How could you grasp something once your mind and body disintegrate? (5)

If my birth were up to me, I would not have come to this dwelling place.
If my becoming were up to me, why would I have done it so bleakly?
The best choice in this old and decaying world would have been
Not to come, not to become, not to be. (17)

What is the use of my addition to and subtraction from this world?
Where is the trace of our existence stored or seen?
In this spinning wheel of existence, at every turn, through the lives of all,
Burned and turned into ash - any trace of smoke anywhere? (18)

It is disheartening that all our toiling fades away,
And that we exit the cycle of existence
In disillusionment and discontentment, in the blink of an eye.
We will crumble away and all our delights will disintegrate. (19)

It seems as though humans in this two-doored world
Experience nothing but anxiety and dying at the end.
In this case, blissful is the entity who never came to life even for a moment,
Liberated is the one who was never born from a mother! (23)

The revolving world adds nothing to our life but grief.
It does not construct anything new unless it has demolished something else.
If those yet to arrive could know what disappointments we harbor from this
   material world,
They would prefer not to come into existence. (28)

In the constellations above there is the bull and the seven sisters,
And also, a hidden bull believed to be holding up the earth from below.
If you have true insight, imagine:
Bulls above and below, and in between, a horde of donkeys! (15)

The spinning world silently whispered a voice in my heart:
'Are you aware of the rules that were laid down?'
If this spinning had been in my control,
I would have liberated myself from its pointless revolving. (33)

The good and evil in human life,
The low and high moments in our mood which create our destiny—
Don't ask the world to resolve them, sound reason should know better.
The world is a thousand times less intrusive than you. (34)

***

Death: The law of the land

When we were children, we attended the teachings of the masters.
For a time, we took a delight in our high knowledge.
But now, hear the end of the story:
We soared like a water fountain and were blown away like the wind. (37)

It is disappointing that the book of our youth comes to an end so soon.
The spring of life quickly becomes winter,
And the stage that is called the youth of life
Remains obscure at the beginning, along its course, and at its end. (35)

Even though all your life you may have savored the company of a loved one
And enjoyed all the sensual pleasures of the world,
At the end, all will vanish and you must prepare for departure.
It is as if you have lived all your life in a dream. (20)

We wish for a point in life when all becomes quiet,
For this long journey to reach its final destination.
We wish that after a hundred thousand years from the heart of the earth
There would be the hope of growing back in full greenness, like grass. (22)

The asset of our life slips from our hand.
When death nears, moods are ruined and hearts are broken.
No one has come back from the other world for us to ask,
What in fact happened to the travelers from this world who went over there? (36)

Whoever laid the foundation of the earth and the spinning cosmos
Didn't anticipate that hearts can be broken.
Darlings with wine-colored lips and musk-scented hair
Are buried in the hollow ground and the coffin of dust. (24)

The cordial friends all expired.
The agent of death took them down one by one.
We were in the celebration of life sharing wine,
Whilst those before us had already gotten drunk on the same wine. (38)

Since this spinning wheel did not even give priority to the wise ones,
Why should it matter whether there are seven or eight planets in our astrology?
Since death and the suspension of all desires is the final destiny,
It doesn't matter if we are consumed by ants in the grave or a wolf in the wild. (40)

On the tablet of existence, what must be has been shown.
The world's pen has been worn down from constantly writing 'good' and 'bad'.
From the dawning day all the forces were laid down.
Our grief and exhausting struggle are pointless. (26)

Since the length of our life cannot be prolonged or condensed,
We ought to circumvent the stress of a long or short life.
As much as we control our own affairs,
Many things cannot, unlike clay, be molded in the hand. (27)

*** *** ***

When I die, dispose of my corpse.
Make the destiny of my life an exemplary model for people;
Soak the dust of my corpse in wine,
And from it make a stopper for a wine flask. (78)

When I pass away, wash my corpse with wine,
And in the funeral procession, read to me more about the precious wine.
Want to find me on resurrection day?
Look for me in the dust of the wine-tavern's doorway. (79)

On the day when my life is uprooted
And its branches and splinters are dispersed,
If a cup is crafted from my clay,
It will come to life again once it is filled with wine. (81)

Dear friends, when you meet in congenial companionship,
Toast to the memory of friends who are absent among you.
Clink your wine cups together,
And when the next one's turn comes, turn over his cup. (83)

I may drink so much wine that its fragrance
Will emanate from my grave, even when I lie deep in the ground.
And if a drunken man stops by my tomb,
The scent of my wine may intoxicate him even more. (80)

When I have to surrender to the message of death
And the hope of living beyond is abandoned,
Make sure to use the clay of my body for a wine cup.
The scent of wine can bring me back to life. (82)

*** *** ***

Oh wise master, rise at dawn and
Look at the youth digging the soil.
Give him some guidance; tell him to dig very gently,
Because of the brain of King Kaykobad and the eyes of King Parviz. (59)

II. The riddle of the world

The world is a mystery. In this section, the focus is on the mystery of the very existence of the world as a one-time experience for everyone. Khayyam explores the question more than offering any 'answers.' As much as Khayyam is intrigued by this enigma and its self-operation, he refuses to engage in speculation about the source or destination of the world, unlike theologians and many philosophers. He is not deceived by the mechanism of the world with the appearance and disappearance in the natural scene, yet he remains optimistic about the more important issues like the joy of existence. In some quatrains, he focuses on the mechanism of interdependency with the demise of one thing enabling the rise of another. He presents the life of grass and plants, for example, as ultimately dependent on the corpses that we supply, buried in the ground—a parade of the opposite forces of rise and demise that move the river of existence.

This sea of existence emerged out of its own shrouded source;
No one person can know the true nature of life.
Every person justifies it according to their ability
But no one really knows the story of reality. (8)

The conundrum of existence is known neither to you nor to me;
We can neither read nor speak of the mysterious world.
We tell each other stories on our side of the curtain,
But once the curtain falls, you and I and our stories no longer remain. (7)

The spinning wheel of our awe-inspiring cosmos
Can only be known by envisioning it in our imagination:
The sun as candle and the world as lantern.
We are just shadow images that revolve inside it. (105)

The wildness of heaven and earth
Leads scholars to debate their appearing and disappearing.
Stay focused without losing sight of your intuition;
The knowledgeable scholars themselves are still bewildered. (9)

Even those who seemed enlightened in the circle of knowers
And had mastered the sciences, holding a small candle of knowledge among
  their peers,
Could not escape the Darkness to gain a glimpse of real daylight.
They all told their stories, and then fell asleep in the Darkness. (12)

The short-sighted thinkers tried to philosophize the process of existence,
Delivering their interpretations of this spinning wheel.
They pondered in uncertainty on the mysteries of the world.
They boasted, before becoming numb and muted. (14)

Since our station in this world is impermanent,
To live without wine and romance is a grave mistake.
How long should we preoccupy ourselves with questions about whether the world was created or has always been?
When I pass away it makes no difference, since created and everlasting will be identical. (93)

You might ask, 'What is the nature of this illusory and ephemeral pattern?'
If I want to share the exactitude of this reality, it will be a long story.
It is a pattern that has emerged from the tides of an ocean,
And the ebbing tides shall return it to the sea floor. (42)

The elegance of the cup overwhelms the power of reason;
It deserves a hundred affectionate kisses on its face.
It is a wonder that the potter of the world crafts such an elegant cup
And then throws it back to the ground time and again! (43)

The custodian of the world beautifies all,
But why would this same custodian then bring ruin and decay?
If things are beautiful, why should they be demolished?
If they are distasteful and ugly, whose fault is it? (11)

If I were in control of the world instead of God,
I would demolish this world and remove it from its misery.
I would construct a world anew
In which one could attain what hearts long for. (25)

III. Wine... The change of perception... Pleasure of life... Enjoying impermanency

With growing awareness, Khayyam begins to create a framework of understanding for accepting the lawful cosmos and the way nature operates. According to him, clarity of mind coming from this understanding is the prerequisite for experiencing the core of life. The highest awareness means savoring the transitory days. After all the despair and confusion, Khayyam has now found the key to happiness; he feels a kind of joy when he looks around his world each moment. Cultivating pleasure becomes the highest goal.

His intuitive framework for a constructive life not only prevents us from being drowned in endless and unanswerable questions about the purpose of life, but also reminds us in the grand scheme of time to live an ever-positive life without endeavoring even for a moment to personalize the reason behind life. To Khayyam, life is not a private celebration but a public one, along with everyone and everything else around us. The cultivation of delight is at its best with music, poetry and a sensible mind. All worldly identities and states of mind are transient; the foundation of life is freedom and joy.

Khayyam's uses allegories to represent such an attitude, including metaphors such as 'wine' and a 'drunken state' and '*Sāqi*.' *Sāqi* is a very common Persian poetical metaphor referring to the 'wine server,' a powerful metaphor since wine represents joy, fearlessness, and connection to one's natural self. Poets like Khayyam use *Sāqi* to represent the imaginary half of oneself, the 'drunken' half that pledges and safeguards joyfulness. It is as if the sober half is carrying on a dialogue with the wise drunken half. In using *Sāqi*, Khayyam is making a reference to the source of parallel intelligence, one's awareness that goes beyond conventional intelligence.[2] This guards one against self-harming anxieties and deluded decisions. *Sāqi*, who serves the wine of joy, thus represents a responsive awareness that participates in life pragmatically and warmly.

The cycles of life without wine are futile,
Without the music, the Iraqi flute is worthless;
The more I meditate on the affairs of the world,
The harvest is pleasure; the rest is waste to toss away. (136)

Look at how much of your life is spent in worshipping yourself,
Focused on well-being and comfort.
Enjoy wine, because a life which will end in aching cruelty
Is better spent in daydreaming or drunkenness. (143)

Since coming to the world was not my own choice,
Then the choice of departure is surely also out of my hands.
Get on your feet and make a firm decision, oh *Sāqi*
That I shall wash down worldly despair with wine. (94)

Since no one has any clue about tomorrow,
Cultivate joy here and now and transform your sad heart.
Drink wine by honoring the moonlight, this moon that
Shall appear many times but one day will not find us anymore. (112)

The going away of winter and the coming of spring
Is like turning the pages of our existence.
"Drink wine, don't be sad," said the wise sage:
All the griefs of the world are poison, and wine is the antidote. (128)

It seems 'happy heart' are just words, echoing over and over,
But a mature companion exists in reality: the pure wine of true happiness.
Do not let go of the cheerful state that your wine jug generates.
The only thing that remains today is your wine cup! (21)

---

[2] See Part II Chapter 8 of this book for the topic of Parallel Intelligence.

Today is my turn to feel happy and young;
I drink wine to let joy inhabit my life.
Do not slander me for my rebellious choice, which brings pleasure to my life.
Although an adventurist choice, it's my way of rewriting life. (16)

If I am drunk from the Magian wine, so I am.
If I am an atheist, pagan or an idolater, so I am.
Every group is suspicious of my position,
But I am my natural self, so I am. (74)

It is morning, let us begin our first moment with glowing wine,
Let us smash the glass-like pride of power and fame,
Let us revoke our desirous cravings and long yearnings,
Let our fingers play in long tresses, and then on the strings of the harp. (117)

Today is a wonderful day, neither too hot nor too cold;
The tender clouds will wash the dust off the face of the flowers.
The nightingale sings to the yellow rose in the old language of Pahlavi;[3]
The wine is to be consumed! (118)

It is the season of flowers and lush streams on the edge of the meadow.
With two or three delightful companions
Bring to the fore the cup, since the wine-drinkers of early morning
Are exempt from going to the mosque and unfettered by promises of Paradise. (119)

Tonight, I shall stockpile casks of wine,
And boost my mood with a cup or two.
First, I shall fully divorce religion and an analytical mind,
Then take the daughter of the grapevine as my partner. (77)

I am acquainted with the appearance of the world of existence and non-existence;
I know the interior of the highs and lows.
Despite this bank of knowledge, I am humbled,
Because I know of no state better than that of drunkenness. (99)

Since the time that Venus and the Moon first appeared in the sky,
No one has appreciated anything better than precious wine.
I am just wondering about those wine sellers.
What better thing could be bought with the proceeds from their sale? (110)

I want a jug of precious wine and a book of poetry,
Strength to breathe, and a half loaf of bread to eat.

---

[3] Persian language (Pahlavi is also the Middle Persian script).

This way you and I find ourselves together, seemingly destitute-
But actually happier than the wealthiest king of the land. (98)

Do not tread any path other than toward the wine-tavern, like the unruly Qalandars,[4]
Do not seek anything other than wine, music, and companionship.
With a wine cup in hand and a full jug on your shoulder,
Drink, my dear, and stop your nonsensical chatter. (96)

Those who are confined by intellectuality and hair-splitting matters,
Worried about living or not living, will go extinct nonetheless.
You, the wise ones, get hold of the fresh juice of the vine:
The unripe ones dried up before they were even seasoned. (84)

Drinking and cultivating pleasure in life is my creed;
Being emancipated from religion and irreligion is my conviction.
I asked the material world, disguised as a bride, "What would you wish for a dowry?"
She answered: 'Your blissful heart.' (75)

In each round, the pansies dip their skirts in violet dye,
And the morning breeze blows on the dresses of the flowers.
Clearheaded is he who with a shining face
Drinks wine and then smashes his wine glass on stone. (123)

My existence will be in jeopardy without precious wine;
Without wine it is hard to bear the burden of physical existence.
I adore the moment when the *Sāqi* whispers:
'Take another cup,' and I am satiated, unable to do so. (76)

I am still breathing due to the work of *Sāqi*.
From the gossip of the masses there is nothing left but ingratitude,
But from the wine of last night, there is still a cup left.
And from the years of my life, I don't know what is left! (100)

Oh, *Sāqi*, as my nagging about the end echoes,
My drunkenness breaks down the boundaries.
Even in my grey-haired state, I am delighted with your wine.
Despite old age, my heart has found the spring of life. (97)

***

---

[4] Qalandaris were the unconventional mystics with many antinomian practices who emerged around the eleventh century Khurasan and Central Asia and then spread to many lands in Western Asia.

Enjoying impermanency

The moonlight slashes the darkness of the sky.
Drink wine, for one cannot find a better moment than now.
Live a delightful life and bear in mind that the moonlight
Will glow on our graves, lying next to each other. (111)

Look how the years of life pass by like a caravan!
Seize the moment and spend it exquisitely;
Oh, *Sāqi*, why despair over tomorrow's distress?
Bring out the cup - the night is passing quickly. (113)

The true and undying moment consists of nothing other than sipping wine.
Since the labor of youth aimed to prepare you for this,
The time is ripe for blossoms and happy-headed friends to sit together.
Be happy in this moment, which reveals the true face of life. (133)

Make wine your companion, as if you have Mahmoud's empire,[5]
And listen to the sounds of the harp, like David's melodic psalms;
Do not reminisce about those who have come and gone.
Make here and now your celebration; this is the utmost aspiration. (134)

Pretend the world flowed according to your wishes- then what at the end?
Pretend you lived your life story again- then what at the end?
Let us imagine living to be a hundred just to fulfill the desires of the heart,
And that you still had another hundred years to live- then what at the end? (103)

When life comes to its end, whether we are in Baghdad or in Balkh,
Whether the goblet is full or empty, sweet or bitter,
Cultivate pleasure
Since after you and I depart, the moon over and over
Will wax mature and then wane back again. (95)

Today you have no access to tomorrow;
Your perpetual dwelling on tomorrow is conspicuously perverse.
Do not spoil the nowness of life if your heart is enlightened;
There is no assurance how much longer we will keep on living! (135)

Dear Heart, the reality of the world is fleeting and illusive
And you won't benefit by complaining about this long and taxing ride.
Instead, allow your body to sail freely with the flow, and dodge trouble.
The direction of your destiny cannot be reversed and there is no point of return. (32)

---

[5] "Mahmud's empire" refers to the powerful Ghaznavid dynasty in Central Asia and Eastern Iran from the late tenth through twelfth centuries.

It takes the teaming up of two hands to clap.
It is the force of a joyful mind that empowers the feet to squash torment.
Be heedful: we simply rise to inhale and exhale at the morning dawn,
Mornings shall continue inhaling and exhaling but we will not. (138)

I question the threshold of my torment whether I have enough or not,
And whether to spend my life cheerfully or not.
Pour wine in my cup, since I am not really confident
Whether or not the breath I draw in will come out again. (137)

Tomorrow, I'll take down the flag of hypocrisy.
Despite my grey hair, I intend to make the most out of wine.
The years of my life have added up to be seventy;
If I don't live delightfully now, then when? (141)

Oh *Sāqi*, the flowers and meadows have become lush and moist.
But grab the moment, because by next week they will have turned into dust.
Drink wine and pluck a flower, since before you even realize it
The flower has withered and the grass has turned into straw. (121)

Do as the spring tulip does: unfold like a cup in hand.
Spend your time with a tulip-faced beauty in every turn;
Drink wine felicitously since this violet-colored cosmic wheel
Converts you into dust suddenly, before you realize it. (122)

Cultivate pleasure, because life only provides us this moment.
Each floating atom comes from the disintegrated dust of kings like Jamshid
    and Kayqubad.
The state of the world, with its fluid foundations for our impermanent life
Is more like an imagination, a deception, a transitory moment, a dream. (109)

From unbelief to religion is only a breath,
From skepticism to certainty is only a breath.
Value this precious breath;
The fruit of our life is only this single breath. (108)

At dawn the morning rooster crows.
Is there a meaning in its call?
It hints at the morning echo which reverberates with the message:
One more night has expired, yet you remain negligent. (114)

The breeze of spring is soothing on the face of the flower,
The open meadow and the face of heart-stirring ones is delightful.
But what you say about the bygones of yesterday is not heartwarming.
Be cheerful and put yesterday's chatter behind you. Today is pleasurable. (120)

Oh friend, let us not grieve the tomorrow that has not arrived.
Let us treasure the life at hand now,
For when we depart from this ancient lodge
We shall join those who departed seven thousand years ago. (130)

****

IV. The nature of the world - - The potter recycles... No return ... Jurists of religion... False hope of heaven and hell

Khayyam now depicts the dynamic world as a self-organized phenomenon. The mechanism that governs the world completely lacks the mix of human emotions, cultures, religions and moralities. The impersonal dynamic of nature is uncompromising; it crafts beautiful things and then demolishes them and forgets them permanently. This craftsmanship of nature is dependent on the recycled dust and clay recovered from corpses.

Khayyam shows a more refined way to see this cycle which produces plants, animals, humans—even wine jugs. His lines remind us that the work of nature ('the potter') is egalitarian. The clay of all corpses, whether noble or poor, amalgamate in one single universal and immortal clay as material for new generations of 'pots.'[6] The cycle goes on and on. This natural process is rather traumatic to human emotions, so Khayyam attempts to detach from emotions by bringing the mind closer to nature and its neutrality.

In light of the ephemeral state of the human condition and the surrounding world, Khayyam deems it fitting to participate in the world joyously with a wine cup in hand all the time, metaphorically speaking. Liberation means dropping all firm expectations of what might lie in the future and living for today. He also radically shatters any dreams of a return to existence. The promises of heaven arise out of blind and desperate hope; knowing there's no heaven helps one live a fuller and more joyful life today.

The brilliant ones are those who keep this perspective in mind and grab their share of joy before they are "sacked"—Khayyam's euphemism for death, being removed from the scene of existence. The clarity of this cycle should leave no doubt and thus no room for belief in an unseen reality which would deflect our attention from the beauty of this world and our precious existence in it.

We are the marionettes and the world is the puppeteer:
Even though it seems real, it is transitory and ephemeral.
We each play a protagonist role for a brief time and
Then go back into the booth of oblivion, one by one. (50)

---

[6] This collection of poems of pottery allegory is known in Persian as *Kuze-Nāmeh*, 'the Book of Pots.'

Cultivate joy and drink wine, since the world is fully primed
For the demolition of your and my splendid life.
Sit in a green garden and drink enlightening wine,
Knowing that the green of this garden someday shall grow from your and my corpse! (64)

Remember that each green plant growing near the streams
Grows from the lips of an irresistible darling.
Do not stomp on these plants in contempt;
They have sprouted from the dust of the tulip-faced. (63)

Since the clouds sprinkle rain on the petals of the tulip in the new day of spring,
You also rise up confidently and grab your wine cup.
Bear in mind, this grass that is staring at you
Will one day be growing from the dust of your corpse. (62)

Clouds coalesce and sprinkle the meadow with rain.
For us, there is no real living without the rose-hued drink.
The grass of the meadow gazes at us today.
I wonder, the grass which grows from our dust will gaze at whom one day? (61)

Observe how the morning breeze has split open the bud of the flower,
And how the nightingale delights in its company.
Sit in the transitory company of such a rose bush.
It has arisen from the soil and shall to the soil return. (60)

Pour from that innocent wine jug.
Drink a cup, and pass it on to me,
Since before long, in some backroads,
The potter will use your and my clay for his jugs. (68)

This mud jug was once like me who also had a yearning after love,
To be passionately involved and entangled in her curls.
The handle you see on the curve of this jug
Was a hand once curved around the neck of a beloved. (72)

It was the day before yesterday that I passed by a pottery workshop.
The potter in each moment curved a creative form.
I saw for myself what non-discerning eyes could not see:
The dust of my father's corpse in every turn of the wheel. (69)

As I passed by a pottery workplace,
I witnessed the master's foot on the wheel,
Meticulously fashioning the jug's lid and handle
From a king's skull and a beggar's finger. (71)

I smashed my ceramic jug against a rock last night.
This oblivious act had to do with my drunken state;
I still can hear the jug telling me,
'I was you once, and you shall indeed be like me!' (67)

Once I saw a solitary worker in a construction site,
Stamping the clay as if it was worthless.
The clay was uttering damning words to the man:
'Just wait! You, like me, will someday be stamped on by others!' (65)

The elegance of the cup overwhelms the power of reason;
It deserves a hundred affectionate kisses on its face.
It is a wonder that the potter of the world crafts such an elegant cup
And then throws it back to the ground time and again! (43)

Oh you potter, stop if you have a sensible mind!
How long shall you continue denigrating people's clay?
You have used the finger of King Fereydoun and the hand of Kaykhosro[7]
At your spinning wheel; what do you think you're doing? (70)

When the pieces of a cup are sculpted together,
Even a drunk man would not deign to shatter it.
So many wonderful parts, head, base, and handle
Caringly put together, who would break it in such fury? (44)

Every atom that has appeared on the ground
Has been the Sun-faced and Venus-faced—a once-glowing beauty.
Beware: even the dust you shake off your sleeve
Has come from a beautiful girl. (58)

I passed by the pottery shop last night
And noticed two thousand jugs, some sitting silently, some speaking;
Each began to whisper to me,
"Where is the pot-maker, the pot-seller, the pot-buyer?" (73)

***

Oh, spinning wheel, demolition is your intrinsic nature.
Injustice is your practice from time immemorial.
Unfeeling earth, if we dig you open,
There are deposits of precious mind buried in your coffer. (39)

---

[7] Legendary kings who ruled Iran recorded in the eleventh century Ferdowsi's epical poems of Book of Kings (*Shahnameh*).

During the time when my body was fashioned,
Many repulsive elements were mixed in.
I could not have become better than what I am.
I came into the world like a shrub growing out of nowhere. (30)

There will come a time when we will not be, but the world shall continue,
No name nor any trace of us will be left.
Before our birth the world was not deficient,
And after our departure things will be the same as they were. (51)

This old guesthouse whose name is 'The World'
Is a colorful resting place for our days and nights.
It has been a place of entertainment for hundreds of kings like Jamshid.
It is also a graveyard where hundreds of kings like Bahram rest. (53)

That glorious palace where Bahram held his cup high
Was where the deer bore babies, and the fox found harmony.
But look at the hunter Bahram, who all his life pursued zebras;
How is it that this time around the grave hunted him down? (54)

I once saw a bird sitting on the city gate of Tus,
Its claws holding the skull of the king Kaykavous.
It was whispering to the skull: 'How sad, how sad!'
What happened to the sound of trumpets and the bang of the drums? (55)

At the palace which once rivaled the heavenly spheres,
Through whose gates glorious kings made their entrances with grandeur,
I once saw a dove on the ruins of its once-fortified wall
Perched and whistling: 'Where are they...? Kookoo, kookoo[8]... (56)

Take your cup and jug, oh seeker of pleasure,
Walk in joy around the meadows near a stream,
Knowing that this spinning wheel has given birth to many beautiful darlings
But then turned them into cups and jugs hundreds of times. (66)

It is morning, oh my brilliant sweetheart,
Compose me a new melody and bring out wine.
As for the world, it has thrown to the ground tens of thousands of kings,
Like summer months thrown out by the winter. (116)

---

[8] 'Koo' in Persian means 'where' – the double connotation of koo koo is both the sound that a bird makes, as well as conveying the meaning of 'where...where?'

Rise up decisively and let go of the distresses of the impermanent world,
Be joyful and wonder about the moment spent in laughter.
If the nature of the world had a shred of trustworthiness,
You would not be next in line after so many before you. (124)

The world may seem lavishly decorated for you,
But this surely would not distract the wise ones.
So many like you would come through, and so many will go.
Grab your ration before you are sacked. (45)

In this wheel of existence with impenetrable frontiers,
Drink wine with a joyful heart, because the circle around you is just right.
And when it's your turn, don't sigh in despair.
It is a cup that everyone is given a chance to taste in their turn. (125)

It is best to evade pedantic learning;
Even better if you caress the Beloved's curl.
Before the world sheds your blood,
It is best to empty your cup of the red drink of the bottle. (126)

The days of life look down on those
Who sit with a tight chest, grieving about the transient world.
At the melody of the harp, drink the wine in your crystal glass,
Before it is smashed on stone. (127)

When precious life has left our bodies
Clay will be put in both our graves.
And then in digging the graves of others,
The dust of your body and mine will be tossed and made into new clay. (57)

Before the universe moves to erase your name
Drink the wine that in its deep power overturns unhappiness in your heart.
Undo the locks of the sweetheart, curl by curl,
Before your own joints come loose piece by piece! (129)

Be cautious, since you live below some treacherous heavens.
Drink your wine since you exist in the world of mishaps.
Because your beginning and end is only dust,
Visualize yourself not lying on the ground but under it. (131)

**

No return ...

From those who have disappeared from this long road,
Who has re-entered to share with us the secret?
Take heed of entering and exiting this road; don't let your craving obstruct it.
Leave no trace behind, since you will not return. (46)

You who are the result of the four elements and influenced by the seven planets, beware:
These are all in constant motion, fluctuating time and again.
Remember my advice to you, given a thousand times: loosen up and drink wine.
You shall not come back. Once you are gone, you are gone forever. (29)

I saw an old man at a local tavern
And asked him: 'Can you share any news about those who left before us?'
He said: 'Drink more wine, because so many like us have exited
And indeed, none have come back.' (48)

I have journeyed and wandered in distant lands,
Almost covered horizon to horizon,
And I never heard a single person
Say whether anyone had returned on this one-way path. (49)

Out of desire, I put my lips to the lip of the jug,
And asked whether I could be given a long-lasting life.
It put its lip to mine and privately whispered:
Put your lips to the wine instead, since you shall not visit this world again. (139)

It is morning, get up gracefully.
Drink your wine gently, and play the harp melodiously,
Those who are with us will not be around afterward,
And of those who departed, none shall come back. (115)

Drink wine, because you will be sleeping a long way under the ground,
A place of solitude without any companion, friend or partner.
Be mindful, do not share this veiled clue with anyone:
A withered tulip will never blossom again. (47)

***

Jurists of religion...

Oh jurists of *fatwa*, we get more things done than you.
Despite our drunkenness, we are more sober than you;
You drink the blood of people; we the grapes.
Let's be fair: who is more bloodthirsty between us? (85)

A religious leader accused a prostitute, saying: 'You're drunk,
And in every turn, you are caught in somebody's hook.'
She sighed: 'Oh, pious man, I am whatever you say about me.
But are you what you appear and claim to be yourself?' (86)

I saw a vagrant sitting on the rough ground,
Oblivious of disbelief and Islam, uncaring about the world or religion,
No god, no truth, no holy laws, no conviction.
Who would dare in this and the next world to be like this man? (104)

False hope of heaven and fear of hell ...

It is said that there is a hell for drunkards and lovers,
But this is an unfounded claim, hard to believe:
If all the drunkards and lovers went to hell,
The next day paradise would be plane and empty. (87)

Oh heart, since you do not know the underlying reasons for this world,
And the arguments of the clever theorists may not be convincing either,
Then perceive this earth as Paradise. Relax like a drunkard, because
Nobody knows about the Paradise of the other world. The promises sound
   quite dubious! (4)

They promise that heaven is filled with angel-eyed beauties,
And pure wine, and honey.
But if I prefer my wine and a lover here - what's the problem?
Wouldn't these be the final reward in heaven? (88)

Paradise will have rivers and beauties, they say,
And streams of wine and sugar, milk and honey.
Pour the wine and put the cup in my hand today!
Cash in the hand right now is a thousand times better than credit in the future. (89)

Nobody has seen heaven and hell, oh heart.
Tell me, has anyone come back from the other world, oh heart?
Our hopes and fears are aimed at things which
Are nothing but invented words, oh heart! (91)

How long should I continue to lay bricks, trying to drop an anchor in the
   unstable ocean of existence?
I abominate outward worshipping and am bored with temples.
Khayyam, ask who is the originator of the belief of hell?
And ask who indeed went to hell or who returned from heaven? (6)

How much longer, visions of the chandeliers of the mosques and the sacrificial smoke of the synagogues?
How much longer, thoughts of the fires of hell and the delights of heaven?
Go and see for yourself:
The unfaltering laws of nature remain unchanged from the beginning of time. (31)

I know nothing about who molded me,
Or whether the substance of my existence is from a glorious heaven or a dreadful hell.
Only a cup, a sweetheart, and a melody are at hand.
I take these three today, and leave to you the promises of heaven. (92)

Some say the virtuous angels in the garden of paradise are wonderful.
But I say that the juice of the vine is wonderful.
Take this cash now and let go of future payment,
Oh brother, the beating of the drum only sounds good from afar. (90)

Oh, delightful *Sāqi* those who departed before us
Have been sleeping in the ground despite their original claims of self-importance.
Listen to my practical advice: lighten up, drink wine!
Their puffed-up assertions were nothing but hot air. (13)

The cosmos in commotion is an echo of our degenerating body;
The Oxus River is an expression of our untainted tears;
Purgatory is but a flare of our futile anguishes;
And paradise is made up of the moments of our tranquility. (142)

V. Nothingness

Figure 2: *Hich* – Nothingness.

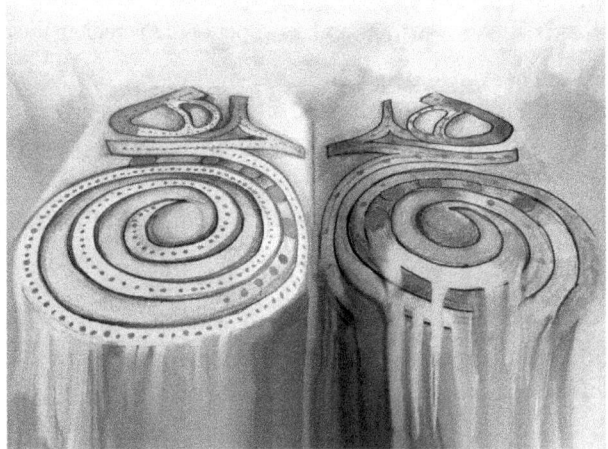

By appreciating life and death as Inseparable phenomena, Khayyam makes an important point not just about the decline and inevitable death of all living entities, but also about the complete dissolution of the mind and memory and anything attributed to the divine. Instead, change and demise are signs of the inherent emptiness of permanence of all phenomena—the only permanence is nothingness itself. Everything has the same destination—nothing. Just like before our birth, 'we' inhabited in the realm of complete nothingness without a bit of memory remaining. A life of pleasure, aging and death all ends in the total and irreversible dissolution of the human constitution, body and mind. All births and deaths take place in an empty space, in which things only come and go; the end effect is empty. All entities end in the nothingness of empty space as if they never were, and yet they become a part of all.

In between this two-ended nothingness, Khayyam finds a delicate and impermanent niche moment by moment in which one can live enthusiastically and freely while looking far back into the past and far ahead into the future, viewing the nothingness of space without us as well as within.

Look! What have I gained from this worldly life? Nothing,
What have I stored from my life experiences? Nothing,
I may be a joyful candlelight, but when I wane, nothing.
I may be a magic cup, but when I am shattered, nothing. (107)

On the face of the earth I only see sleepwalkers;
Under it, I see those consumed and sealed off.
When I visualize the landscape of nothingness,
I see the unborn and the expired ones. (52)

The harmony in which all are born and die, time and again,
Seems an endless parade without a beginning or end.
No one has a clue whether this has any hidden message or not,
Or why we come into being and then disappear into a void. (10)

A drop of water unified with the ocean.
A particle of dust merged and became one with the earth.
What is the purpose of your coming to this world,
Like a fly that appears and then vanishes. (41)

You have seen the world, but whatever you saw has turned into nothing,
And whatever you have heard and recounted has turned into nothing,
You ran from one horizon to another, and all were rendered into nothing,
And even relaxing in your house has turned into nothing. (102)

Oh oblivious ones, physical appearance is nothing but emptiness,
And this nine-sphered cosmos is also empty.
Just cultivate a delightful heart now in the midst of a decaying existence.
We live precariously dependent on the next breath, and even that may soon be empty! (101)

Since obliteration is the outcome of everything,
Whatever exists will have the same fate as sand blown by the wind.
Since the fate of whatever exists is decay and collapse,
Let us visualize the world containing all the things it has already lost,
And imagine the loss of all the things the world already contains. (106)

For my tormented heart, put wine in my hand.
These fast-fleeting days of life are so capricious,
And I confess that the fire-like enthusiasm of youth is just water.
Beware, your epiphany will also fall into the domain of dreams. (132)

Khayyam, if you have become a drunkard, savor it;
If you spend your time with a tulip-faced lovely one, savor it.
Since the terminus of this world is nonexistence
Pretend you don't exist. But since you do exist, savor it. (140)

Bibliography

Abdel-Halim, Rabie El-Said. "The role of Ibn Sina (*Avicenna*)'s medical poem in the transmission of medical knowledge to medieval Europe." *Urology Annals* 6, no. 1 (Jan-Mar 2014): 1-12. https://www.ncbi.nlm.nih.gov/pmc/articles/PMC3963335/.

Afnan, Soheil. *Avicenna: His Life and Work*. London: George Allen & Unwin LTD, 1958.

Alghani, Jalal Abd. "Medieval Arabic Love Theory Between Dissonance and Consonance: Abu Bakr Muhammad Ibn Zakariyya al-Razi and His Argument Against 'Ishq." *Acta Orientalia Academiae Scientiarum Hungaricae* 67, no. 3 (2014): 273-287.

Ames, Roger T., and James Hamilton Ware. "Zhuangzi." https://www.britannica.com/biography/Zhuangzi. (Accessed May 12, 2020).

Aminrazavi, Mehdi. *The Wine of Wisdom: The Life, Poetry and Philosophy of Omar Khayyam*. Oxford: OneWorld, 2007.

Aminrazavi, Mehdi. "Reading the Rubā'iyyāt as "Resistance Literature"." In *The Great 'Umar Khayyām: A Global Reception of the Rubáiyát*, edited by A. A. Seyed Ghorab, 39-53. Leiden: Leiden University Press, 2012.

Aminrazavi, Mehdi and Glen van Brummelen. "Umar Khayyam." *The Stanford Encyclopedia of Philosophy* (Spring 2017 Edition), Edward N. Zalta (ed.), https://plato.stanford.edu/archives/spr2017/entries/umar-khayyam. (Accessed November 25, 2020).

Ansari, A. S. Bazmee. "Philosophical and Religious Views of Muhammad Ibn Zakariyya al-Razi." *Islamic Studies* 16, no. 3 (Autumn 1977): 157-177.

Araj Khodaie, Mostafa et al., "Avicenna (980-1037CE): The Pioneer in Treatment of Depression." *Transylvanian Review* 25, no. 17 (May 2017): 4377-4389.

Attār, Farīd al-Dīn. *Taḏkirat ul-Aulīyā*. Edited by Mohammad Este'lami. Tehran: Entesharat Zavvar, 8th edition, 1374/1995.

Avery, Peter and John Heath-Stubbs. *The Ruba'iyat of Omar Khayyam*. London: Penguin Books, 1981.

Avicenna. al-Ur Juza fi al-Tibb or *Poème de la Médicine*. Avec Introductions, notes, et index. Etabli et présenté par Henri Jahier et AbdulKader Noureddine, Paris: Société d'édition "Les Belles Lettres," 1956.

Baffioni, Carmela. "Pre-Socratics in the Arab World." In: Lagerlund H. (eds) *Encyclopedia of Medieval Philosophy*. Springer, Dordrecht, 2011. https://doi.org/10.1007/978-1-4020-9729-4_416.

Barrett, T. H. "Tang Taoism and the Mention of Jesus and Mani in Tibetan Zen: A Comment on Recent Work by Rong Xinjiang." *Bulletin of the School of Oriental and African Studies* 66, no. 1 (Feb. 2003): 56-58.

----- *Taoism Under the T'ang: Religion and Empire During the Golden Age of Chinese History*. Reviewed by Chan, Alan K. L. *China Review International* 7, no 2 (Fall 2000): 392-395.

Berger, Douglas. "Nagarjuna (c. 150—c. 250)." *Internet Encyclopedia of Philosophy*. https://www.iep.utm.edu/nagarjun/ (Accessed April 25, 2020).

Bodenstedt, Friedrich. *Die Lieder und Sprüche des Omar Chajjam*. 1881.

Bowen, C.E. "The Rubā'iyyāt of Omar Khayyam: A Critical Assessment of Robert Graves' and Omar Ali Shah's Translation." *Iran: British Institute of Persian Studies* 11 (1973): 63-73.

Brereton, Joel P. "'Tat Tvam Asi' in Context." *Zeitschrift der Deutschen Morgenländischen Gesellschaft* 136 (1986): 99–109.

Broughton, Jeffrey L. *The Bodhidharma Anthology: The Earliest Records of Zen*. Los Angeles, Berkeley: University of California Press, 1999.

"Buddhism: Central Asia." https://www.britannica.com/topic/Buddhism/Central-Asia-and-China. (Accessed November 23, 2020).

Bulliet, Richard. *The Patricians of Nishapur: A Study in Medieval Islamic Social History*. Cambridge: Harvard University Press, 1972.

Burrell, David B. "Ghazali and Aquinas on the Names of God." *Literature and Theology* 3, no. 2 (July 1989): 173-180.

Castaing, A. "Vernacularizing Rubaiyat: The Politics of Madhushala in the Context of the Indian Nationalism." In *The Great 'Umar Khayyām: A Global Reception of the Rubáiyát*, edited by A. A. Seyed Ghorab, 215-232. Leiden: Leiden University Press, 2012.

Chawoshi, Ja'afar Aghyani. "Āyā Khayyam va Abul 'Alā Ma'arrī Zandīq Budehand?" In *Nineteen Maqāleh dar bāreh Hakim Omar Khayyam Neishaburī*, Khurasan: Neishabur Shenasi, n.d.

Cook, David. "Apostasy from Islam: A Historical Perspective." *Jerusalem Studies in Arabic and Islam* 31 (2006): 248-288.

D'Ambroso, Vinnie-Marie. *Eliot Possessed: T. S. Eliot and Fitzgerald's "Rubaiyat"*. (Gotham Library of the New York University Press), New York: New York University Press: 1988, 1991.

Diogenes Laertius. *Lives of Eminent Philosophers*. Translated by R. D. Hicks, London: William Heinemann and New York: G. P. Putnam's Sons, 1925.

Donnelly, Gary. "To What Extent is Madhyamaka a Reassertion of Original Buddhism?" *British Journal of Undergraduate Philosophy*, 6, no. 1 (Heythrop Spring Conference 2013): 70-81.

Druart, Thbrbse-Anne. "Al-Razi's Conception of the Soul: Psychological Background to his Ethics." *Medieval Philosophy and Theology* 5 (1996): 245-263.

Dyslin, Christopher W. and Thomsen, Cynthia. "Religiosity of Young Adults: Does Childhood Maltreatment Make a Difference." *Mental Health Religion & Culture Religion & Culture* 7 (Sept. 2011): 625-631.

Elphinstone, Mountstuart. *An Account of the Kingdom of Caboul, and Its Dependencies, in Persia, Tartary, and India*. New and revised edition, vol. 1 (two-volumes) London, 1815; 1842.

Fattal, Michel. "Le logos d'Héraclite: un essai de traduction." *Revue des Études Grecques*, tome 99, fascicule 470-71 (Janvier-Juin 1986): 142-152.

Fragments by Heraclitus. Translated by John Burnet, Arthur Fairbanks, and Kath-leen Freeman, 10. https://antilogicalism.files.wordpress.com/2016/12/heraclitus_fragments_final.pdf.

Fragner, Bert G. "Iran, Zentralasien und die Seidenstraße—universalgeschichtliche Überlegungen." Vol. 6, fasc. 4 *Spektrum Iran* (1993): 34-62.

Frank, Daniel. "Hiwi al-Balkhi EBR." *Encyclopedia of the Bible and Its Reception* 11 (2015): 1199-1200.

Frye, Richard N. *Bukhara: The Medieval Achievement*. Norman: University of Oklahoma Press, 1965.

Ganjoor. https://ganjoor.net. (Collection of Persian Poetry).

Gernet, Jacques. *A History of Chinese Civilization*. New York: Cambridge University Press, 1982.

Goddemeier, Christof. "Groddeck: 'Fanatiker der Heilkunst'." *Ärzteblatt* (Juni, 2009).

Goodman, Russell. "William James." *The Stanford Encyclopedia of Philosophy* (Winter 2017 Edition), Edward N. Zalta (ed.), https://plato.stanford.edu/archives/win2017/entries/james. (Accessed August 3, 2020).

Goodwin, William W. *Plutarch's Morals*. Vol. 1, with an Introduction by Ralph Waldo Emerson, Boston: Little Brown and Co., 1871.

Graham, A. C. *Chuang-Tzu: The Inner Chapters*. London: Unwin Hayman Limited:1981, 1989.

Graham, Daniel W. "Heraclitus." *The Stanford Encyclopedia of Philosophy* (Fall 2019 Edition), Edward N. Zalta (ed.), https://plato.stanford.edu/archives/fall2019/entries/heraclitus/. (Accessed January 5, 2020).

Griffel, Frank. *Apostasie und Toleranz im Islam: Die Entwicklung zu al-Gazālīs Urteil gegen die Philosophie und die Reaktion der Philosophen*. Leiden: Brill, 2000.

----- "Toleration and exclusion: al-Shāfiʿī and al-Ghazālī on the treatment of apostates." *Bulletin of the School of Oriental and African Studies* 64, no. 3 (Oct. 2001): 339-354.

----- "al-Ghazali," *The Stanford Encyclopedia of Philosophy* (Summer 2020 Edition), Edward N. Zalta (ed.), https://plato.stanford.edu/archives/sum2020/entries/al-ghazali. (Accessed November 25, 2020).

Grimm, R. E. "Horace's "Carpe Diem"." *The Classical Journal* 58, no. 7 (April 1963): 313-318.

Halabi, Ali Asghar. *Gozīdeh Rasā'il Ikhwān al-Safā*. Tehran: Entesharat Asātir, 1380/2001.

Hannibal, Kara E. and Bishop, Mark D. "Chronic Stress, Cortisol Dysfunction, and Pain: A Psychoneuroendocrine Rationale for Stress Management in Pain Rehabilitation." *Physical Therapy* 94, no. 12 (2014): 1816–1825. Published online July 17, 2014. https://www.ncbi.nlm.nih.gov/pmc/articles/PMC4263906/.

Häfner, Steffen. "Georg Groddeck—Vater der Psychosomatik." *Zeitschrift für Psychosomatische Medizin und Psychoanalyse* 40, no. 3 (1994): 249-265.

Haussig, Hans Wilhelm. *Die Geschichte Zentralasiens und der Seidenstraße in islamischer Zeit*. Darmstadt: Wissenschaftliche Buchgesellschaft,1988.

Hedaayat, Sādiq. *Tarāneh-hāye Khayyam*. Tehran: Entesharat Javidan, 1313/1934.

----- "Muqqadame-yee bar Rubāʿīyyāt-i Khayyam." In *Neveshtehā-ye Farāmoush Shodeh-i Sādiq Hedāyat*, edited by Maryam Dānāʾī Boromand, Tehran: Mo'asseseh Entesharat Negah, 1376/1997.

Hristeva, Galina and Mark F Poster. "Georg Groddeck's Maternal Turn: Its Evolution and Influence on Early Psychoanalysts." *American Journal of Psychoanalysis* 73, no. 3 (Sept. 2013): 228-53.

Hülsz, Enrique. "Heraclitus on Logos: Language, Rationality and the Real." In *Doctrine and Doxography: Studies on Heraclitus and Pythagoras*, edited by David Sider and Dirk Obbink, 281-301. Berlin: De Gruyter, 2013.

Ibnou Zahir, Ilham. "Hippocrates: Philosophy and Medicine." *European Scientific Journal*, 12, no. 26 (September 2016): 199-210.

Imperio, Paolo. "Omar Khayyam il vino mistico della conoscenza." *Secreta Magazine* 1 (2013): 20-30.

Ivry, Alfred. "Arabic and Islamic Psychology and Philosophy of Mind." *The Stanford Encyclopedia of Philosophy* (Summer 2012 Edition), Edward N. Zalta (ed.), https://plato.stanford.edu/archives/sum2012/entries/arabic-islamic-mind. (Accessed July 29, 2020).

Izutsu, Toshihiko. *Sufism and Taoism: The Key Philosophical Concepts.* Berkeley & Los Angeles: California University Press, 1984.

Johanna, Seibt. "Process Philosophy." *The Stanford Encyclopedia of Philosophy* (Summer 2020 Edition), Edward N. Zalta (ed.), https://plato.stanford.edu/archives/sum2020/entries/process-philosophy/. (Accessed April 18, 2020).

Joukovsky, Françoise. *Le Feu et le Fleuve: Héraclite et la Renaissance française.* Genève: Librairie Droz, S.A., 1991.

Kahn, Charles H. *The Art and Thought of Heraclitus: An Edition of the Fragments with Translation and Commentary.* New York: Cambridge Univ. Press, 1979; 1999.

Kahneman, Daniel. *Thinking, Fast and Slow.* New York: Farrar, Straus and Giroux, 2011.

Kemal, Salim. *The Philosophical Poetics of Alfarabi, Avicenna and Averroës: The Aristotelian Reception.* New York: Routledge, 2003.

Kirk, G. S. *The Cosmic Fragments: A Critical Study with Introduction, Text and Translation.* London: Cambridge Univ. Press, 1954; 1975.

Kohl, Christian Thomas. *Denkweisen aus Asien und Europa: Nagarjuna, Albert Einstein, Niels Bohr, Roger Penrose, Ein Bilderbuch.* Saarbrücken: Akademiker Verlag, 2012.

Kohler, Kaufmann and Ludwig Blau. "Gehenna: Sin and Merit." *Jewish Encyclopedia* (1906). http://www.jewishencyclopedia.com/articles/6558-gehenna#345.

Kossaifi, Christine. "Bois du vin, cueille la rose et pense: Variation d'Omar Khayyam sur le Carpe Diem horatien." *Bulletin de l'Association Guillaume Budé* 2 (Juin 2001): 171-194.

Krishnananda, Swami. *The Chhandogya Upanishad.* https://www.swamikrishnananda.org/chhand/Chhandogya_Upanishad.pdf

Krznaric, Roman. *Carpe Diem Regained: The Vanishing Art of Seizing the Day.* London: 2017. Kindle.

Lao Tzu. *Tao Te Ching.* Translated by Ch'u Ta-Kao. New York: Samuel Weiser, 1973.

"Latin Averroism." *Encyclopædia Britannica* (April 2009). https://www.britannica.com/topic/Latin-Averroism. (Accessed November 30, 2020).

Lieu, Sammuel L.C. "Manicheism vi. in China." *Encyclopædia Iranica*, online edition, 2002, available at http://www.iranicaonline.org/articles/manicheism-v-in-china-1. (Accessed on 4 December 2020).

Linden, Michael. "Promoting Resilience and Well-being with Wisdom and Wisdom Therapy." In *Increasing Psychological Well-being in Clinical and Educational Settings*, edited by Giovanni A. Fava and Chiara Ruini, *Cross-Cultural Advancements in Positive Psychology*, Springer, Dordrecht. vol. 8 (2014). https://doi.org/10.1007/978-94-017-8669-0_5.

Lindstedt, Ilkka. "Anti-Religious Views in the Works of Ibn al-Rawandi and Abul 'Ala al-Ma'arri." *Studia Orientalia* 111, Helsinki: Published by Finnish Oriental Society (2011): 131-158.

Lucretius. *The Nature of Things*. Translated by A. E. Stallings, introduction by Richard Jenkyns, London: Penguin Classics, 2007.

Luper, Steven. "Death." *The Stanford Encyclopedia of Philosophy* (Winter 2019 Edition), Edward N. Zalta (ed.), https://plato.stanford.edu/archives/win2019/entries/death/>.

Lyle Jennings Virginia, Howard. "Nietzsche and Heraclitus." Master Thesis, Louisiana State University, Department of Philosophy Spring 4-13-1992. Louisiana State University LSU Digital Commons.

Majjhima Nikaya: The Middle Length Discourses of the Buddha. Translated by Bhikkhu Ñāṇamoli and Bhikkhu Bodhi, Somerville, MA: Wisdom Publications, 1994.

Marcus Aurelius. *Meditations*. A New Translation, with an Introduction by Gregory Hays, New York: The Modern Library. http://seinfeld.co/library/meditations.pdf.

Margreiter, Reinhard. *Erfahrung und Mystik: Grenzen der Symbolisierung*. Berlin: Akademie Verlag, 1997.

McEvilley, Thomas. *The Shape of Ancient Thought: Comparative Studies in Greek and Indian Philosophies*. New York: Allworth Press, 2002.

Merton, Thomas. *The Way of Chuang Tzu*. New York: New Directions Publishing Corporation, 1965; 2010.

Meschnig, Oliver. *Der indische Heraklit: Die moderne Rezeptionsgeschichte der Vorsokratiker im Lichte interkultureller Betrachtung*. https://www.academia.edu/12176599/Der_indische_Heraklit. (Accessed February 6, 2020).

Meshram, Manish. "The Significance of Heart Sutra in Mahayana Buddhism." *Shabd Braham - International Research Journal of Indian languages* 2, no. 12 (2014): 75-82.

Mohammadian, Mohammad. "Der oblique Blick: Zum Verhältnis von Philosophie und Religion in den Robâ'iyât von Omar Khayyâm." In *Atheismus im Mittelalter und in der Renaissance*, edited by Friedrich Niewöhner, 95-114. Wiesbaden: Harrassowitz Verlag, 1999.

Mojtabai, Fatullah. *Nahv Hindī va Nahv 'Arabī*. Tehran: Nashr Karnameh, 1383/2004.

Moreno, M. Martino. "Mistica musulmana e mistica indiana." *Annali Lateranensi* 10 (1946): 103–212.

Morony, Michael. "Iraq i. In the Late Sasanid and Early Islamic Eras." *Encyclopædia Iranica*. Vol. XIII, Fasc. 5, pp. 543-550. https://www.iranicaonline.org/articles/iraq-i-late-sasanid-early-islamic. (Accessed March 15, 2021).

Naficy, Parvin. "Poetry Therapy with Rumi in the Clinical Treatment of Frail Persian Immigrants in Late Adulthood." *Online* (January 2016).

Nagarjuna. *The Fundamental Wisdom of the Middle Way, Nagarjuna's Mūlamadhyamakakārikā*. Translation and commentary by Jay L. Garfield, Oxford: Oxford University Press, 1995.

Nicholas, J. B. *Les Quatrains de Khèyam, traduit de Persan*, Paris, 1867.

Nicholson, Reynold A. *A Literary History of the Arabs*. New York, 1907.

Nietzsche, Friedrich. *Thus Spoke Zarathustra: A Book for Everyone and Nobody*. Translated with an Introduction and Notes by Graham Parkes, Oxford: Oxford University Press, 2005.

Nimrouzi, Majid et al., "Avicenna's Medical Didactic Poem: *Urjuzhe Tibbi*." *Acta Med Hist Adriat* 13, Supl. 2 (2015): 45-56.

Obert, Mathias. "Rückzug und Freiheit im Zhuangzi: Ansätze zu einer komparativen Ethik." *Perspektiven der Philosophie, Neues Jahrbuch Online*, Band 28 (2002): 359-382.

Olivelle, Patrick, trans. *The Early Upanishads*. New York & Oxford: Oxford University Press, 1998.

Özkan-Rashed, Zahide. *Die Psychosomatische Medizin bei Abu Zaid al-Balhi*. Düren: Shaker Verlag, 2019.

Parchizadeh, Reza. *The Myth of Xayyam: A Study of Monologism in Persian Discourse*. Saarbrücken: VDM Verlag Dr. Müller GMbH & Co. KG, 2010.

Parkes, Graham. "Death and Detachment: Montaigne, Zen, Heidegger and the Rest." In *Death and Philosophy*, edited by Jeff Malpas and Robert C. Solomon, 75-87. London & New York: Routledge, 1998.

----- "Confucian and Daoist, Stoic and Epicurean. Some Parallels in Ways of Living." In *Confucius and Cicero: Old Ideas for a New World, New Ideas for an Old World*. 43-58, edited by Andrea Balbo and Jaewon Ahn, 43-58. Leck: De Gruyter, 2019.

Peseschkian, Nossrat. *Angst und Depression im Alltag: Eine Anleitung zu Selbsthilfe und positiver Psychotherapie*. Frankfurt: Fischer Verlag, 1998.

----- *Psychosomatik und Positive Psychotherapie*. Frankfurt: Fischer Verlag, 1993.

----- *Positive Psychotherapie: Theorie und Praxis einer neuen Methode*. Frankfurt: Fischer Verlag, 1985.

----- *Der Kaufmann und der Papagei: Orientalische Geschichten in der Positiven Psychotherapie*. Frankfurt: Fischer Verlag, 1979.

Pines, Shlomo. "A Study of the Impact of Indian, Mainly Buddhist, Thought on Some Aspects of Kalām Doctrines." *Jerusalem Studies in Arabic and Islam* 17 (1994): 182-203.

Prajñāpāramitā-Hṛdayam The Heart of the Perfection of Wisdom. Edited by Edward Conze, translated by Ānandajoti Bhikkhu. *https://www.ancient-buddhist-texts.net/Texts-and-Translations/Short-Pieces-in-Sanskrit/Prajnaparamita-Hrdaya.pdf*.

Prajna Paramita Heart Sutra. Translated from Sanskrit into Chinese by Tripitaka Master Hsuan Tsang. Commentary by Grand Master T'an Hsu. Translated into English by Venerable Dharma Master Lok To. Edited by K'un Li, Shih and Dr.

Frank G. French. New York, San Francisco, Toronto: Sutra Translation Committee, 1995; 2000.

Przybyslawski, Artur. "Nietzsche Contra Heraclitus." *Journal of Nietzsche Studies* 23 (Spring 2002): 88-95.

Pulleyblank, Edwin G. "Chinese-Iranian Relations i. In Pre-Islamic Times." *Encyclopedia Iranica*, Vol. V, Fasc. 4, (December 15, 1991; October 14, 2011): 424-431.

Qaragozlu, Alireza. *Omar Khayyam*. Tehran: Entesharate Tarhe Nou, 1381/2000.

Rangarajan, A. "Attempts at Locating the *Rubáiyát* in Indian Philosophical Thought." In *The Great 'Umar Khayyām: A Global Reception of the Rubáiyát*, edited by A. A. Seyed Ghorab, 233-243. Leiden: Leiden University Press, 2012.

Rempis, Christian. *Beiträge Zur Hayyam-Forschung*. Leipzig: Deutsche Morgenländische Gesellschaft, 1937.

Rezakhani, Khodadad. "The Road That Never Was: The Silk Road and Trans-Eurasian Exchange." *Comparative of South Asia, Africa and the Middle East* 30, no. 3 (2010): 420-433.

Robertson, Donald. *The Philosophy of Cognitive-Behavioural Therapy (CBT): Stoic Philosophy as Rational and Cognitive Psychotherapy*. London: Routledge, 2nd edition, 2019.

Rogers, J. M. "Chinese-Iranian Relations ii. Islamic Period to the Mongols." *Encyclopedia Iranica* Vol. V, Fasc. 4 (December 15, 1991, October 14, 2011): 431-434.

Rosen, Friedrich. *Die Sinnsprüche Omars des Zeltmachers*. Berlin 1919; Wiesbaden, 2008.

Rosenthal, Judah. "Hiwi al-Balkhi: A Comparative Study." *Jewish Quarterly Review* 38, no. 3 (January 1948): 317-342.

----- "Hiwi al-Balkhi: A Comparative Study: Christian Heretics Continued." *Jewish Quarterly Review* 39, no. 1 (July 1948): 79-94.

Rothfeld, Otto. *Umar Khayyam and His Age*. Bombay: D.B. Taraporevala Sons & Co. 1922.

Sánchez-Álvarez, Nicolás. "The relation between emotional intelligence and subjective well-being: A meta-analytic investigation." *The Journal of Positive Psychology* 11, no. 3 (2016): 276–285.

Sartwell, Crispin. "Beauty." *The Stanford Encyclopedia of Philosophy* (Winter 2017 Edition), Edward N. Zalta (ed.), https://plato.stanford.edu/archives/win2017/entries/beauty/.

Schutte, Nicola, Edward Schuettpelz, and John M. Malouff. "Emotional Intelligence and Task Performance," *Imagination, Cognition and Personality* (June 2001). https://journals.sagepub.com/doi/10.2190/J0X6-BHTG-KPV6-2UXX.

Scott, David. "Manichaean Views of Buddhism." *History of Religion* 25, no. 2 (November 1985): 99–115.

Segal, Eliezer. *Ask Now of the Days That Are Past*. Calgary: The University of Calgary Press, 2005.

Selye, Hans. *The Stress of Life*. New York: McGraw Hill, 1956;1978.

Shahbazi, A. Shapur. "Shiraz i. History to 1940." *Encyclopædia Iranica*, online edition, 2016. http://www.iranicaonline.org/articles/shiraz-i-history-to-1940. (Accessed March 31, 2021).

Shahristānī, Abdulkarim. *al-Milal wal Nihal (Tozih al-Milal)*. Translated by Seyed M. R. Jalali Naini, vol. II, Tehran 1387/2008.

Shirazi, J. K. M. *Life of Omar Al-Khayyami*. London & Edinburgh: T.N. Foulis, 1905.

Specter, Michael. "Drool: Ivan Pavlov's Real Quest." *New Yorker* (November 24, 2014).

Shanmuganathan, Vitthiyeswary. *"Introduction of Heraclitus." Philosophy Writing.* https://www.academia.edu/29801328/INTRODUCTION_OF_HERACLITUS. (Accessed February 5, 2020).

Starr, Frederick. *Lost Enlightenment: Central Asia's Golden Age from the Arab Conquest to Tamerlane*. Princeton, New Jersey: Princeton University Press, 2015.

Straface, A. "Abū Bakr al-Rāzī, Muḥammad ibn Zakarīyā' (Rhazes)." In *Encyclopedia of Medieval Philosophy*, edited by Lagerlund H. Dordrecht: Springer, 2011.

Stroumsa, Sara. *Freethinkers of Medieval Islam: Ibn al-Rawandi, Abu Bakr al-Razi and Their Impact on Islamic Thought*. Leiden/Boston/Koln: Brill, 1999.

----- "From Muslim heresy to Jewish-Muslim polemics: Ibn al-Rawandi's Kitab al-Damigh." *Journal of the American Oriental Society* 107, no. 4 (Oct.-Dec. 1987): 767-772.

Sundermann, Werner. "Dīnāvarīya." *Encyclopaedia Iranica*, (1995/ Last Updated: November 28, 2011). (Accessed December 2010/ and November 25, 2020).

Taran, Leonardo. "Heraclitus: The River Fragments." *The Society for Ancient Greek Philosophy Newsletter*. 253 (1989). https://orb.binghamton.edu/sagp/253.

----- "Heraclitus: The River Fragments and Their Implications." *Elenchos* 20 (1999): 9–52.

Tavakoli, Mohammad Hadi. "Barresi Ede'âye Yeksân Engâri 'Fatakunu anta dhaka' dar Bayân Bâyazid Bastâmi va 'Tat tvam asi' dar Chandogya Upanishad." (Investigation of the claim on the identical "takunu anta Dhaka" in Bayazid Bastami's statement and "Tat tvam asi" in Chandogya Upanishad), *Journal of Motale'at Erfani* 27 (Spring-Summer 1397/ 2018- Kashan, Iran): 5-30.

Tejomayananda, Swami. *Ganapati Atharvashirsha Upanishad*. Mumbai: Central Chinmaya Trust, digitized, no date.

The Fihrist of al-Nadīm. Vol. 1, translated and edited by Bayard Dodge, New York: Columbia University Press, 1970.

"The Chhandogya Upanishad by Swami Krishnananda." Chapter Two: Uddalaka's Teaching Concerning the Oneness of the Self. https://www.swami krishnananda.org/chhand/ch_2.html. (Accessed May 28, 2020).

The Principal Upanishads. Translated and edited by Swami Nikhilananda, New York: Dover Publications, Inc., 1963; 2003.

The Upanishads. Translations from the Sanskrit with an introduction by Juan Mascaró, Delhi: Penguin Books, 1965; 1994.

Trattker, Ernest. "Umar Khayyām-Poet Against al-Ghazali." *The Muslim World* 53, no. 2 (April 1963): 120-126.

Tubbs, R. Shane et al. "Abubakr Muhammad Ibn Zakaria Razi, Rhazes (865-925 AD)." *Child's Nervous System* 23, no. 11 (December 2007): 1225-26.

Vafai, Mohammad Afshin. "نویافته رباعی دو - غزّالی محمد امام و خیّام عمر رابطۀ از تازه‌های آگاهی" ,"غزّالی رثای در خیّام از" (New Information Concerning the Relationship between

Omar Khayyam and Imam Mohammad al-Ghazzali: Two Newly Found Quatrains by Khayyam Elegizing Ghazzali), *Pazhoheshhaye Iranshenasi* 2, no. 7 (Fall 1396/2018): 1-14.

Vajda, Georges. "À propos de perpétuité de la rétribution d'outre-tombe en théologie musulmane." *Studia Islamica* 11 (1959): 29–38.

Van Bladel, Kevin. "Eighth-Century Indian Astronomy in the Two Cities of Peace." In *Islamic Cultures, Islamic Contexts: Essays in Honor of Professor Patricia Crone*, edited by Behnam Sadeghi, Asad Q. Ahmed, Adam Silverstein, Robert Hoyland, 257-294. Leiden: Brill, 2014.

----- "The Bactrian Background of the Barmakids." In *Islam and Tibet— Interactions along the Musk Routes*, edited by Anna Akasoy, Charles Burnett, and Ronit Yoeli-Tlalim, 43–88. Surrey: Ashgate, 2011.

Van Ess, Joseph. "Jahm b. Ṣafwān." *Encyclopædia Iranica*, XIV/4, 389-390. http://www.iranicaonline.org/articles/jahm-b-safwan. (Accessed 6 January, 2021).

Vaziri, Mostafa. *Liberation Philosophy: From the Buddha to Omar Khayyam*. Willmington, DE: Vernon Press, 2019.

----- "Das Zeitverständnis im Sufismus." In *Chronos - Kairos - Aion, alles eine Frage der Zeit?* Edited by Paul Danler (Hrsg.), 71-80. Würzburg: Königshausen & Neumann, 2019.

----- *Rumi and Shams' Silent Rebellion: Parallels with Vedanta, Buddhism, and Shaivism*. New York & London: Palgrave Macmillan, 2015.

----- *Buddhism in Iran: An Anthropological Approach to Traces and Influences*. New York & London: Palgrave Macmillan, 2012.

----- *Iran as Imagined Nation: The Construction of National Identity*. New York: Paragon House, 1993; New Jersey: Gorgias Press, 2013.

Vetter, Tilmann and Anne MacDonald. "Once Again on the Origin of Mahāyāna Buddhism." *Wiener Zeitschrift für die Kunde Südasiens* 45 (2001): 59-9.

Viévard, Ludovic. "La vacuité et sa valeur instrumentale." *Journal Asiatique* 288.2 (July 2000): 411-429.

Vivenza, Jean-Marc. *Nâgârjuna et la doctrine de la vacuité*. Paris: Albin Michel, 2001.

Von Schack, Adolf Friedrich. *Strophen des Omar Chijam*. Stuttgart, 1878.

Vykoukal, Elisabeth. *Georg Groddeck: Krankheit als Symbol - Schriften zur Psychosomatik*. Frankfurt: Fischer Taschenbuch, 1983.

Walker Donald. F. et al., "Changes in Personal Religion/Spirituality During and After Childhood Abuse: A Review and Synthesis." *Psychological Trauma Theory Research Practice and Policy* 1, no. 2, (2009): 130-145.

Watson, Burton. (Translator and Editor). *The Complete Works of Zhuangzi*, New York: Columbia University Press, 1968; 2013. https://archive.org/details/thecompleteworksofzhuangzi/page/n5/mode/2up.

Watt, W. M. "The Political Attitudes of Mu'tazilah." *Journal of Royal Asiatic Society* 1, no. 2 (April 1963): 38-57.

Westerhoff, Jan Christoph. "Nāgārjuna." *The Stanford Encyclopedia of Philosophy* (Spring 2019 Edition), Edward N. Zalta (ed.). https://plato.stanford.edu/archives/spr2019/entries/nagarjuna. (Accessed April 27, 2020).

Williams, Howard. "Heraclitus' Philosophy and Hegel's Dialectic." *History of Political Thought* 6, no. 3 (Winter 1985): 381-404.

Willke, Elke. "Tanz in der Psychotherapie Entwicklung eines integrierenden Konzeptes zu einem kreativitätstherapeutischen Zugang in der Rehabilitation." Ph.D. Dissertation an der Universität Dortmund, 2005.

Wujastyk, Dominik. "From Balkh to Baghdad: Indian Science and the Birth of the Islamic Golden Age in the Eighth Century." *Indian Journal of History of Science* (December 2016): 1-18.

Yalom, Irvin D. *Existential Psychotherapy*. New York: Basic Books, 1980.

Yao, Zhihua. "Typology of Nothing: Heidegger, Daoism and Buddhism." *Comparative Philosophy* 1, no. 1 (2010): 78-89.

Yogananda, Sri Sri Paramahansa. *The Wine of the Mystic: The Rubaiyat of Omar Khayyam—A Spiritual Interpretation*. Delhi: Macmillan Limited, 1997.

Zaehner, R. C. *Hindu and Muslim Mysticism*. London: University of London, The Athlone Press, 1960.

Zahabi, Seyed Abbas. "Avicenna's Approach to Health: A Reciprocal Interaction Between Medicine and Islamic Philosophy." *Journal of Religion and Health* 58 (2019): 1698-1712.

Ziporyn, Brook (Translation and Introduction). *Zhuangzi: The Essential Writings, With Selections from Traditional Commentaries*. Indianapolis: Hackett Publishing Company, Inc., 2009.

Zonta, Mauro. "Influence of Arabic and Islamic Philosophy on Judaic Thought", *The Stanford Encyclopedia of Philosophy* (Winter 2016 Edition), Edward N. Zalta (ed.), https://plato.stanford.edu/archives/win2016/entries/arabic-islamic-judaic. (Accessed November 24, 2020).

Index

A

Abbasid caliph-Caliphate, 14, 17, 18
Abu Ali Sindhi, 37
Abu Sahl (astronomer), 14
Achaemenid-Persian, 40
Afghanistan, 8, 13, 27
al-Biruni, 5, 17, 32
al-Dāmigh (the book of al-Rawandi), 27
al-Farabi, 15, 17, 103
al-Ghazali, 20, 21-4, 30
al-Khwarizmi, 17
al-Kindi, 15
al-Mamun, 17
al-Mansur, 15
al-Qifti, 7, 29
al-Rawandi, (Ibn Rawandi), 27
al-Warraq, Abu Isa, 27
Allegory, 36, 45, 83, 89, 165n6
Aminrazavi, Mehdi, 3n1, 146
Anthropology/anthropological, xiii, xv, 17, 33, 36, 105n12, 125
Anxiety, 34, 38, 54, 57, 61, 75-6, 84, 85, 87, 99, 101, 104, 109, 114-15, 117, 125, 129, 130, 132, 133n15, 135, 150, 153-55
Apostate, 20, 24, 29, 30
Apostasy (in Islam), 20, 21, 20n42, 23, 38, 46
Aquinas, Thomas, 22
Arabian Peninsula, 19
Arabic, 3, 5, 15, 17, 18, 18n39, 19, 28, 105n14, 124, 136n17
Aristotle, 15, 30, 31, 42n17, 103, 106
Aristotelian, xiii, 4n2, 22, 31, 40n4, 106, 149
Aromatherapy, 104
Arzhang (Book of paintings of Mani), 25
Asanga, 13
Atheism, 25, 28, 147
Atman, 89, 90, 91, 92, 94
Atomism, 25, 82n40
Averroes (Ibn Rushd), 22, 103
Averroism, 22
Avicenna (Ibn Sina), 15, 17, 22, 27, 30, 31, 103, 104, 105, 105n12, 105n14, 106, 106n15
Avicennian, xiii, 4n2, 5, 22, 29, 31, 40n4, 106, 149
Aurelius, Marcus, 43n21, 134

B

Baghdad, 5, 13-18, 21, 26, 27, 163
Bahmanyar, 31
Balkh, 7n6, 13, 14, 16, 18, 27, 35, 163
Barmakid/Barmakid family, 14
Bayazid, 37
Bayt al-Hikam (the Center of Knowledge), 15
Bhagavad Gita, 143
Bid'ah (innovation), 19-20
Biruni (see al-Biruni)

Bodhidharma, 11-12, 12n22
Brahman, 29n73, 36, 37, 89-93, 94
Buddha, 13, 15, 24-5, 25n57, 28, 35, 68-71, 73, 73n21, 75-6, 79-80, 79n34, 84-7, 88, 125, 143, 143n6
Buddhism, xiii, 4, 5, 10, 11, 11n20, 12, 12n23, 13, 14, 16, 32, 34, 35, 36, 68, 69, 70, 71, 71n13, 73, 76, 82n40, 88
Bukhara, 5, 16, 18, 28

C

Carpe diem (*Carpe diem* therapy), xiv, 124, 132-3, 132n14, 134-7, 137n19
Central Asia/n, xiv, 4-6, 8, 10-12, 12n22, 13-17, 16n33, 18-21, 23-4, 26-8, 31-2, 34-7, 40, 40n4, 65, 71, 104-5, 105n12, 142, 162n4, 163n5
Central Asian Enlightenment, 18, 40n4
Chandogya Upanishad (Upanishads), xiii, xiv, 4, 32, 36, 37-8, 37n94, 90n3, 89-96,
China, xii, xvi, 8-13, 12n22, 12n23, 14, 17, 21, 34, 52, 65, 71
Chinese philosophy-thought (Daoism), xiii, 4, 5, 6, 32, 104
Chinese medicine, 104
Christianity, 10
'Clay' metaphor, 36, 46, 83, 89-90, 92-6, 109, 109n29, 128, 157, 165-67, 169
Clubs (Omar Khayyam Clubs), xi, 141, 146
Confucianist, 57
Corona pandemic, xi
Counterintuitive, 46, 54, 64, 127, 129

Cowell, Edward, 144

D

Damascus, 13
Dance (Rumi), 111
Dao (Way), Daoistic, 33, 51-3, 55, 60
Daoism, xii, xiii, 4, 11, 12, 12n23, 32-4, 34n84, 51-3, 57, 62, 64, 65, 71n13, 104
Daoist philosopher, xvi, 11, 12, 24, 33-4, 51-2, 54, 58, 122, 138
Dara Shukoh, 37, 37n94, 38
Dashti, Ali, 146
Death dilemma-anxiety, 54, 57, 61, 75, 76, 84, 85, 87, 101, 104, 125, 129, 130, 130n10, 133, 153, 154
Delusion, 47
Democritus, 32, 82n40, 102
Depression, 101, 104, 118
Despotism, 149
Detachment, 58
Dharma, 70, 74, 76
Dialectics/dialectical, 28, 31, 32, 36, 47, 69
Dinavariya (Manichaean groups in Central Asia), 27
Dopamine, 111, 117-19, 118n12, 127
'Drunken state' 'drunkard' metaphors, 30, 33, 34, 45, 51-5, 57-60, 61, 65, 66, 84, 133, 156, 157, 160-1, 167, 170, 171, 174
Duality, 44, 59, 85, 135
'Dust' metaphor, 47, 61-2, 69, 76-7, 90, 92-4, 96, 128, 130, 147, 156, 157, 161, 164-6, 7, 169, 173

E

East India Company, 142

Index 187

Ego/egocentric/egoistic, 33, 51, 53, 54, 119, 127, 134
Einstein, Albert, 43
Eliot, T. S., 146
Elphinstone, Mountstuart, 142, 142n3, 144
Emerson, Ralph Waldo, 146
Emotion/emotional, xiv, 33, 47, 53, 59, 62-5, 76, 81-2, 84, 88, 94, 96, 99, 100-102, 107-9, 113, 116-19, 121-3, 125, 127-8, 131, 133, 138, 149, 153, 165
Emotional intelligence, 126-8
Emptiness (Buddhist-Daoist-Khayyamian), 34-6, 63, 67-70, 72-4, 73n21, 76, 79, 83, 85-6, 88, 127, 173
Enlightenment (Central Asian), 18, 40n4
Epicurus, 32, 38, 82n40, 133
Epicurean, xii, 33, 107, 122, 132, 138, 144, 144n7, 149
Equanimity, 56, 58, 59, 60, 85, 118, 133
ertidād (apostasy), 20
Euclid/Euclidean, 6
Europe/European, 9, 22, 28, 46, 105, 105n12, 106n14, 144, 144n7

F

False hope, 47, 75, 165, 171
Fatwas, 20, 23, 170
Fear of Missing out (FoMo), 133
FitzGerald, Edward, 132, 144, 145
Foroughi, Mohammad Ali, 146
Freedom (existential), 23, 35, 58, 61, 75, 87, 123, 130, 135, 144, 149, 159, 160
Freethinkers, xiii, 4, 6, 21, 27, 31, 38, 71

Freud, Sigmund, 114

G

Gandhara, 13
General Adaptation Syndrome (GAS) (Selye), 116
Gnosticism, 28, 147
"Golden Age" of Islam or Central Asian, 15n31, 16-20
Gospels (of Jesus), 143
Greed/greedy, 58, 74, 76, 84, 85, 86, 110, 134
Greek (see also Hellenic), xiv, 4, 5, 6, 13, 15, 17, 19, 25, 29, 30, 32, 40, 43, 103, 124
Groddeck, Georg, 113-14

H

Hafiz, 108-110
Hanbali, 20
Happiness, xiv, 38, 55, 56, 61, 84-6, 108, 129, 132, 147, 159, 160
Harun al-Rashid, 17
Haussig, H. W., 10
Healing, xiii, 53, 99, 106, 107, 108, 114, 118n13, 119
Heaven and Hell, 46, 47, 81, 82, 86, 133, 135, 136, 142, 153, 165, 171, 172
Hedayat, Sadiq, xvn1, 3, 3n1, 154n1
Hegel, Wilhelm Friedrich, 40
Hellenic (see also Greek), xiii, 5, 8, 15, 21, 25, 28, 32, 33, 40, 82n40, 103, 122n1, 124, 131
Heraclitus, xiii, xiv, 4, 8, 25, 32, 33, 38, 40, 40n1, 41-4, 41n15, 42n18, 45-9, 69, 73, 124
Heraclitan, 4, 26, 33, 41, 44, 47
Herat, 16, 18

Hîch (nothingness), xvi, 82, 172
Hindu/Hinduism, 5, 6, 21, 37, 90, 147
Hippocrates, 103, 118n13
Hiwi al-Balkhi, 27-8
Horace, 132, 137, 137n19

I

Iatrike (medicine), 103
Ibn Hanbal Ahmad, 20
Ibn Rushd (see also Averroes), 22
Id ("es") (Groddeck and Freud), 114
Ignorance, 38, 69, 79n34, 85
Ikhwan al-Safa (Brethren of Purity), 21
Illusion, 37, 42, 44, 45, 55, 68, 72, 74, 128
Impermanency/Impermanent, xv, 8, 31, 36, 38, 45, 55, 61, 65, 67-9, 73-4, 76, 79-81, 85, 92-3, 108-9, 126, 129, 130, 133, 135, 137-9, 153, 159, 163, 164, 173
Incoherence of the Incoherence (*Tahafut al-tahafut*), 22
Incoherence of the Philosophers (*Tahafut al-falasifa*), 22
India/Indian, xiv, 5, 6, 8, 9, 12-14, 15, 17, 26, 28, 32, 35, 36, 37, 78, 90, 142-3, 144, 147
Indian philosophy, xiii, xiv, 4-6, 14-16, 25, 26n59, 32, 37, 78, 82n40, 122n1, 143
Intermediate state (Madhyamika), 34, 35, 68, 72-3, 76, 88
Iran, 3, 5, 8-10, 11, 17, 20, 21, 25, 26, 27, 37, 109, 141, 141n1, 144, 147, 163n5, 167n7
Iranian, xiv, 5, 6, 10, 11, 15, 16, 19, 37, 142, 146

Islam, 6, 7, 16, 18-21, 22-5, 27, 20n42, 26, 38, 136n17, 142, 171
"Islamic Golden Age", 17-18
"Islamic Civilization" 16
Islamization, 21

J

Jahm b. Safwan, 26
Jahmiyya, 26
James, William, 113
Jewish, 16, 28
Judaic, 27, 28, 136n17

K

Kabul, 142, 147
Kāfir, 20
Kahneman, Daniel ('illusion of certainty'), 128
Kamkars Ensemble, 147
Kapisa, 13
Kashgar, 5, 13
Kashmir, 8, 12, 14, 37
Khayyamian perspective, xiii, 3n1, 32, 34-6, 59, 64, 67,69, 76-7, 82, 93, 102, 128, 130, 132-4, 139, 141, 142, 144n7, 145, 146, 149
Khurasan, 3, 5, 6, 26, 27, 29, 36, 37, 162n4
Koran, 19, 24, 26, 27, 136n17
kufr (unbelief), 20, 21, 29

L

Laertius, Diogenes, 40, 44n28
Laozi (Lao Tzu), xii, 11, 33, 52, 56, 58, 60, 64
Liberation, 35, 67, 68, 69, 71, 71n12, 72, 82, 86, 113, 122, 122n1, 153, 165
Life anxiety, 130

Logic/logical, xiv, 8, 20, 21, 23, 31, 42, 45, 46, 48, 74, 75, 76, 78, 80, 119, 123, 143
Logos, 41-4
Longfellow, Henry Wadsworth, 146
Lotus Sutra, 88
Lucretian, 33, 132, 144, 144n7
Lucretius, xii, 82n40, 133, 138, 149

M

Madhyamika (Middle Way), 13, 34, 70-1, 71n13
Mahayana (Buddhism), xiii, 13, 36, 70-1, 71n13, 73, 79n34
Malamati (mystics), 35
Manichaean/Manichaeism, 5, 10, 11, 11n20, 16, 21, 24, 25, 27, 28, 65
Maya (changing phenomenon), 37, 89, 92
Materialism, 23, 25, 26, 33
Mathematics/mathematician, xii 3, 6, 6n4, 8, 15, 17, 20, 23, 44, 49, 77, 105n11, 106
Mazdakism, 16, 21
Mecca, 29
Metaphor/metaphorical, 9, 12, 33, 39, 40, 46, 51-2, 54, 76, 90, 91, 92, 103, 109n29, 122, 125, 133, 160, 165
Middle Ages, 22
Middle Way (*Madhyamika*), 34, 70, 71, 72
Mithraism, 21
Mongols, 18, 12n23, 141n1
Monotheism, 18, 23, 25, 27, 46
Mūlamadhyamakakārikā (Nagarjuna), 67, 71
murtadd (apostate), 20

Muslim(s), 6, 7, 13, 16, 17, 18, 19, 21, 22, 24, 25, 26, 29, 30, 37, 38, 46, 64, 147

N

Nagarjuna, xiii, xiv, 13, 4, 8, 32, 34, 35, 38, 67-88
Nagarjunian, 68, 73, 76, 82
Naturalism, 23, 32, 33, 59, 62
Nawbakht (astronomer), 14
Near East, 13-14, 15, 105n12
Neoplatonism, 16, 149
New England, 146, 147
Nietzsche, Friedrich, xvi, 40, 42, 130, 130n10, 131
Nirvana, 35, 69, 71, 72, 74, 75, 79, 82, 86, 87, 88
Nishapur, xiv, 3, 4, 5, 8, 10, 11, 16, 18, 21, 27, 28, 31, 32, 34, 35, 36, 37, 65
Non-Islamic, 15, 25
Non-self, 68, 75-6, 80, 85
Nothingness, xvi, 35, 49, 63, 69, 75, 76, 77, 82, 122, 128, 130, 138, 145, 150, 153, 172, 173
Nowness, 73, 85, 86, 88, 129, 137, 163

O

Ouseley, William, 144

P

Padmasambhava, 13
Pantheism, 16
Paradigm (shift), xi, 18, 69, 75, 114, 123
Paradise, 48, 136, 161, 171, 172
Parallel intelligence, 117, 126-8, 160

Pari-nirvana, 79
Pavlov, Ivan, 100-2
Persian (poetry, literature), xv, 3, 5, 13, 15, 18n39, 31, 34, 35, 37, 40, 86, 105n12, 108, 109, 116, 124, 141, 142, 143, 144, 160, 161n3, 165n6, 168n8
Peseschkian, Nossrat, 116-17
Peshawar, 13
Plato/Platonic, 39n1, 47, 149
Plutarch, 39n1, 49n36, 131
Poeticize, 45, 84
Poetry as medicine, 99, 100, 102-6, 109, 111, 113, 118-19
'Pot', 'pot-maker- potter' metaphors, 27, 36, 46, 83, 84, 89-93, 95, 109, 130, 153, 159, 165, 166, 167
Prajnaparamita-Sutra (Perfection of Wisdom-Sutra), 36, 70, 71, 74, 74n24, 75, 86, 87
Pre-Socratic, 24, 25, 26, 32, 33, 40
Process Philosophy, 8, 41, 69
Prophet(s), 10, 11, 23, 25, 26, 27, 107, 142
Psychoanalysis, 113-14
Psychoneuroimmunology (PNI), 101, 115
Psychosomatic, 99, 104, 106, 113-14
Psychotherapy/psychotherapeutic, 100, 109, 116

Q

Qalandari, 35, 162n4

R

Racism, 149
Rationalism, 19, 25, 26, 27
Rayy, 17, 26, 37

Razi, Muhammad ibn Zakariya al-, 26-7, 106-8
Razi's books, 106-8
Reincarnation, 29, 45, 75, 76, 79, 80, 81, 90, 91
Renaissance, 22, 40
Richthofen, Ferdinand von (*Seidenstraße*), 9
Rumi, 110-11

S

Saadi, 108, 109, 110, 116
Saadia Gaon, 28
Sāqi ('wine server,' intelligence self), 52, 55, 160, 162, 163, 164, 172
Samarqand, 5, 6, 11, 13, 16, 18, 27, 28
Samsara, 73-5, 82, 86, 88
Sanskrit, 5, 14, 15, 28, 32, 34, 37, 69, 73, 91
Sassanid Empire, 5, 10, 11, 13, 15
Second Buddha (Nagarjuna), 69-70
Self-rule, 35, 67
Seljuq dynasty, xii, 6, 16
Selye, Hans, 115, 115n8, 116
Serotonin, 111, 118-19
Shafei, 20
Shafi'i, Imam, 20
Shahrastani, 32
Shahrazuri, 30
Shiites, 25
Shiraz, 141, 141n1, 142, 147
Siddhartha, Gautama (astrologer), 14
Sirr-e Akbar (Dara Shukoh), 37
Skepticism, 123, 141, 142, 147, 164
"sleep-walkers" (Heraclitus, Khayyam), 42, 49
Sociology, 105n12, 110

Social psychology, 101, 110
Socratic, 149
Soghdian, 5, 10, 15
Spice Route, 25
Spinoza, 28
Stoics, 82, 104, 122, 123, 134
Sufi, 7n6, 20, 21, 29, 34, 37, 73n22, 149
Sufism, 109, 143
Swat Valley, 13

T

Tajikistan, 8, 27
Talas (Taraz), 13
Tang dynasty, 11, 12, 13, 34
Tantra-Tantric, 13, 86, 143
"Tat Tvam Asi" ('You Are That'), 37
Tathagata, 85-6, 88
Taxila, 13
Techne (art), 103
Thoreau, Henry David, 146
Tibet, 11, 13, 71
Tibetan Buddhism, 71n13
Tirmidh, 26
Torah, 28
Transcendentalism, 146
Turkish (Seljuq), 16
Turkistan, 8, 13
Twain, Mark, 145

U

Uighur, 5, 8, 10, 11
Ultranationalism, 149
Umayyad Caliphate, 13

Upanishads, xiii, xiv, 4, 32, 36-8, 89-92, 93, 94-6

V

Vajrayana Buddhism, 13
Vasubandhu, 13
Vedanta, 16, 29n73, 32, 36, 37, 91
Vedantic-philosophy, 37, 38, 89, 92
Vegetarian, 7, 29, 30, 106

W

Wang Fuzhi, 57
Whitehead, Alfred N., 69
Wilde, Oscar, 124
Wu wei ('non-disruptive activity'), 53, 57, 58, 60

Y

Yin-yang, 58
Yogacara, 13, 71n13
Yogananda, Paramahansa, 143-5

Z

Zen, xiii, xvi, 11, 12, 34, 71n13, 73
Zhuangzi (Chuang Tzu), xii, xiii, xiv, 4, 8, 32, 33, 34n84, 38, 51-9, 61-4, 65, 133
Ziran ('self so'), 57-8
Zoroastrian/Zoroastrianism, 7, 10, 16, 21
Zouwang ('forgetting self'), 57-8

www.ingramcontent.com/pod-product-compliance
Lightning Source LLC
Chambersburg PA
CBHW070259230426
43664CB00014B/2584